Dr. Mom's

PRESCRIPTION FOR

PRESCHOOLERS

Dr. Mom's

PRESCRIPTION FOR

PRESCHOOLERS

Seven
Essentials
—— *for the* ——
Formative
Years

Marianne Neifert, M.D.

GRAND RAPIDS, MICHIGAN 49530

Dr. Mom's Prescription for Preschoolers
Copyright © 2001 by Marianne Neifert
Requests for information should be addressed to:
Zondervan, *Grand Rapids, Michigan 49530*

Library of Congress Cataloging-in-Publication Data
Neifert, Marianne R.
  Dr. Mom's prescription for preschoolers : seven essentials for the formative years
/ Marianne Neifert.
    p. cm.
  ISBN 0-310-22876-X
  1. Preschool children. 2. Child rearing. 3. Parenting. 4. Parenting—Religious aspects—Christianity. I. Title: Doctor Mom's prescription for preschoolers.
II. Title.

HQ774.5 .N447 2001
649'.123—dc21

2001017805

Interior design by Melissa Elenbaas

Printed in the United States of America

01 02 03 04 05 06 /❖ DC/ 10 9 8 7 6 5 4 3 2 1

To the glory and honor
of our Lord and Savior, Jesus Christ,
who "called the children to him and said,
'Let the little children come to me,
and do not hinder them,
for the kingdom of God belongs
to such as these'" (Luke 18:16).

Contents

Acknowledgments

I gratefully acknowledge the following individuals who contributed directly to this manuscript or who indirectly influenced the work by their significant impact on me:

My extraordinary children—Peter, Paige, Tricie, Heather, and Mark—for being my earthly crown of jewels and for sustaining and inspiring me with an unquenchable outpouring of love.

My precious daughters- and sons-in-law—Courtney, Becky, Phil, and Craig—who have become my bonus children and integral members of our family.

My husband, Larry, with whom I have shared the exhilarating journey of raising our magnificent children.

My father, Andrew M. Egeland, and my late mother, Mary Annabel Egeland, for admirably filling all my essential needs and nurturing me for a lifetime.

My beloved brothers, sisters, and marvelous extended family who have uplifted me with their steadfast love and prayers.

My esteemed brother-in-law, Pastor Charles Poncelow, for his keen theological insights and special contributions to this work.

My capable editor at Zondervan, Cindy Hays, for her astute critique and invaluable input.

My literary agent, Faith Hamlin, at Sanford J. Greenburger Associates, for her unfailing faith in me and her unwavering support.

The late eminent child psychiatrist, Rudolf Dreikurs, M.D., for his lifelong work with children that has shaped much of our modern philosophy of discipline.

Parenting magazine, where I initially shared my perspectives on a number of the topics discussed in this book.

And the countless parents and children whose families have enriched my life and inspired my mission.

Introducing Dr. Mom

As a pediatrician and the mother of five adult children, my journeys in medicine and motherhood have been intricately intertwined for more than a quarter-century, giving me a unique perspective and hard-earned wisdom concerning children and families. My first baby was born only a few months before I started medical school, and my fifth child arrived seven years later, on the final day of my pediatric residency training. My busiest child-rearing years were spent attempting to balance the compelling needs of my children with my weighty professional responsibilities. As an author of parenting books, a contributing editor for *Parenting* and *BabyTalk* magazines, and a professional speaker, I have enjoyed both the privilege and the accountability of having a public forum for communicating child-rearing advice. As a Christian woman, my parenting philosophy is imbued with the belief that God is love and that the greatest manifestation of this love is reflected in the perfect life, atoning death, and triumphant resurrection of Jesus Christ. In addressing secular audiences, however, I have necessarily omitted the spiritual dimension to parenting and, thus, have withheld from parents their most effective tools and the most significant measure of their child-rearing role. You see, without the benefit of God's model as our divine parent, the personal example of the life of Jesus Christ, and the comfort and empowerment of the Holy Spirit, parents are not adequately equipped for our sacred obligation of shepherding God's littlest lambs through the perilous paths of childhood. At last I have been given the opportunity to write a parenting guide that incorporates not only my professional parenting knowledge and personal experiences but also my deeply held spiritual convictions.

Your child's preschool years are critically important to his future learning and academic success, behavior and personality, social and coping skills, and emotional well-being and happiness. We call the early years the formative period in a child's life because a child's early experiences and the conclusions she draws about the world will powerfully shape her future and largely determine whether she fulfills her potential. While it is never too late to improve your parenting skills and the way you interact with your child, young children are like clay that readily yields to our touch and can be easily molded and fashioned. Later, when undesirable behaviors and attitudes have hardened into habit, it becomes more difficult to reshape a child's heart and mind.

Thus, our parenting role during our child's preschool years is vital to her future. Not only are the stakes so high, but caring for young children is an arduous task, filled with questions, doubts, concerns, and worries about the adequacy of our efforts. Children develop and change so rapidly during the early years that we constantly must readjust the way we interact with them. Caring for young children with their emerging independence, unique personalities, intense desires, and low frustration levels can be physically and emotionally draining. While a baby can be easily dressed, for example, getting a squirming toddler into his shirt and pants requires skilled distraction and speedy maneuvering. And a dawdling five-year-old can turn your morning rush into maddening slow motion.

Supporting young children's increasing independence by letting them do things for themselves that you can do faster takes enormous patience and encouragement. Remaining calm and choosing the appropriate response to misbehavior requires admirable self-restraint and wisdom.

Fortunately, parenting young children involves more than awesome responsibilities and daunting challenges. It also includes many priceless gifts that little children bring into our lives. We need to be open to recognizing, receiving, and holding these gifts tenderly. Just when we are tempted to take life for granted, young children bring us the gift of joy and wonder in the ordinary. They delight in the simple pleasures of life, marveling at the intricacies of a colorful stone, a rainbow on the horizon, or the dots on a ladybug. Young children are prodigious learners who daily make new discoveries about the world God created and its inhabitants. In their insatiable quest to unravel life's mysteries, they endlessly ask why and prompt us to pause and ponder. A preschooler's fantasy play draws us into his magical world of dreams and imagination, reminding us of life's endless possibilities. In the face of our own hardships and disillusionment, little children radiate joy and happiness in simply being alive and drinking in all the wonders of God's universe. For the preschooler, the glass is never half empty but always half full.

Young children also bring us the gifts of frankness, honesty, lack of guile, and candid observations that often make us smile and become philosophical. When a three-year-old innocently asks, "Grandma, do wrinkles hurt?" we learn something about ourselves in our answer: "Only your feelings, honey, only your feelings." Preschoolers bring us the gift of trusting acceptance of others, as they search for the positives in the people they meet. Each person they encounter represents a potential new friend, rather than a threat. Still free of adult prejudices, the young child does not judge individual differences but readily embraces the wide range of diversity in physical appearance and personality traits.

Young children bring us the gift of humor and boisterous gaiety. Their laughter and giggles fill a room and bring a smile to adult faces as they find something comical about the mundane aspects of life. A glob of food on the tip of their finger, a tuft of Mommy's hair sticking out of place, earmuffs on a man's head, or shaving cream on their daddy's face are all cause for hilarity. Even when children are not intentionally funny, such as the ambivalent big sister who suggested naming her new baby brother "Mr. Nobody," seeing the world from a child's perspective can make us smile inside or laugh out loud.

I wrote this book to help Christian parents fulfill their responsibilities and reap the abundant rewards of nurturing young children. When I recall my own parenting journey, I am reassured that I innately did many positive things, largely because my parents had modeled many positives for me. Despite my numerous successes, however, I now recognize that I lacked vital information about early child behavior and was juggling too many commitments to parent optimally. The year I was a pediatric intern—the most physically and emotionally draining year of my entire life—I had three preschoolers at home and was pregnant with my fourth child. While I was knowledgeable about many medical aspects of pediatric care, I knew too little about the emotional needs of young children. I'm afraid I made many mistakes in parenting my preschoolers, such as beginning toilet training too early, making some unfortunate child-care choices, and not always dealing appropriately with common misbehaviors. As I reflect on the sometimes-chaotic years when my children were preschoolers, I wish I had had the information shared in this book. Such knowledge would have greatly reduced my parenting stresses, increased my effectiveness, and magnified my rewards. Parenting well is not an innate ability. Rather, it involves a complex set of skills that must be taught and practiced.

The seven parenting essentials I discuss in this book will give you specific skills to help you parent well and focus on what matters most during your child's formative years. My prescription for preschoolers outlined in these pages has been distilled from the informed, examined experience of my own parenting pinnacles and perils, along with those of countless other families I have encountered. The foundational essentials are addressed sequentially, as follows:

The Essential Need to Make Parenting a Priority. Effective parenting involves continually reassessing our priorities and consciously choosing to say no to good and glamorous opportunities in order to say yes to our children's compelling needs and our hearts' deepest desires.

The Essentials of Early Child Development. Parents of preschoolers need to understand the basics of early child development, recognize the emotional needs of young children, and know specific strategies for optimizing early brain development and learning.

The Spiritual Essentials: Passing on Your Faith. Parents are called to nurture their children's precious inner spirituality and to share with them the immeasurable gift of God's love, example, guidance, comfort, strength, and hope as we journey through this life and face the life to come.

The Essential Ingredients of Healthy Self-Esteem. To reach their full potential, children need a strong sense of self-worth that comes from feeling loveable and capable—having the assurance of their intrinsic worth and value, along with the conviction that they are competent to handle life's challenges.

The Essentials of Discipline: Love and Limits. Effective discipline is the labor of love by which children learn to handle difficult feelings, distinguish acceptable from unacceptable behavior, make good decisions, and develop responsibility and self-control. It involves both the promotion of desired behavior and the appropriate management of misbehavior.

Those Essential Others: Alternate Caretakers. Because the majority of preschool children receive regular care and education by alternate caretakers, parents need to be able to recognize quality child care that assures your child will be physically safe, emotionally secure, and optimally stimulated during your absences. Too many parents settle for substandard care that can have long-lasting adverse effects.

Essential Answers for Common Concerns. Parents of young children are often perplexed by common, troubling behaviors and habits. Armed with empowering information, you can learn to distinguish normal from problematic behavior and to work with your child in handling the emotional challenges of the preschool years.

Few memories are laced with as much joy and sheer happiness as the recollection of my children's preschool years. What once seemed so laborious was all too fleeting. I always thought there would be more time to relish the simple pleasures of this magical period, but I must have blinked. When I opened my eyes, the precious time I thought would drift like clouds had stolen away on angel's wings. I thank God for the awesome privilege of being responsible for little children and for the immense rewards of that important stewardship. This book is my gift of gratitude offered to a new generation of parents who have accepted God's calling to become the Lord's servant by reflecting his immeasurable love as the parent of a preschooler.

Chapter 1

The Essential Need to Make Parenting a Priority

Parenting has never been an easy endeavor, but today's parents face unique pressures in our high-tech, fast-paced world. Our society has traded traditional sex role stereotypes for expanded role opportunities for both men and women. For many parents, the result is increased performance expectations at the workplace and at home. In these hectic times, when the majority of new mothers in America return to work before their babies turn a year old, parenting often gets sandwiched between a multitude of competing priorities. Yet parenting isn't a subordinate role to be penciled into the available openings in our day planner. Rather, the responsibility of being the caretakers of our children's physical needs, as well as their most influential nurturers, teachers, role models, and mentors, is a high and noble calling.

I don't consider it an overstatement to say that parenting is the most important job a person will ever do. If you don't believe me, just consider the consequences of "blowing it." Nothing else you ever achieve can compensate for failing in this critical role. On the other hand, nothing else you ever accomplish will compare to the joy of raising a responsible, well-adjusted, competent, moral, happy individual, with whom you enjoy a lifelong positive relationship and share a living faith in a loving God. The privilege and responsibility of being a parent are among God's greatest blessings bestowed on humankind and are among the most fulfilling ways we are invited to become cocreators with God.

God — the Perfect Parent

As we contemplate the awesome responsibilities of parenthood, we can take comfort in having a perfect heavenly Father who serves as our model for the ideal parent. When God created Adam and Eve, he placed them in the Garden of Eden, which contained abundant provisions for all their physical needs, serving as a reminder of our commitment to our children's physical care and protection. Just as God created humans for a relationship with him and walked with Adam and Eve in the garden in the cool of the day, we, too, delight in our children and endeavor to build a strong emotional bond. Our relationship with God is so deeply personal that he suffers, weeps, and rejoices with us, modeling the depth of emotional intimacy we seek with our children.

> The privilege and responsibility of being a parent are among God's greatest blessings bestowed on humankind and are among the most fulfilling ways we are invited to become cocreators with God.

God realized that human beings needed a human example of ideal behavior, so he came as the incarnate Jesus to show us how to live. The gracious gift of Jesus' example reminds me of the story about the little boy who was awakened one night by a loud thunderstorm. Terrified, he called out to his daddy in the next room, who came to his son's bedside to comfort him. Embracing his vulnerable little boy within his strong arms, the father spoke tenderly. "Don't be afraid of the storm, Son. Remember, God is here with us," he said reassuringly. "I know," the frightened youngster responded. "It's just that right now, I need someone with skin on!" Just as this child needed the tangible presence of a protective father, our children need parents who are daily and deeply involved in their lives, not distant or emotionally remote. Just as Jesus provides the model for the perfect way to live our lives, parents are the principal role models for our children, who readily imitate our words, attitudes, and actions.

> God's model of unmerited grace and a personal relationship through Jesus Christ serves as our ideal standard of unconditional love and a unique relationship with each of our children.

In the same way that God is moral and just and provides consequences for sin, parents are to establish and enforce rules and boundaries for our children's own good. God also provides the perfect model of sacrificial love in the atoning death of Jesus Christ on our behalf. No sacrifice we ever make for our own children can compare to the willingness of Jesus to bear the sins of the world. God's model of unmerited grace and a personal relationship through Jesus Christ serves as our ideal standard of unconditional love and a unique relationship with each of our children. Finally, no greater example exists of parental love and acceptance than God's perfect example of forgiving and forgetting, seeking the lost, welcoming the prodigal, purifying the unclean, accepting the outcast, uplifting the downcast, redeeming the condemned, and healing the hurting.

The Tyranny of the Urgent

Despite the sacred metaphor of God as our heavenly Father, many people act as if being a mom or dad were an incidental role. We have all heard glamorized accounts of "superwomen" who keep working until their labor begins. Then, seemingly undaunted, they return to high-profile professions a few weeks after delivery, armed with a portable electric breast pump with which they express their milk at scheduled intervals for an alternate caretaker to feed to their baby. The implication is that quality parenting can be fit into an already crammed schedule as easily as a new hobby. The truth is that effective parenting involves continually reranking our priorities and being willing to say no to good opportunities in order to say yes to our children's needs. When we commit to being a parent, we must commit to parenting well.

To parent well, we must rank this responsibility above other priorities and learn to distinguish *important* activities, like spending quality time with our youngsters, from *urgent* demands, like ever-present work deadlines and household tasks. I've discovered that most of us structure our days around urgent priorities, while we ultimately define our lives by important commitments. This tyranny of the urgent often obscures the very things that are truly important. The key is to do something important every day. Yet we tend to live our lives as if there will be endless opportunities to get our priorities straight tomorrow. The seemingly noble psychology of postponement that allows us to achieve lofty career goals by delaying gratification steals our present moments with the convincing lie, "This isn't really it. Life will begin when . . ." We say, "Someday when things slow down, I'll spend more time with my kids." "Someday, when I catch up at work, I'll cut back and focus on my family." Well, someday isn't a day we can designate on our calendars, and it isn't guaranteed to arrive. All we have for certain is now, today, this moment, and we must cherish it. All too often, tomorrow—if it comes at all—tends to arrive after we have missed irretrievable "might have been" opportunities with our loved ones.

> We tend to live our lives as if there will be endless opportunities to get our priorities straight tomorrow.

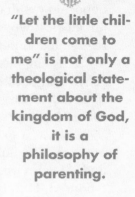

Parents would do well to ponder one of the sweetest stories in the Gospels, which centers around Jesus and children (Matt. 19:14–15; Mark 10:13–14; Luke 18:15–16). Jesus is on his way to Jerusalem, knowing he must suffer and die. Mothers were bringing their babies to Jesus, seeking his blessing on them. The disciples, in a well-meaning attempt to protect Jesus from being bothered, rebuked the women. Seeing this, however, Jesus called the children to him and made time to bless and pray for the little ones, even as he was preparing to face the cross. Jesus gave us this powerful example about making time for the children, even amid our weariness and worries. "Let the little children come to me" is not only a theological statement about the kingdom of God, it is a philosophy of parenting.

> "Let the little children come to me" is not only a theological statement about the kingdom of God, it is a philosophy of parenting.

Living in Sync with Our Values

A few years ago, I was speaking to a group of parents in Texas. A conscientious young father asked me for advice about whether to accept a lucrative job opportunity that would afford his family future financial security. The problem was that he would have to work on an off-shore oil rig at a significant distance from his wife and young children. Although he would miss out on daily involvement with his family, he would earn considerably more money.

Actually, this man's dilemma was not so unique. It's really a universal question that takes a variety of different forms: Do I rank the quality of my present family life higher than the potential for financial rewards or recognition? At that Texas speaking engagement I wondered, Would the man's decision be different if he could foretell the future and know that one of his little girls would die in a car accident in two years? The problem is, none of us can know what the future holds. We have to live in the present, in sync with our values. Remember, "each day is a gift from God. That's why they call it the present."

When I had my first four babies during college, medical school, and internship, I was enamored with the glamorous opportunities that were unfolding for women. I thought I was the luckiest woman in the world to be able to go to medical school in addition to being a wife and mother. I told myself I was relishing the "triumph of having it all" when I did outrageous things, like giving birth Friday evening after class and returning to class Monday morning as a second-year medical student!

Later, as a practicing pediatrician, I would never recommend that a couple integrate their new baby into their family under such circumstances. I hadn't lived out the values I espoused. I realize today that those harried and exhausting years of assuming the responsibilities of motherhood in the middle of arduous medical training weren't as glamorous as I once convinced myself they were. Instead of savoring the journey of life, I was enduring the present, waiting for the future. I hadn't been honest with others or myself about the compromises I was forced to make. I paid a personal price for the professional opportunities I sought, and I missed some of the quiet joys of motherhood. Thankfully, by the grace of God, my family survived intact and my kids grew up to become wonderful adults. But when I recall those frenetic years, I sometimes feel as if I laid my children's babyhoods at the altar of medicine.

Living in accordance with the values we claim is, of course, the challenge of the Christian life. We all struggle to "walk the walk" as well as "talk the talk." This need for harmony between our profession of values and the action of our living is heightened when we become parents. Not only does our walk become the living confession of our faith, it also becomes the most powerful teaching that shapes our children's worldview and personality. Much more than what we say, our preschoolers look to what we do, in their quest to discover what is important, meaningful, and valuable in life. Our behaviors, far beyond our words, tell them whether God should be trusted or ignored, whether life is full of fun or of fear, whether people are to be loved or used. The scriptural observation that "a little child will lead them" has often proven true for parents who have chosen to make changes in their lives to instill deeply held but poorly lived values in their children.

Here is a way to both test your values and make appropriate changes. Picture your child at age ten, seventeen, thirty-five. Do not worry about what she might accomplish in sports, school, or career. Rather, focus on character. What kind of person do you wish for her to be? What do you hope she will value? How will she face the challenges of living? Now, with that picture in mind, what needs to change in your life? Choose to live and act just as you hope she will. We pass more than eye color and property to our children. The most important inheritances they will receive are neither genetic nor financial, but gifts of the heart and spirit.

> **We pass more than eye color and property to our children. The most important inheritances they will receive are neither genetic nor financial, but gifts of the heart and spirit.**

Saying Yes to What Matters Most

The truth about life is that we can't have it all—not all at once. I've concluded that we can play lots of roles sequentially but only a few simultaneously. We get to choose the commitments we make at a given point. When we choose one alternative among several possibilities, we automatically exclude other options. We don't get to homeschool our child the same year we do an internship. We don't get to work full-time *and* parent full-time. Instead, we get to choose. My message to you is, choose well. I advise you to make your tough choices based on who you are and your relationships, rather than on what you do to earn a living.

When I had my babies, I was determined to continue breastfeeding after returning to school or work, even though I knew I would be separated long hours from my infants. Despite my best efforts, however, long-term breastfeeding became one of many casualties of my work demands until I reranked my priorities and made different personal choices when my last child was born. My firstborn, Peter, arrived in the middle of my final semester of college, and I resumed my heavy premedical curriculum only a week later. By scheduling my classes closely together, I managed to miss only one feeding each day. Paige was born at the beginning of my second year of medical school, when I took my now-infamous weekend-long maternity leave. Fortunately, I found a babysitter across the street from the hospital campus. That enabled me to nurse her periodically throughout the day, until the sitter moved away. I was a fourth-year medical student when Tricie was born, and emboldened by personal experience and growing assertiveness, I was able to rearrange my clinical rotations to allow for a glorious ten-week maternity leave of exclusive breastfeeding before returning to my hospital duties.

Few things are as physically and emotionally grueling as having a baby during the internship year of medical training. My one-month maternity leave after Heather's birth virtually sped by, and I returned to an exhaustive workload and call schedule that accentuated the mounting conflict I felt between meeting the needs of my baby and the hospitalized children under my care. Needless to say, breastfeeding under my unique circumstances proved more difficult than I imagined. For one thing, we didn't have fancy electric breast pumps back then, and furthermore, no one would consider letting it be known that you were collecting a body fluid at the workplace! I didn't manage to achieve the ideal breastfeeding duration of at least one year, until I finally learned to say no to some good things in order to say yes to my very best.

While pregnant with my fifth baby, I decided to rank breastfeeding higher than other priorities, to make a different choice. To do this, I declined several attractive professional opportunities at the end of my residency training in order to be available to my last baby for unrestricted breastfeeding. Only by making significant lifestyle changes was I able to fulfill a parenting commitment that previously had been crowded out by other demands. It was one of the best decisions I ever made and one that changed the direction of my career.

It's not my place to rank your priorities or make decisions for you and your family. But I do want to encourage you to examine whether you are living in sync with your governing values. I want to urge you to make the choices about your family life that give you the fewest regrets and the greatest peace of mind—the choices that fulfill God's will for your life.

Sometimes making right choices involves acknowledging that we are off course and need to change our direction to get back on track. For example, a hospital administrator I know often expressed her ambivalence about the long hours required by her prestigious and demanding position. A string of job-related crises left her husband feeling like a single parent and all but eliminated her quality time with her four-year-old. One day, when the frazzled woman picked up her little girl at preschool, the teacher confided, "I thought you would want to know that when your daughter draws a family picture, you're not in it." This brief exchange became a moment of truth for the mother, who deliberated only briefly before giving two-weeks notice and accepting a nonmanagerial nine-to-five position that allowed her to be more available to her family. "The career and financial rewards of the position I left cannot compensate for what I was missing with my family," she concluded. "It simply wasn't worth it."

If we tune in to what our children are telling us, we will find many less-dramatic examples of how our hectic lives affect our parenting in our "struggle to juggle" competing priorities.

Another working mother shared an experience involving her two-year-old daughter as they hurried to get to the child-care center on time. The mother said that as they exited the car and headed toward the building entrance each morning, she would walk behind her daughter on the sidewalk, urging her to go faster by repeating, "Quick, quick . . . quick, quick." One day, the toddler ran ahead a few steps, then stopped and turned to face her mother. "No quick!" she announced sternly, urging her mother to back off with the "hurry up" message.

Another mother decided to leave her position in the corporate world and open a home office in order to be with her young child all day. Although she spent many hours on the telephone, she used a hands-free headset in hopes that her child would be less aware of the time she devoted to clients. Much to her surprise, her son's first sentence was "No phone. No phone."

One of my favorite four-year-old insights came from the daughter of a busy, overwrought mom who was juggling a part-time job and numerous volunteer commitments. A neighbor child told this little girl, "My mom says your mom is going to start baby-sitting me." The insightful youngster retorted, "I don't think so. She doesn't even have time to take care of me!"

Contemporary Challenges of Parenting

In addition to getting our daily priorities straight, today's parents face a host of other challenges. As traditional family roles are discarded, more men and women find themselves suffering from role overload. Not only is the two-earner family a new societal norm, but many women in such households are both the principal breadwinner and the designated home manager. Many fathers are more active participants in child rearing than their own fathers were and are shouldering more household responsibilities. Fewer men today have the support of a homemaker wife. Instead, their partners are likely to be employed outside the home or to run a home business.

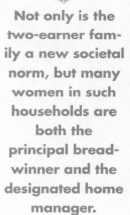

Despite the new dual-earner norm, too many families with young children lack accessible, affordable, quality child care, making substitute care a matter of daily concern. Many school-aged children are left unsupervised and vulnerable to negative influences. Television, video games, movies, and other media bombard our children with values that contradict our own. Children as young as four are learning to use a computer and will ultimately surf the internet, where they can scan the encyclopedia—or find directions for making a bomb.

Not only is the two-earner family a new societal norm, but many women in such households are both the principal breadwinner and the designated home manager.

Births to unwed mothers and high divorce rates, especially among couples with young children, weaken families through the loss of involved fathers. Blended families add a new layer of complexity to family dynamics and relationships. Lack of elder care leaves many adults sandwiched between the needs of their children and the care of their aging parents. A national epidemic of violence threatens our safety and peace of mind, both at home and in the community. Widespread drug and alcohol problems make many parents emotionally unavailable to their children. Amid such societal threats, the responsibilities of parenthood loom more awesome than ever, leaving mothers and fathers to wonder if they are up to the job.

While parenting is certainly not a role for the fainthearted, we needn't approach this sacred responsibility with trepidation. God has promised to equip us for the tasks to which he calls us. Armed by God's example in Jesus Christ and empowered by the Holy Spirit, we can enjoy a rich and rewarding family life as we fulfill our parenting mission. The perspectives, insights, and specific strategies I offer in this book will help you be a more effective and confident parent.

The Perils of Perfectionism

Many parents are additionally burdened by their own unrealistic expectations of themselves and their children. If the house isn't immaculate, their performance appraisal at work isn't flawless, or their Christmas cards aren't mailed on time, they feel inadequate. These parents tend to embrace all-or-nothing thinking. If things aren't perfect, then they must be just awful. Parenting is filled with so many unknowns and factors beyond our control that trying to be a perfect parent is a sure recipe for a sense of failure. To make matters worse, perfectionists sometimes place excessive demands on their children, spouses, and coworkers, thus making life difficult for everyone within their sphere of influence.

Parenting is filled with so many unknowns and factors beyond our control that trying to be a perfect parent is a sure recipe for a sense of failure.

Instead of striving for unattainable perfection, my advice is to aim to be a "good enough" or "fully satisfactory" parent. Actually, a parent who manages to be consistently *adequate* in his or her role is doing a great job! When the demands of work, the call of involvement, or the desire to succeed in some chosen endeavor raise our stress levels and impinge on our parenting, we need to pause, to pray, and to pass, if necessary.

Focus on those relatively few items that are essential to the mental, physical, emotional, and spiritual well-being of your child. When we set priorities, we deliberately rank one thing as more important than something else. If you value quality time with your children and spouse over a clutter-free house, then you are consciously choosing to lower your housekeeping standards in exchange for something you cherish more. This is an example of saying no to something good in order to say yes to something better. Tell yourself it's a choice and stop feeling guilty about it. Enlist more help from your family, hire the Merry Maids, or simply accept that for the time being, your house may not measure up to your mother's standards. Consider, however, that it is a whole lot easier to get another house than to find another family! Years from now, I doubt you will remember the addresses of the homes you struggled to keep clean, but you will never lose the precious memories of reading to your child, watching her achieve a new milestone, going on a picnic together, or playing a game.

I know a woman who learned a lot about priorities and "good enough" parenting after she gave birth to premature triplets. It was her second pregnancy. With her first baby, she had compiled an elaborate baby book, chronicling every detail of her infant's development. The first year of life for her triplets was an exhilarating, overwhelming, exhausting roller-coaster ride, complicated by the babies' need for home oxygen, physical-therapy appointments, and countless doctor's visits. Somehow, the basics got covered and the babies grew up to be healthy, happy, high-achieving youngsters. When the triplets later discovered the older sister's detailed baby book, they accusingly inquired whether their mother had kept journals of their early life. This unflappable woman calmly replied, "Of course I have a baby book for each of you with records of all your important milestones—weights, measurements, immunizations, and development. It's called your medical record, and we keep it at the doctor's office." But their real baby books were actually sealed in her heart—page after page being filled with the sacrificial love and actions she had chosen.

All parents make mistakes and have regrets. What's important is to apologize to our children when we wound

> *Years from now, I doubt you will remember the addresses of the homes you struggled to keep clean, but you will never lose the precious memories of reading to your child, watching her achieve a new milestone, going on a picnic together, or playing a game.*

their spirits, to forgive ourselves for the human frailty of being imperfect, to learn from our mistakes, and to seek God's help to do better. Instead of wallowing in guilt over our shortcomings as parents, tell yourself that you did the best you could with the circumstances and knowledge you had at the time. Even when it wasn't "good enough," doing the best we could at the time is all that can be asked of us.

Strengthen Your Parenting Team

A balanced parenting team can divide the responsibilities and multiply the rewards of child rearing. Because mothers and fathers parent in unique and complementary styles, our children thrive best when they receive the daily involvement of two committed parents. In addition, mothers and fathers are maximally fulfilled when they both share the responsibilities and rewards of parenthood. There are good reasons why God's design for the family is based on two deeply committed parents. Yet in most two-parent families, both parents are employed, leaving less quantity and quality time available for effective parenting. And owing to high rates of divorce and single parenthood, many contemporary families are headed by a lopsided, unbalanced team that makes parenting harder than it might be. Nearly a third of children live with a single parent, usually a mother, who shoulders sole or disproportionate responsibility for her children's welfare and who may lack the physical and emotional reserves for optimal parenting.

Because mothers and fathers parent in unique and complementary styles, our children thrive best when they receive the daily involvement of two committed parents.

Father Hunger

Countless children today are hungering for their father's love and presence in their lives. Although strong scientific evidence supports a two-parent advantage, only half of American children today live in traditional nuclear families.[1] The alarming number of absent fathers leaves children longing for the love of their daddies, places disproportionate responsibility on mothers, and results in missed opportunities for men to become fulfilled in their parenting role. Among children whose parents are divorced, separated, or never married, few see their fathers on a regular basis.

I recall a five-year-old boy who accompanied his mother to my office for his new sister's well-baby visit. Turning to me, the little boy wistfully announced, "My daddy's far away, and I don't know how to find him." This little fellow was voicing what countless young children feel—a longing for their fathers to be involved in their lives. So many children today are impacted by absent fathers that our society has coined the term "father hunger" to describe the void left by men who have abdicated their paternal responsibilities. Children without a father naturally assume that they weren't special enough to keep their daddy around. "What made him leave me?" a child inevitably wonders.

> So many children today are impacted by absent fathers that our society has coined the term "father hunger" to describe the void left by men who have abdicated their paternal responsibilities.

A Father's Unique Contribution

Traditionally, fathers have been viewed principally as providers and protectors. In recent decades, the growing acceptance of unwed motherhood, the impact of divorce on family structure, and the increased economic independence of working women have combined to devalue fatherhood. Indeed, the prevailing conviction that mothers provide what children really need while fathers provide a few extras has created a widespread perception of a father as the superfluous, or "disposable," parent—nice to have around, but no longer essential.[2]

But this perception is false. Numerous studies now confirm the importance of involved fatherhood to the welfare of children. When acknowledging the significance of fathers, we often overemphasize their economic contribution or their failure to pay child support, thus fueling the stereotype of fathers as principally financial, rather than emotional, providers. Certainly fathers greatly improve their children's economic situation, so that children fare better financially in a two-parent home. For example, among two-parent families with children, only 8 percent live in poverty, compared to 46 percent of families with children headed by single mothers.[3]

But we do fathers a huge disservice when we limit their value to the size of their wallet. It is wrong for our society to judge noncustodial fathers solely on whether they pay child support. Just because a man is not labeled a deadbeat dad doesn't mean he is an adequate father. Both absent fathers and fathers in the home can leave their children emotionally impoverished, whether or not they provide for their financial needs. A father's necessary contribution extends far beyond essential financial support to include a unique quality of love and influence. Whether living with their children in traditional nuclear families or living apart as noncustodial parents, fathers need to know they are enormously important to their children's welfare. In his provocative book *Fatherless America*, David Blankenhorn convincingly argues that fatherlessness is the most significant contributor to the decline in well-being among America's children.[4] A father's regular input and guidance significantly buffer a child from our worst social ills, including school dropout, teenage pregnancy, suicide, gangs, drug abuse, violence, and criminal activity.

Thus, fathers are much more than assistant mothers or an extra source of nurturing to augment a mother's love. Fathers parent differently and provide children with unique emotional, intellectual, and social stimulation that significantly enhances a child's outcome. Fathers even play with children differently than mothers, often in a more stimulating way that combines physical activity with teaching new skills and instilling competence.

While mothers generally represent the first continuous nurturing and sheltering presence in their child's life, the father usually is the first important figure in a baby's experience who regularly comes and goes. This coming and going, while the mother traditionally remains with the infant, serves as a child's first connection with the outside world. A father provides for his son an essential model for appropriate anger control. For his daughter, a father models how a man should treat her with respect and represents the first man whose approval she seeks. Typically, mothers are the principal caretakers of children's immediate physical and emotional needs, while fathers tend to focus more on preparing children for the future by building self-reliance and assertiveness. They promote independence and encourage healthy risk-taking and a sense of adventure. Mothers often hover over young charges, urging caution: "Watch out," "Be careful," "Don't get hurt." Fathers, on the other hand, tend to convey confidence in their children's ability to master the task at hand: "You've got it now," "One more time," "Hang on tight," "Don't give up."

Fathers parent differently and provide children with unique emotional, intellectual, and social stimulation that significantly enhances a child's outcome.

I recall our fearless middle daughter learning to swim at the age of four. As Tricie sailed down the water slide, her father, Larry, waited in the pool below, calling out encouragingly, "You can do it," while I stood by and shrieked, "Be careful!"

Another scene I witnessed recently reminds me how mothers and fathers parent in unique ways. I overheard the dialogue between a father and his young son as the two were leaving a medical office building, where the boy had just received several stitches for a cut forehead. The father, shepherding his son through this new experience, patiently and calmly explained why the stitches were necessary (to stop bleeding and reduce scarring) and praised his little boy for enduring the procedure. As I observed this interaction, I realized that I would have responded to my son much differently, based on my overriding need to protect and shelter him. Instead of providing such a rational explanation, I could imagine myself being frightened about my child's injury and admonishing him, "I told you not to climb so high on the jungle gym! That's why you fell and got hurt." Then, as consolation, I probably would have added, "Come on, we'll get some ice cream, and you'll feel better." Each of these differing parental responses communicates an important message about love, protection, problem-solving, and coping. When a child receives both kinds of messages from two loving parents, together they best prepare a youngster to interpret life's circumstances.

The High Calling of Fatherhood

When performed well, fathering not only enriches the lives of children and families, it is potentially the most rewarding, creative, and fulfilling endeavor of a man's life and the ultimate manifestation of masculinity.

A few years ago, I encountered a young father who was a fourth-year medical student approaching graduation. He and his classmates were present at an annual "Match Day" ceremony in which the students would learn where they would be completing their internship during the coming year. "Matching" with a coveted internship program is a highly competitive process. Students apply to numerous programs and rank them in order of preference. Likewise, the programs evaluate and rank their applicants. Students hope to match with one of their top choices. When this man's name was called, he approached the podium and made the surprising announcement that he had applied to only one internship program—the one in the same city where the mother of his little boy now resided with his son. This program, he had learned, didn't accept him, so he would not be doing an internship next year. He explained that it didn't make sense to devote himself to caring for other people's children if he couldn't be the kind of father he wanted to be to his own little boy. After putting his most important priority first and moving to be near his son, this man happily discovered things fell into place. Ironically, a residency position unexpectedly became available in the training program to which he had originally applied, and he was able to complete his pediatric training while remaining in proximity to his child.

> **When performed well, fathering not only enriches the lives of children and families, it is potentially the most rewarding, creative, and fulfilling endeavor of a man's life and the ultimate manifestation of masculinity.**

Solo Parenting

My arguments about the advantages to children of living in a two-parent family are not meant to disparage the nearly one-third of families today that are headed by a single parent. Acknowledging there is a two-parent advantage is not intended as an indictment of single parenthood. Many of these solo parents—women and men—do an absolutely heroic job of raising their children while shouldering enormous responsibility. While children with absent fathers are at greater risk for various social problems—from poverty to poor academic achievement—one must not conclude that the single-parent home is automatically a curse.

Yet the fact remains that single parents face daunting challenges; many children miss out on a parent's influence; and absent parents miss out on the joys of responsible parenthood.

Women who punish men by denying them access to their children are doing their youngsters a great disservice since children thrive best when they receive nurturing, guidance, and discipline from both parents. Whether just across town or out-of-state, noncustodial fathers still can cultivate a special relationship with their children. Involved fathers not only feel better about themselves and their masculinity, but they end up spending more time with their children and voluntarily paying more support.

All single parents can use practical help and emotional support from others, whether in the form of baby-sitting, car and home repairs, financial support, or friendship. If you are a single mother (or father), I commend you for the extra responsibility you carry on behalf of your child. I urge you to ask for the help you need and to arrange for periodic breaks from parenting. I also encourage single mothers to provide your children with positive and trustworthy male role models. Often, a grandfather or uncle can serve as a loving and effective father figure, along with teachers, pastors, and coaches. Unless your child's safety would be jeopardized by a relationship with his father, I urge you to go the extra mile in promoting a positive father-child bond.

Stepfathers

For many children, a stepfather serves as their father figure. A stepfather's commitment to a child is contingent upon the man's alliance with the youngster's mother. Often the stepfather is in the awkward situation of living with his wife and her children, while his own children live with their mother. His present wife may resent the financial support paid to his "other family," while his ex-wife and children may resent his commitment to his new family. There's no doubt that stepfathers

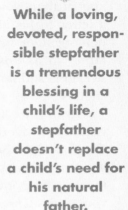

play a critical role in reducing "father hunger" and providing positive male role models for many children with absent fathers. The willingness to graciously love another person's child is a truly honorable commitment, and the stepparents who do this are to be commended.

While a loving, devoted, responsible stepfather is a tremendous blessing in a child's life, a stepfather doesn't replace a child's need for his natural father. Even if the stepfather is a splendid guy and a child's birth father has glaring faults, it doesn't mean a child won't long for his father's involvement in his life. This is not to diminish the very real contribution that a loving stepfather makes to a child's well-being. I only want to emphasize that a substitute father—no matter how wonderful and loving—cannot completely fill the void left by an absent father.

> While a loving, devoted, responsible stepfather is a tremendous blessing in a child's life, a stepfather doesn't replace a child's need for his natural father.

When a Child's Father Is Permanently Absent

If your child's father has died or is permanently absent or has severe emotional deficits that prevent him from showing love to your child, it is best to be honest about the facts. Let your child know that his father will not be returning. It is preferable for a youngster to grieve the loss of his father and get on with his life than to continue to hold out futile hope that an inaccessible parent will return or reform. Explain repeatedly that his father's absence or inability to express love for the child has nothing to do with your youngster's worthiness of love. Emphasize that many other people, including yourself, love the child and that he surely will establish many other loving relationships in the future. Give your child permission to grieve the loss of his father and express his legitimate sadness over not having two involved parents. At the same time, help your child appreciate that prolonged anger does no good and only makes him unhappier. Help him accept the situation instead of stewing about it.

If feasible, make a scrapbook commemorating what is known about your child's father. Let your child dictate or write a letter to his absent father expressing his sadness, disappointment, or anger. Always go out of your way to present his father in as positive a light as possible, emphasizing his strengths and downplaying his shortcomings. After all, your child is biologically related to him.

Do all you can to help your child cultivate meaningful relationships with other loving men in his environment. Be aware that a mother's boyfriend might develop a special relationship with her fatherless child. However, if the couple breaks up and the man drifts out of the child's life, this could accentuate a youngster's sense of father-loss. Children who experience such broken relationships understandably might become reluctant to risk forming another strong bond in the future.

Lopsided Two-Parent Families

Even in two-parent households, lopsided parenting teams are common, now that the dual-earner family has become a new norm. Despite all the rhetoric about changing sex role stereotypes, it is the mother who typically retains major responsibility for the daily welfare of children, while the father "helps" his partner with her awesome responsibility. In his practical and insightful book *Why Parents Disagree* (New York: William Morrow, 1994), Dr. Ron Taffel explains how this all-too-common family arrangement restricts the contribution of men in the child-rearing arena and leaves women feeling exhausted and resentful about their oppressive role overload.

Even in two-parent households, lopsided parenting teams are common, now that the dual-earner family has become a new norm.

This pattern of unequal participation gets perpetuated both by women's reluctance to relinquish their power as gatekeepers of family life and kinship work and by men's reluctance to take greater ownership for daily, seemingly mundane parenting chores. Women accept this imbalance that creates nearly intolerable role overload because it pays off in increased intimacy with our children. Meanwhile, men pay the personal price of feeling emotionally distanced and less involved in their children's lives.

> **A big difference exists between asking for help and sharing ownership for all that it takes to run a family.**

Enlightened mothers are willing to relinquish some family control in exchange for more shared responsibility by fathers. Because child care traditionally has been women's domain, we must resist the temptation to ask our partners to "help us" with "our" enormous responsibilities. Instead, we must invite men to take ownership for some aspects of parenting. A big difference exists between asking for help and sharing ownership for all that it takes to run a family. Only by redistributing child-care responsibilities does everyone benefit. Fathers win by becoming more connected to their children, and mothers win because their heavy burden is reduced. The simple secret is that more balanced participation results in more balanced rewards—for both parents and children.

How to Help Fathers Become More Involved Parents

Not only are fathers immeasurably important in their own right, but the growing number of employed mothers makes it mandatory that contemporary fathers more equitably share the daily responsibilities of caring for children. Yet few men have a realistic role model for how to be an involved father. Many children who live with their fathers feel emotionally distanced from them, instead of enjoying a warm and loving bond. A father's presence in the home does not guarantee an emotionally nurturing parent-child relationship. Such a bond results from a father's active participation in ordinary child-rearing duties. Special and intimate moments with children usually aren't scheduled events. Rather, such experiences emerge from sheer quantity of time spent together, often engaging in mundane daily activities like doing homework, enjoying a cozy bedtime story, or walking the dog together.

A woman should convey to her husband from the outset that she considers parenthood to be a joint endeavor and that she views his participation as critically important. The best way to begin promoting an enduring father-child relationship is to stop worrying about whether your child's father is "doing things right." Focus instead on whether he is "doing the right things." Men soon lose interest in assuming responsibility for children's care if mothers constantly look over their shoulder to see whether things are being done right or insist on "coming to the rescue." Encourage your child's father to share responsibility for routine duties, such as buying and wrapping a birthday present, preparing a meal together, taking a child to the doctor, or buying new shoes. The more fathers become intimately involved in the daily, seemingly mundane aspects of their children's lives, the more rewarding, creative, and fulfilling they find fathering to be.

> The best way to begin promoting an enduring father-child relationship is to stop worrying about whether your child's father is "doing things right."

Finally, I want to urge involved fathers to consider expanding your commitment beyond your own families to include those children in your sphere of influence who desperately need a father figure or admirable male role model. The magnitude of father hunger in our nation and the toll it is exacting on our children cries out for responsible fathers to help fill the void left by absent fathers. God can use your example of responsible fatherhood to motivate other dads to fulfill their duties to their families and to reap the rewards of involved parenthood. Many of you can become fathers to the fatherless by serving as caring stepfathers, coaches, Scout leaders, Sunday school teachers, mentors, and friends to children with father hunger.

Additional Strategies to Make Parenting Your High Priority

It's hard enough to be at peak performance as a parent when things are going relatively well in our lives. However, our parenting effectiveness diminishes whenever we become physically and emotionally depleted, whether due to marital discord, financial pressures, lack of self-care, or other stress factors. We can't make parenting the high priority it deserves to be when we are preoccupied with ongoing crises in our personal life. Keeping other aspects of your family life healthy will help assure that you have sufficient emotional reserves to parent well.

Strengthen Your Marriage

Parenting is easier and more effective when a couple has a strong marriage and a loving relationship. When our marriage is going great, we are healthier, happier, more energetic, and are more effective in nurturing our children. Since pain tends to create a wedge between partners instead of serving as glue, a strong marital relationship is necessary to help couples successfully weather the inevitable crises of parenthood. A successful marriage is the foundation of a strong parenting team.

Today in America, however, half of all marriages end in divorce. Because the median length of dissolved marriages is seven years, young children are often affected. Among couples who remain married, only half are truly happy, and divorce rates are 10 percent higher for remarriages than first marriages. The major problems in most divorces are not profound, intractable differences, such as physical abuse, drug or alcohol problems, or long-standing patterns of infidelity. The majority of divorces are due to poor communication, poor conflict-resolution skills, and the gradual loss of love and affection. Although romantic love is needed to get a relationship started, effective communication skills are needed to keep it going. In their encouraging guidebook on why couples succeed, *We Can Work It Out* (New York: Putnam, 1993), Dr. Clifford I. Notarius and Dr. Howard J. Markman explain that every relationship has an emotional bank account. Happy couples are those who have built up a healthy reserve of emotional goodwill upon which to draw. Both grand gestures and little acts of kindness toward your partner count as deposits in your relationship bank account, while huge grievances, as well as small irritations, will deplete your balance. Couples with strong relationships take care to keep a generous balance in their relationship bank account by promoting mutual goodwill and reducing the number of emotional barbs that erase multiple acts of kindness.

Most Americans believe that love is a feeling and that when "you've lost that loving feeling," the relationship is doomed. In truth, love is a choice you make—a commitment. When you choose to treat your spouse in a loving manner, you begin to feel more loving toward him or her. If you find that anger is deadening your relationship, I urge you to seek professional help for your marriage, just as you would seek expert help for a medical problem. Learn constructive ways to deal with conflict and practice these relationship skills. You will be surprised how even small changes in the way you interact with your partner can make a large, positive difference in your relationship. Meanwhile, choose to honor your spouse with your actions and words of affection, whether you feel like it or not, and refuse to deplete your relationship bank account by making nasty remarks, which prove to be very emotionally expensive.

Most couples spend more time maintaining a new car— with oil changes, tire rotations, tune-ups, and so on—than they spend maintaining their marriage—with date nights, compliments, meaningful communication, and worshipping and praying together. Couples who successfully nurture their marriage discover that our deepest needs are not satisfied by accomplishments. Instead, most of our joys in life come from our relationships—with God, spouse, children, extended family, and friends.

Live within Your Means

Few things put a greater damper on family life than chronic money worries. For all income groups, money—and its related issues of power and control—is the major source of marital conflict among American couples. The easy availability of credit and our national consumer mentality combine to seduce Americans into spending more than we earn. Learning to budget and use credit wisely is one of the most essential family-life skills. Unfortunately, sound money management is a skill that too many people learn the hard way, sometimes after spending years in the stifling vise grip of money woes. Living beyond our means is such a common condition that 800,000 Americans file for protection under the federal bankruptcy laws each year and millions more worry excessively about their financial situation. In addition to provoking marital conflict, financial concerns can leave well-meaning parents too preoccupied to nurture their children effectively. Children who overhear parental arguments about money and expressed fears about the family's financial security can become chronically anxious about adult problems beyond their control.

If you and your mate often argue about money, or if you must juggle creditors each pay period, and find you have nothing left at the end of the month, I urge you to meet with a credit counselor. Credit counseling can help you figure where your money has been going, create a realistic budget, trim your expenses, increase your spending power, make a debt reduction plan, and even save money for your family's dreams. Credit counselors can help you make a comprehensive assessment of your financial situation and develop an appropriate action plan.

You would be surprised how relatively small changes in spending patterns can significantly reduce your expenses. Credit counselors usually can make arrangements with your creditors to reduce your interest rate and develop a realistic payment schedule to eliminate your debt within five years.

Don't be ashamed or embarrassed about getting overextended financially. It's a common pitfall, and you are certainly not alone. The key is to get expert help as soon as you realize you have a problem and to change the way you manage your money. Hoping to win the lottery is not an adequate financial plan! Facing your problem and getting control of your personal finances can change your whole outlook and your family dynamics.

Downscale and Simplify Your Life

For much of my adult life, I have felt as if I had a ten-pound load in a five-pound sack. No matter how many ways I have tried to rearrange the contents, my sack of commitments has been overly full and has weighed me down. A woman I know recalled her mother's childhood advice to her: "Don't ask for a lighter pack. Ask for a stronger back." Yet the faster we race on the treadmill of life, the higher someone cranks the speed: "Every day do a little more than people expect, and soon they expect a little more."

The biblical story of Mary and Martha (Luke 10:38–42) serves as a powerful illustration of the unnecessary personal stress we create by trying to do too much. As Jesus traveled to Jerusalem, he stopped in Bethany to rest at the home of his friends, Mary and Martha. Martha, eager to lay out a great spread and showcase her hospitality, fussed and fretted with her elaborate preparations. Meanwhile, her sister, Mary, sat blissfully at the Lord's feet listening to his teaching. While Martha was distracted and troubled by her self-imposed serving agenda, a simple meal would have sufficed. In her overworked state, Martha became resentful and complained to

Jesus that Mary had left her to serve alone. Instead of defending Martha's flurry of activity, Jesus quietly explained that Mary had chosen what is better.

One day as I was contemplating my own role overload, I identified with Martha's predicament. I wanted to rail at God: "Lord, don't you care that I have too much to do?" Then I was struck by the insight that most of the responsibilities in my sack of commitments were not God-given assignments. Rather, they were self-imposed priorities I had accepted out of my mistaken belief that the more I do, the more I am. God hadn't given me more than I could handle. I had willingly taken on too much responsibility in pursuit of significance and out of my need for approval from others.

You, too, may be overscheduled, overstimulated, overworked, over budget, and just plain overwhelmed. Too many commitments, activities, decisions, expenses, and material possessions—too much stuff—can crowd out the simple joys of life, including the rewards of parenthood. If this is true for you, I invite you to downscale your materialism, your commitments, and the flurry of activity that obscures the "one thing that is needed."

As we increase our material possessions, we soon discover that the more we accumulate, the more anxiety we feel about protecting and maintaining our things. Not only do we need bigger safe-deposit boxes, more storage space, larger insurance policies, and more elaborate security systems to safeguard our possessions, but there are entire stores devoted to selling us even more items to help us organize all our stuff. Just as we pay a personal price to maintain our material things, we also expend time and physical and emotional energy protecting our titles,

Too many commitments, activities, decisions, expenses, and material possessions—too much stuff—can crowd out the simple joys of life, including the rewards of parenthood.

volunteer commitments, children's activities, elaborate traditions, and housekeeping standards. We literally give our lives away hour by hour and day by day to the priorities we fill in on our day planners.

Could you move closer to your work, live in a smaller house, get by with one vehicle, simplify your hair and wardrobe, or discontinue elaborate traditions that make holidays more a burden than a blessing? One way to simplify our lives is to keep both our material possessions and our activities in balance. Just as you give some of your clothing away as you acquire new outfits, consider not taking on any new commitments without relinquishing a current responsibility. Resist the temptation to inflict a pattern of frenetic activity on your children like a genetic disease. Ask yourself whether your child has enough unstructured free time to "just be a kid." To capture more quality family time, try turning off the TV and doing an activity together. Watching one less hour of television each day will save you the equivalent of nine work weeks annually. Imagine what you could harvest if that much time were devoted to strengthening your relationship with your child or your spouse, pursuing an educational or career goal, cultivating a hobby, or taking better care of yourself.

Celebrate Family Traditions

Familiar routines and family traditions provide children with a comforting sense of security and predictability. Daily routines, weekly activities, annual rituals, and special celebrations provide essential structure and reassurance that reduce childhood uncertainty and anxiety. Dependable routines simplify a young child's life, impart a sense of timing, and increase a youngster's confidence and perception of control.

Family traditions provide the social glue that bonds one generation to another, creating a sense of acceptance and belonging, family continuity, and cultural heritage. Familiar traditions generate many of the "anchor" memories in a family's history.

A decade-old tradition in our own family involved a multigenerational Thanksgiving family reunion which gave our children a strong family identity and connection to their past. Some of the most meaningful traditions for children involve regular routines like sharing the events of their day around the dinner table, being tucked into bed at night, reciting grace and eating together as a family, worshipping together, having Sunday dinner at Grandma's house, or singing the same old songs around a family campfire.

> *Just as Christians draw spiritual strength from the biblical stories that chronicle the "faith of our fathers," children draw inspiration and hopeful expectation from family stories of struggle and triumph.*

Sharing family stories about your childhood, your relatives, and ancestors from past generations can have a positive influence on children. Learning about another family member who overcame adversity, achieved a measure of success, served our country with distinction, or acted courageously in a crisis instills pride and confidence in children, who feel a biologic connection with their forebears. Just as Christians draw spiritual strength from the biblical stories that chronicle the "faith of our fathers," children draw inspiration and hopeful expectation from family stories of struggle and triumph.

Holiday celebrations, religious rituals, daily routines, family vacations, and even beloved pets become a key part of the cherished memories our kids carry from their childhood. Uniquely personalized family experiences communicate a powerful message of acceptance and belonging that reduces anxiety in young children and helps buffer older children from negative peer pressure and the allure of gangs.

Renew Your Energies

Being an effective parent involves nurturing our children from our own emotional overflow. Chronic sleep deprivation, isolation, and self-neglect can leave parents physically depleted and emotionally discouraged. Such "martyr parents" soon lose their efficiency and enthusiasm and become highly ineffective in their role. Trying to parent as a martyr only leaves us more drained and diminished, and it takes the fun out of parenting. As the adage goes, "If Momma ain't happy, ain't nobody happy." Don't let home be the place where you go when you are tired of taking care of others and being nice. Today, I recall with sadness how many times I arrived home "on empty" after a long, exhausting day of meeting other people's needs. Three-year-old Mark would greet me expectantly and—in his childlike attempt to assess my emotional availability to my own family— innocently ask, "Are you cwanky?"

To parent effectively, it's important to give yourself permission to periodically recharge your batteries by taking good care of yourself.

In contrast to parenting like a martyr, if we manage to get our own needs met through appropriate self-care, we are enabled to function as "altruist parents," rather than as martyrs. Nurturing from our own emotional abundance no longer depletes us. Instead, we discover that by taking better care of ourselves, we are energized and replenished in the process of giving to our children.

To parent effectively, it's important to give yourself permission to periodically recharge your batteries by taking good care of yourself. Regular Bible study and prayer, a little extra sleep, an afternoon alone, an evening with your spouse, regular exercise, the chance to pursue a hobby—doing something nice for yourself—isn't selfish. These self-renewal practices are essential in order to brighten your perspective, maintain your energy and effectiveness, and provide a healthy model of self-care for your children. Yet many parents have difficulty asking for what they need and accepting help from others. They can't accept the fact that to take better care of yourself, you have to be willing to "take."

To help meet some of your own needs for friendship and emotional support, personal growth, spiritual development, and creativity, I strongly urge you to seek out a group like MOPS (Mothers of Preschoolers) at a local church. At monthly MOPS meetings, you will be nurtured by Christian fellowship with other mothers of young children, enriched by opportunities for creative expression, and equipped for your parenting and family responsibilities with biblically based instruction. Your little ones will enjoy a loving, learning experience through their participation in the MOP-PETS program. Contact MOPS International (303-733-5353) to find out if there is a MOPS group near you or to learn how to start one in your community.

I once met a woman and her mother-in-law, who had become a second mom to her after her own mother's death. She explained that the older woman had lovingly counseled, encouraged, and helped her raise her children and preserve her marriage. "I never could have done it without her support," she insisted. Her mother-in-law just smiled and modestly acknowledged, "Everybody needs somebody to steady things up." *That's it,* I thought. A virtual parade of helpers crossed my memory, individuals who had steadied things up for Larry and me when we were overwhelmed with responsibility for five children. In fact, we hadn't done it alone. We were aided every step of the way by the experience and generosity of grandparents, aunts and uncles, baby-sitters, educators, mentors, coaches, pastors, Sunday school teachers, Scout leaders, soccer moms, neighbors, and friends. We had taken care of our children because we had taken care of ourselves and

> **Yet many parents have difficulty asking for what they need and accepting help from others. They can't accept the fact that, to take better care of yourself, you have to be willing to "take."**

accepted help from others—gifts of time, baby-sitting, material possessions, financial support, chauffeuring, counseling, mentoring, cooking, housecleaning, companionship, prayers, and love. We discovered that sometimes the ultimate form of giving is to be a gracious recipient of care from others. The apostle Paul reminds us that Jesus Christ is the source of the comfort that overflows from us to others when he writes, "We can comfort those in any trouble with the comfort we ourselves have received from God" (2 Cor. 1:4).

When God commanded, "Remember the Sabbath day by keeping it holy" (Exod. 20:8), he gave us the model of work followed by rest and recreation. God used the Sabbath to teach us that life is an alternating rhythm of serving and being filled. Even Jesus alternated between periods of intense activity and solitude and prayer. His example provides a model for acknowledging our human limits, our need for God, and our recognition that we are not in charge. By taking time for periodic rest and reflection, by renewing our sense of God's presence with us, we restore our energies, broaden our perspective, and become more effective parents to our children.

Being a parent is both an awesome responsibility and a sacred opportunity to become a cocreator with God in shaping the life of the child entrusted to our care. Parenting is not just an incidental role among many competing priorities but is the most important job we will ever do. Effective parenting involves identifying our governing values and then making daily choices that enable us to say yes to our highest priorities and fulfill God's will for our family life. Children thrive best when they are privileged to have two committed parents who jointly share the responsibilities and reap the rewards of child rearing. Yet the present crisis of father hunger in our nation leaves countless children vulnerable to a host of social ills. Committed men are needed to help fill the void left by absent fathers. Nurturing your marriage, living within your means, avoiding overcommitment, sharing family traditions, and practicing self-care are helpful ways to protect your emotional reserves and enable you to parent well. In the next chapter, you will learn the basics of early child development that will clarify your child's essential emotional needs and equip you to facilitate her optimal development.

Chapter 2

The Essentials of Early Child Development

Your child's preschool years are a remarkable period of rapid development and change, inspired by a sense of wonder. Not only does your child between two and five undergo highly visible physical changes and increasing motor skills, she also develops at an amazing rate mentally, socially, and emotionally. Among the most dramatic changes from infancy are her emerging independence and autonomy that will inevitably alter your parent-child relationship. In a few short years, she is transformed from a helpless, dependent newborn who views herself as part of her mother to an independent, self-aware, exuberant, talkative, social youngster who is capable of most aspects of self-care with minimal assistance.

Although children follow the same predictable sequence in their development, each child progresses at her own pace. Thus, no two children of the same age have identical skills and abilities. One may be more advanced in motor development, while another possesses greater language skills. Being knowledgeable about the progression of child development can prepare you for what to expect and equip you to facilitate your child through each stage.

A child's particular stage of development powerfully influences his behavior. Yet many parents have minimal knowledge about the stages of early childhood. In addition, just as they get comfortable with one stage, their child has morphed into another. All too often, this information gap contributes to two problems: unrealistic expectations about the abilities of young children, and the failure of parents to meet children's essential emotional needs. This chapter will summarize the basics of early child development from infancy through the years before a child starts first grade. In addition, it will help you provide experiences and interactions that can optimize your child's intellectual, emotional, and social development. Finally, it will set the stage for understanding much of the information presented in subsequent chapters dealing with the spiritual development of preschoolers, promotion of healthy self-esteem, discipline of young children, and common behaviors in early childhood.

> **Although children follow the same predictable sequence in their development, each child progresses at her own pace.**

Infancy

Each stage of a child's life has a set of developmental tasks that shape the child's self-perception. Babies come into the world dependent on their parents and other adult caregivers to meet their needs. Infancy is the period when a baby develops an orientation of either trust or mistrust toward the world that will powerfully impact his social and emotional well-being. A baby who concludes that the world is a safe and friendly place develops a positive orientation toward oneself and others. This critical sense of trust is engendered when a baby's adult caregivers provide the following essential components of infant care.

Attentive Care

The most important way to help an infant learn to trust is to meet the baby's needs in a consistent and loving way. The parent's regular attentiveness teaches an infant about his worth. On the other hand, when an infant's needs are not recognized or are neglected, the baby's world is unreliable and chaotic. He concludes that his needs are not important and that he can't get them met. The result is a negative self-concept, self-defeating behavior patterns, reduced quality of relationships, and negative feelings such as fear and insecurity.

The most important way to help an infant learn to trust is to meet the baby's needs in a consistent and loving way.

Warm, Loving Relationships

A baby has an essential need for a close relationship with her mother and a few other key adults. This strong love bond with parents is critical to develop the capacity to love others. When a mother strokes and smiles at her infant during feeding, a relationship is being forged, the quality of which has long-lasting implications. A baby draws conclusions about her worth from the way she perceives herself reflected in her mother's eyes. Your warm, tender, loving responses to your baby's cries tell her that you are glad she is here, that she is worthy and loved, and that her needs are legitimate and are going to be met. Simple things like talking to, singing to, or playing with your baby convey your high opinion of her. She feels delight in your enthusiastic approval when she smiles, rolls, sits, and crawls. Your demeanor, words, and actions tell her that you cherish her existence, that you are pleased with her gender, that you like to hold her, that she doesn't have to hurry to grow up, and that you will meet all her needs. This core message is the first step in building trust and instilling a sense of self-worth.

Touch

Of the five senses, touch is the most sensitive, and of all the baby's organs, the skin is the largest. Touch is a major way that parents get to know their new babies, and infants thrive best when parents use liberal quantities of touching, stroking, and massaging to convey their love and protection. The tactile system provides the earliest information about the world, and the bonding fostered by human touch is essential for social and emotional development. New babies can only be helped, not spoiled, by liberal amounts of carrying, cuddling, caressing, and rocking. In addition to providing ideal nutrition, breastfeeding offers plenty of skin-to-skin contact. Wearing your baby in a sling or carrier is another way to guarantee lots of physical intimacy.

Protection

The assurance of physical safety is basic to the healthy development of trust. A child needs to feel safe, protected, and free from fear of physical harm. In addition to securing your child's physical welfare, showing concern when he expresses fear will convince him that he can count on his parents: "The kitty's tongue licked you. I know it feels funny. He just wants to be friends."

Baby-proofing your house and putting away dangerous and breakable items gives your baby an environment where he is free to explore. Parents who refuse to create a safe, inviting environment and who insist that their baby must learn not to touch their things may unwittingly thwart their baby's natural drive to explore and may undermine the baby's confidence. An excessive number of "no-no's" will inhibit exploration and invite passivity.

Infancy Milestones

Babies quickly develop specific skills and control over their body (such as rolling, reaching, sitting, and crawling) and discover comforting behaviors (such as thumb sucking) that help them self-soothe. Late in the first year, most babies develop an attachment to a "security object," such as a blanket or stuffed animal, that provides comfort when the baby is anxious or separated from her mother. As babies learn to play with appropriate toys, they develop fine motor skills, learn eye-hand coordination, and gain increased competence. Games like pat-a-cake and bye-bye begin to teach a baby about reciprocal social skills. Playing peek-a-boo helps him remember that something out of sight still exists.

Toddlers and Twos

The chief developmental task of toddlerhood is establishing autonomy, or separateness, from the mother. Meeting a baby's dependency needs gives him confidence and freedom to try out his emerging independence as a toddler. After a full year of near total dependence on his parents, the toddler's increased mobility rapidly accelerates his independence.

The chief developmental task of toddlerhood is establishing autonomy, or separateness, from the mother.

Learning to walk unassisted expands dramatically a toddler's ability to explore his world and gives him a genuine sense of accomplishment. His new mobility brings a change in self-concept and requires him to balance two contrasting impulses: the urge for unrestricted exploration and the longing to feel safe in the presence of his parent. To support a toddler's emerging sense of self, parents need to recognize his competing drives—both to explore and remain close to Mom—and balance their dual parental urges to protect their child and simultaneously promote his budding independence.

A Secure Home Base

The drive to explore the world and learn new skills results from a basic feeling of trust and security. A child's curiosity cannot flourish if he is preoccupied with fear. In order to be free to pursue the allure of exploration and to gain a sense of competence, power, and independence, a toddler must have the enduring love, protection, and emotional security of a trusted adult.

Parents and caregivers of toddlers must be prepared to alternately offer "letting go" behaviors and "protective" behaviors, depending on the child's cues at the moment. Respecting a toddler's needs to alternately cling or roam—to seek reassuring proximity to you or the excitement of exploration, depending on the circumstances—is one way to honor his unique needs and provide an atmosphere conducive to learning. During this period of intense exploration, the protective parent represents a safe haven to which the child can retreat when tired, overwhelmed, or afraid. Typically, a toddler will wander away from his mother for brief moments, while taking frequent glances to reassure himself of her presence, then periodically return to show off something that interests him. After a toddler has been held on your lap during an airplane flight, for example, you can expect him to want to run around for a while once you disembark, before needing to touch base again.

The Drive for Independence

After establishing his separate identity, the young child proceeds to master his environment as he struggles to learn new tasks. A toddler takes enormous delight in his accomplishments and has an almost insatiable craving for recognition of his milestones: "Lookee me!" "Dood it myself!" As he succeeds in his new endeavors (feeding, using the potty, dressing, manipulating toys), his sense of competence is nurtured. His unlimited drive for learning is reflected in his boundless curiosity. We provide additional confidence boosters when we praise his new milestones, admire his creations, listen intently when he speaks, paraphrase what he has said, and answer his questions.

We nurture our toddler's increasing independence when we let him do things for himself, even if we can do them faster. Instead of taking over for him when he struggles with a task, we can offer patient help as he triumphantly completes it himself. Some days, however, being grown up may feel like too much pressure, causing him to regress temporarily. Respect this need and don't make him feel inadequate by insisting that he act like a "big boy."

> We nurture our toddler's increasing independence when we let him do things for himself, even if we can do them faster.

The Power of Language

At the same time the toddler is gaining independence through mobility, his expanding vocabulary and increased mastery of language give him the power to convey his wants and needs. Now, instead of crying or pointing, he can communicate his desires and convey information more effectively with two- and three-word phrases: "More juice." "Go outside." "Where's Daddy?" "All gone." "Dat's mine." "I go potty." Although his speech is still limited, a toddler understands much of what is said to him in clear, simple words. The two-year-old is more likely to talk with adults than with children, and most of his talk is self-initiated, rather than a response to your question.

Naming games are very important to toddlers who take great delight in creating meaning by the ability to name things. When giving toddlers names for body parts, be prepared to name the genitals. We should help young children feel comfortable with their whole bodies instead of implying that certain parts are unnamed, untouchable, or even "dirty."

The Importance of Play

Play is a powerful teaching tool for toddlers and provides a way for them to practice new skills in a controlled situation and to deal with developmental issues. Games like hide-and-seek, mutual chasing, and tag help toddlers gain mastery over their conflicting drives to explore and to remain close. For example, between twelve and eighteen months, a toddler loves to run off and have his parent chase after him. This taunting behavior that can be so frustrating for the parent has great significance for the toddler. Each time his mother catches up to him and picks him up, he gains the reassurance he craves that both independence and a close relationship can coexist. When a toddler stacks a tower of blocks and then deliberately makes them fall, he is using such play to gain a sense of control over his own tumbles that accompany his increasing mobility.

Self-Awareness

Between eighteen and twenty-four months, toddlers become more self-aware. They take an interest in their own appearance and have opinions about what to wear. They also develop a strong identity as a boy or girl. Toddlers begin using pronouns, especially "I" and "me," and are quick to assert their possessiveness: "Mine!" Don't scold your child for his inability to share graciously at this young age. Instead, temporarily put his favorite toys aside if another toddler is coming over, and be prepared to distract a playmate who takes something of his. A toddler's increased self-awareness involves learning to describe what he is feeling, including happy, sad, mad, tired, or hungry. You can help your child develop emotional awareness and feel valued by reflecting and validating his feelings: "You're upset because Jevon has to go now. You wish he could stay longer."

The toddler's emerging sense of identity and confidence is strongly influenced by his perceptions of his body. Between two and three years, as children gain increased bowel and bladder control, they become more aware of their genitals and take pride in their body. They love to run naked and are fascinated with their body's products, including urine, feces, nostril contents, and gas. Parental rejection over genital touching not only can erode a child's self-image, it can have a negative impact on the child's future ability to derive pleasure from his body. Again, a balance is required in the parental response—celebrating your child's increased body awareness while teaching about private versus public behavior. (See discussion of masturbation in chapter 7.)

Negativism

Typically between eighteen months and three years of age, toddlers will respond negatively to many requests and act stubborn, giving rise to the unfortunate label Terrible Twos. This temporary phase is normal and necessary to help a child begin to establish her own identity and decide what she does and doesn't like. Saying no to parental requests and choices helps the toddler feel more in control in a world orchestrated by adults. After all, consider how often your toddler hears you tell her no in response to her behavior, "No, you can't touch that!" Don't be surprised if she says no to something she really wants just to feel more powerful. Parents should not take this negativism too seriously or overreact. Try to ignore most of your child's no's or view them as, "Do I really have to?" Instead of asking a question that can be answered no, such as, "Do you want to put your jacket on now?" phrase your request in a way that lets her emphasize her preferences: "Do you want to wear your jacket or your sweatshirt?" "Shall I read *Harold's Purple Crayon* or *Mama, Do You Love Me?*" Building simple choices like these into your child's daily routine is an effective way to support her desire for independence.

Saying no to parental requests and choices helps the toddler feel more in control in a world orchestrated by adults.

Frustration

Toddlers have high expectations of their abilities and want to do things for themselves instead of depending on adults.

When their abilities disappoint them, they are easily frustrated. Lacking the verbal skills to express their stress, they may experience an emotional meltdown for seemingly trivial reasons. A tantrum is a primitive form of communication used by young children who have not yet acquired the language skills to talk about their frustrations. Tantrums typically occur when a toddler is frustrated by his inability to do something—when he can't manipulate a toy as desired, when his parents can't understand his speech, or when they refuse to grant his requests. Toddlers are more likely to react to frustration by having a tantrum when they are tired, hungry, excited, or bored. Tantrums also can be triggered when a toddler has to stop an enjoyable activity, like playing at the park, without being given ample warning.

During this vulnerable time, your child needs your support and encouragement, not your disapproval. You can hold your child lovingly, or if he objects to being physically restrained, simply remain nearby quietly or talk in a soothing manner. The tantrum is an outward manifestation of his internal conflict between wanting to be independent and wanting to depend on you. Your presence and calm response will be much more helpful to your child than your anger or emotional withdrawal. Give him words to express what has frustrated him and what he is feeling. Don't give in to your child's demands or you will reinforce the tantrum behavior. Treat your child as usual afterward and give him a hug to convey your love. With a parent's support, toddlers eventually can learn to handle hard feelings without losing control. (See the discussion on tantrums in chapter 5.)

A toddler cries easily when she falls down, gets picked on, or can't manipulate a toy the way she wants. It's important not to call her a crybaby or demean her by trivializing her very real frustration. Instead, say something like "Let's see what happens if we try it this way." And don't jump in too quickly to rescue her from common frustrating situations. Although your actions may restore calm for the moment, your little one may conclude that she is helpless and needs you to intervene whenever things get challenging. Instead, show her how to assert herself and ask for what she needs without crying: "Why don't you tell Missy to share the crayons with you? I'll stay right here in case you need me." If you want to learn more about the rapidly changing emotions of toddlers, their drive for independence, and their need for a secure base, I highly recommend Dr. Alicia Lieberman's interesting, useful, and elegantly written guide *The Emotional Life of the Toddler* (New York: The Free Press, 1993).

The Preschool Years

While trust is the foundation of babyhood, and independence and autonomy define toddlerhood, the preschool years are characterized by interdependence and mastery. After establishing a separate identity, the three-year-old proceeds to gain mastery over his environment and struggles to learn new tasks and feel capable. The rapid increase in awareness and abilities (speaking, reasoning, dressing, feeding, using the toilet) between three and six years generates new demands and responsibilities. Now better able to control their bodies and their physical environment and to express their ideas, preschoolers are eager to learn and work cooperatively to reach their goals. Their enhanced sense of power, however, is coupled with the recognition that they cannot always do what they want, making it necessary to develop self-control and responsibility so as not to feel guilty.

While trust is the foundation of babyhood, and independence and autonomy define toddlerhood, the preschool years are characterized by interdependence and mastery.

Preschoolers are highly social. They seek friends as they move from parallel play and associative play to enjoy cooperative or interactive play, imagination, and role-playing. Their creative

> **Increased predictability in a child's daily activities results in better compliance, less frustration, and the sense of belonging that children crave.**

play, art, and the use of make-believe represent their daily work, as they practice adult roles, master language and motor skills, and learn to relate to others, to share, and to empathize.

Preschoolers benefit from predictable daily routines. When meals, naps, and playtime are structured around established routines, children learn what to expect and what is expected of them. Increased predictability in a child's daily activities results in better compliance, less frustration, and the sense of belonging that children crave. Thus, structure and routine become the framework around which the young child organizes his learning and his life.

Three-Year-Olds

Three-year-olds are delightful children—generally cooperative, eager to please, and motivated to master what is required of them. They love receiving recognition for their achievements. Threes are learning to separate from the adults in their lives, and many are ready for a preschool experience. While physical and motor development slow down in comparison with infancy, three-year-olds experience a spurt of intellectual, social, and emotional growth. In their eagerness to act more grown-up, they imitate our behavior (sometimes to our embarrassment!).

Social and Emotional Characteristics

One of the most dramatic areas of development evident in the three-year-old is her obvious pleasure interacting with other children. Her rapidly expanding verbal skills and increased emotional awareness help prepare her for learning to take turns, share, make friends, and play cooperatively. Threes are interested in their own and other families and love playing with and imitating adults, including roles such as firefighter, police officer, and cowboy. They are becoming aware of their feelings, their needs and wants, and their body parts. Imaginary companions are common, along with fears of the dark, animals, clowns, and other costumed characters. Threes have trouble distinguishing fantasy from reality and may innocently stretch the truth and "tell stories." They may still need the security of a transitional object, such as a treasured blanket, or a habit to relieve tension, like thumb sucking, to help them reduce anxiety in unfamiliar surroundings. Threes are eager to help out at home and at preschool, and their slow, inexpert "help" contributes to their feelings of worth and importance.

Language

Language skills continue to be acquired at a rapid pace and include communications with other children, as well as with adults. Stuttering may appear and should be ignored (see chapter 7). While mispronunciations are common, the majority of the child's speech should be understandable. Threes are learning to control their tantrum impulses by using words to express hard feelings. With their expanded vocabulary, three-year-olds can tell a story about their artwork and enjoy simple songs and rhymes. They love to learn new words, and favorites are "surprise" and "secret." Many parents allow threes to overhear inappropriate conversations and television programming, forgetting that they can understand many more words than they can speak. Threes are learning about writing, can scribble, and may be able to write the first letter of their name. They can speak to a group of their peers and listen to a simple story.

Self-Care

Three-year-olds are eager to master various aspects of self-care to demonstrate their independence. Children this age can feed themselves efficiently. Most are toilet-trained and are genuinely disappointed about "accidents." Bedwetting is still common, however. Threes may still need help with wiping themselves and reminders about hand-washing. A child's foot-stool at the sink will promote the practice by allowing a young-ster to reach the faucet. A three-year-old can dress herself in simple clothing, with minimal assistance. She can manage shoes with Velcro flaps, unbutton easy buttons, and unzip a zipper.

Gross Motor Skills

A three-year-old walks more gracefully than a toddler and loves to run, jump, climb, and participate in movement activi-ties with other children, such as passing a beanbag or rolling and bouncing a ball. Threes also enjoy performing silly motions that make them laugh. Children usually learn to pedal a tricy-cle at three and love to ride wheeled toys. A typical three-year-old can walk up stairs alternating her feet but may still come down one step at a time, placing the same foot first. She enjoys kicking and playing with a ball but has trouble catching it.

Fine Motor Skills

Three-year-olds make rapid progress manipulating objects with their hands. They can learn to cut, although imprecisely, with scissors and are able to draw a circle. Threes enjoy shap-ing play dough and clay, making puzzles, using fat crayons and markers, stringing beads, building with large blocks or Legos, and fitting together other toys that allow them to practice their fine motor skills. A three-year-old can copy a circle and imi-tate a cross.

Intellectual Abilities

Three-year-olds are learning about colors and shapes, and about identifying things that are alike and dissimilar. They love sorting objects by size, shape, color, and category. They are interested in the world and nature, including animals, plants, and the weather. They can count by rote from one to ten. Threes are learning about spatial relations and can follow one-step directions ("Put the book on the table"). A three-year-old has acquired enough confidence about how things should be that she readily finds humor in the ridiculous. She enjoys funny faces, clowning movements, and the silly use of language, and can go from the brink of tears to laughter if encouraged to see the humor in a stressful predicament.

Four-Year-Olds

Four-year-olds are boisterous and exuberant, testing the energy level of their parents and other adults who care for them. They are curious and imaginative, endlessly asking "Why?" Fours are beginning to display initiative, for example taking responsibility for putting toys away. They enjoy fantasy, like believing in Santa Claus and the Easter Bunny, and they often have an imaginary friend. They are gaining more self-control and are able to plan ahead, for example in play activities ("I'm going to make a house and a fence around it"). They are in love with life and all its excitement, as their thoughts run from scary monsters to silly riddles.

Four-year-olds are boisterous and exuberant, testing the energy level of their parents and other adults who care for them.

Social and Emotional Characteristics

Four-year-olds are highly social beings who love playing with their peers, especially same-sex playmates. They are now better able to work and play cooperatively, take turns, express empathy, and help others. Fours are beginning to grasp the concept of fairness and the reason behind a rule. They can identify and boldly express their likes and dislikes, and their emotions often run to extremes. They are interested in family roles, gender differences, and physical attributes. Fours readily identify with superheroes as a way of coping with their own fears and sense of vulnerability. Aggressive language and, to a lesser degree, aggressive behavior may be observed. Fours love dramatic, or pretend, play, where they create settings and take on imaginative roles. This type of fantasy play allows young children to rehearse for later life roles and to practice getting along with others.

Language

Four-year-olds still are rapidly expanding their vocabulary and use of language. They enjoy the power of words, modulating their voice, or experimenting with swear words, bathroom language, wild boasting, silly word use, giggles, and bossiness. They are more comfortable using words to talk about hard feelings and to solve their social problems ("It's supposed to be my turn now"). Fours can converse easily and love to tell a story as well as hear one. They can follow a plot and draw a picture to illustrate a story. They enjoy singing songs and being part of a discussion.

Self-Care

A four-year-old can handle all aspects of using the bathroom, including washing afterward. Bathrooms and bathroom language fascinate him, and he is naturally curious about physical differences between the sexes. A four-year-old usually can button and unbutton, zip, and lace—but not tie—his shoes. He loves to do things for himself, like comb his hair, pour his own milk, and brush his teeth (although he will need your supervision with brushing for several more years). Fours love to help out and feel important by being useful and having a daily chore.

Gross Motor Skills

A four-year-old is a bundle of energy and requires ample opportunity to play outdoors. She is more coordinated than at three, and enjoys running, jumping, climbing, galloping, whirling, and dancing. Her motor skills are more refined, and she can skip, hop, balance on one foot briefly, and pump a swing. She can use her hands more than her arms in catching a small ball.

Fine Motor Skills

Fours are more dexterous and can manipulate small objects with better control. A four-year-old can cut on a line with scissors and is more skilled in handling crayons, markers, and brushes. Fours can copy a square and a cross and draw a recognizable stick person. They display greater dexterity in stringing beads, matching shapes, making puzzles, and building with blocks and Legos. They enjoy drawing and coloring and love to finger-paint.

Intellectual Abilities

Fours are learning more about sorting by color, size, and category. They have an understanding of yesterday and tomorrow and the sequence of events, distinguishing what comes before and after. Although they can grasp the concept of cause and effect ("If I pour milk too fast, it might spill"), much of their thinking remains "magical." For example, they may conclude that their baby brother got sick as a result of their bad thoughts about him. They are now more interested in trying to make letters and numbers, and some fours can print their name. Many can count by rote to twenty.

Five-Year-Olds

Five-year-olds are more restrained, pleasant, self-controlled, and focused. They are delightfully positive, compliant, and eager to please. Fives are more cooperative, social, and comfortable within boundaries. The five-year-old is a good judge of his abilities and is generally satisfied with himself. He is proud of his vast knowledge and can come across as a know-it-all. Fives are able to play more organized games and in larger groups. Rules of the game are important to him. Friendships are even more important to the

Five-year-olds are more restrained, pleasant, self-controlled, and focused. They are delightfully positive, compliant, and eager to please.

five-year-old, and he makes a cooperative playmate. From a parent's perspective, five is usually a golden age, although sometimes, around five-and-a-half, children may become more demanding and volatile.

Social and Emotional Characteristics

Five-year-olds usually love their mother more than anyone and want to be in her presence and please her. They are eager to help and able to take responsibility for simple chores at home and at school. They are better at cooperating, settling differences, expressing their emotions, controlling their impulses, and displaying empathy for others. Fives are refining their unique self-concept, while embracing a strong sense of family. They usually are kind to and protective of younger siblings. Dramatic play with props, playing house, dolls, and building elaborate constructions are favorite pastimes. Television is very popular with five-year-olds and should be monitored by parents and limited to two hours of educational programming daily.

Language

The five-year-old's language skills are well developed, and he may seem to talk constantly. Fives enjoy books more than younger preschoolers and have personal favorite authors and subjects. They often know the letters of the alphabet, can spell their own name, and like to spell out signs. They can tell a story and anticipate what follows. Fives can wait to speak in a class setting until they are called upon.

Self-Care

Fives can dress with minimal assistance, including fastening buttons and zipping, but still may not be able to tie shoelaces. Many fives dawdle, however, and need reminders about dressing themselves. Most take full responsibility for using the toilet and washing their hands. A five-year-old can use a dinner knife for spreading but still needs help with cutting.

Gross Motor Skills

Five-year-olds love all kinds of gross motor play, especially riding a tricycle, a bike with training wheels, and wheeled riding toys. They love to swing, climb, jump, and skip. The five-year-old has improved motor skills reflected in better kicking, catching, and throwing. Fives enjoy group games with rules.

Fine Motor Skills

By five, left- or right-handedness has been established. Fives can cut on a line with scissors and manipulate smaller crayons, markers, and puzzle pieces. They are more skillful at coloring within outlines, can draw a circle, square, and triangle, as well as a representational person. They can build more elaborate constructions with blocks and Legos, including planning their project.

Intellectual Abilities

Most five-year-olds can count by rote to thirty or higher, write some numbers, and appreciate concepts like greater than and less than. The five-year-old takes pride in his work and is proud of his intellectual abilities. He enjoys practicing writing his name, spelling words, or printing numbers. He may be able to identify word signs and recognize his own name. Fives have a more developed sense of time and know when daily events take place in relation to one another. They know the days of the week, are learning calendar concepts, and are interested in the clock but still cannot tell time. Fives love to learn about science and how the world works.

For parents who want to read more about early child development, I recommend Karen Miller's superb guide, *Ages and Stages* (Telshare, 10th printing, 1999). Additional helpful resources include sequential guides to understanding children of different ages, written by Dr. Louise Bates Ames and Dr. Frances L. Ilg. The Gesell Institute of Human Development publishes this series of books for parents.

How to Enhance Your Child's Learning During Preschool Years

Recent media coverage has highlighted the critical importance of early childhood experiences on a youngster's brain development, personality, and emotions.[1] We now appreciate that long-term patterns of behavior, learning, and problem-solving typically are established in early childhood. Previously, we thought a baby's brain was a blank slate at birth, waiting to be filled with information, and that her potential for development was mainly shaped by genetics. Instead, the evidence shows that a child's total environment—including the interaction between parent and child—combines with genetics to influence early brain development. Although learning begins at birth and continues throughout life, the brain undergoes its most rapid development during the first three years or so, when patterns of interacting with the world are established. Nerve connections that relate to specific skills, such as language, are being made or lost during critical early periods. Your efforts to promote your child's early brain development are guaranteed to pay off later in terms of her social, academic, and emotional well-being.

> A child can learn only so much at a given age and level of development, since basic skills are necessary before new abilities can be acquired.

The essential requirements for young children to thrive include the need to:

- feel special and irreplaceable;
- feel protected and secure;
- have a sense of predictability and routine;
- explore their environment safely;
- know the rules and limits on their behavior; and
- have access to a variety of stimulating toys and educational opportunities.

Of course, each child is a unique individual whose development is never identical to that of other children. A child can learn only so much at a given age and level of development, since basic skills are necessary before new abilities can be acquired. Overstimulating your child will not promote more rapid brain development; it will only frustrate both of you. Although much of the emphasis on early brain development has focused on the first three years, please remember that learning is a lifelong process, and brain development does not stop after age three. Fortunately, it is never too late to provide positive learning opportunities for your child.

Brain Circuitry

New brain-imaging technologies, such as Positron Emission Tomography (PET) scans, have allowed medical scientists to map the growth of the human brain. A baby's brain at birth weighs about 25 percent of its approximate adult weight and has about 100 billion brain cells.[2] However, these cells are not yet connected, or "wired," in a way that allows thinking and learning to take place. After birth, extraordinary numbers of brain connections (known as brain circuitry) are formed in response to your child's interactions with you and his world. By the time your child is two years old, he will have about 1,000 trillion connections—many more than adults. Brain cells, known as neurons, send out signals in the form of electrical impulses and receive input from other brain cells. Learning happens when a particular experience activates certain nerve cells and changes the pattern of brain connections, or synapses. Repeated use strengthens some connections, while others that go unused are eventually lost. Thus, practice and repetition shapes the structure of the brain.

The synapses, or brain connections, that affect the way we function are continually being made, refined, and reorganized. Although the vast majority of synapses are formed during the first three years of life when a child's every waking moment involves new experiences, the formation of neuronal connections continues at a slower rate until about the age of ten.

Thereafter, synapses that are not used are pared down, a process known as pruning. A child's early experiences powerfully impact the structure of his brain by influencing which synapses will survive and which will be eliminated. Brain circuitry that is used repeatedly becomes permanent, while connections that go unused are lost, or pruned. The resulting architecture of the brain creates patterns of thinking that not only influence a child's intellectual development but also determine the way he interprets social situations and handles his emotions.

Windows of Opportunity

Critical periods in the development of a child's brain are like windows of opportunity that are opened briefly to allow maximal development of certain skills. Although learning continues lifelong, there are "prime times" for learning—especially in the first three years or so—during which the brain is most effective in processing certain types of experiences. Once a "window of opportunity" has passed, the potential for that particular area of development will be restricted compared to what it might have been.[3] For example, we know that visual and language areas of the brain develop maximally early in life. This knowledge has changed the way medical professionals treat children born with impaired vision or hearing. Delayed detection of hearing loss in an infant can result in permanent impairment of language development in the child. Similarly, the failure to recognize and correct visual problems during the early years of life can interfere with the development of normal visual pathways in the brain and lead to permanent loss of vision in the weak or unused eye. Thus, the child's brain has critical periods of development that represent "use it or lose it" opportunities. While these windows of opportunity aren't necessarily slammed shut at a certain point in time, they are partially closed.

Early experiences are so influential to guiding the growth and architecture of the brain because they tell the brain which connections between neurons to form and keep. Remember only the brain connections that are frequently activated are retained, while those that are not activated are eventually pruned. The resulting brain circuitry determines how we think, feel, relate, and behave. Structural and chemical nerve connections that relate to specific skills, such as language and math and logic, are ready to be either strengthened or lost, based on positive or negative experiences in the child's life. For example, talking to and reading to your child daily promotes further mastery of language skills, while young children who receive little language stimulation will have subsequent trouble acquiring these skills.

The Adverse Effects of Early Stress

Responding to your child in a consistent loving way actually affects the biological systems that help your child later handle his emotions and cope with stress. Early learning opportunities provided in a nurturing environment result in more complex brain function in later childhood. On the other hand, early stress, such as inconsistent care, exposure to violence, or lack of stimulation, can change brain chemistry in a way that negatively impacts brain functioning.

Children who are neglected and not stimulated properly have brains that are smaller than normal for their age and are developmentally delayed. Traumatic events, such as chronic neglect and physical and emotional abuse, increase the production of a hormone in the brain called cortisol. This hormone can cause destruction of brain cells and reduction in synapse formation that alters brain function. The result can be impaired brain development that is significant and long-lasting. Indeed, children

> Early stress, such as inconsistent care, exposure to violence, or lack of stimulation, can change brain chemistry in a way that negatively impacts brain functioning.

with chronically high levels of cortisol as a result of stress have more cognitive, motor, and social delays than other children. Chronic stress can also alter the balance of other hormones in the brain, including serotonin (which aids in the management of emotions) and noradrenaline (which regulates responses to fear and anger). This can result in behavioral, emotional, and cognitive problems. For example, a chronically stressed child may function in a persistent state of fear and hypervigilance that causes the child to act more aggressively. Fortunately, quality child-care programs that provide consistent, nurturing relationships and individualized, attentive care can help overcome deficits in the home environment, thus mitigating some of the effects of stress.

What Parents Can Do

One of the most critical ways the brain is influenced early in life is through the quality of our relationship with our baby and young child. Learning takes place in the context of relationships—with parents and other key caregivers, like child-care workers. Providing loving, consistent care strengthens the brain connections that help a youngster handle emotions, adapt to stress, and control impulses. The most important way to program your child's brain for optimal functioning is to provide a loving, stable, emotionally supportive, and predictable environment.

The more stimulating your child's environment during the early years, the more connections are formed in her brain, and the effects are long-lasting. However, you don't need a lot of expensive toys or formal classes to promote your child's learning. Simply talking and singing to your baby during routine daily care stimulates language development, as does lively face-to-face conversation involving reciprocal verbal exchanges. Use your child's name and modulate your voice as you tell her what is going on around you. Respond to her movements and facial expressions. Learn to be sensitive to her moods, laughing with her when she is happy and attempting to soothe her when she is upset. Studies have shown that toddlers whose mothers talk to them more have larger vocabularies than babies of less talkative mothers.

Watching television or hearing a video of different foreign languages does not stimulate language in the same way ordinary conversation does, because babies need human interaction to attach meaning to words. In fact, television is not recommended for children under two years, and those over two should watch no more than one to two hours of educational programming daily. If you speak a second language, don't hesitate to use it with your child. You'll discover how easily she can learn both. Children exposed to different languages early in life are able to learn them more readily than children who don't study a foreign language until middle or junior high school.

The most important way to program your child's brain for optimal functioning is to provide a loving, stable, emotionally supportive, and predictable environment.

In addition to daily conversations with your child, reading to her—beginning in early infancy—helps stimulate optimal language development. Daily reading to your child demonstrates the importance of communication and encourages her to become a lifelong reader. The closeness fostered by reading together will spur discussions about a book's message and strengthen your relationship. Other daily activities that promote early learning include simple things like playtime with stimulating toys and playmates; dancing; listening to music; drawing pictures; playing games together; taking a nature walk; and being free to explore in a safe environment. Children who are helped to have enriching early experiences are being groomed for later academic success, healthy emotional adjustment, and greater responsibility and impulse control. *Opening Your Child's Nine Learning Windows,* by educator Cheri Fuller (Zondervan,

1999), offers powerful insights into how children learn and suggests practical brain-building activities to maximize your child's learning potential.

The first step in optimizing your child's intellectual, social, and emotional development is resolving to make parenting a high priority. The importance of strengthening your parenting commitment and your parenting team are covered in chapter 1. Strategies for beginning in the early years to teach children about God and spirituality are discussed in chapter 3. Giving your child plenty of love and focused attention and promoting positive communication between parent and child lay the foundation for learning. Strategies for providing a healthy, safe, emotionally stable, and loving home are presented in chapter 4. Setting appropriate limits and enforcing them consistently, thoroughly addressed in chapter 5, helps provide essential structure and order in your child's life that promotes problem-solving and self-responsibility.

Daily reading to your child demonstrates the importance of communication and encourages her to become a lifelong reader.

Brain development continues to occur whether you are present or absent from your child. Therefore, you will need to assure that the other key caretakers who impact your child's development will provide not only a safe environment but also high-quality learning experiences and affectionate interactions. Recommendations for choosing quality child care that will enhance your child's brain development are covered in chapter 6.

As a parent, you will powerfully influence your child's intellectual, emotional, and spiritual development, but this heavy responsibility need not be the source of undue anxiety. An understanding of the basic emotional needs and developmental abilities of young children, combined with a warm and enduring parent-child bond, will equip you to provide the quality experiences that will positively shape your child's mind.

Chapter 3

The Spiritual Essentials: Passing On Your Faith

Within the pages of this book, you will find many practical parenting lessons and advice to help you bring out the best in your child. Yet I would be remiss if I did not share my deep conviction that the greatest parenting lesson of all is the essential need to nurture our child's precious inner spirituality. In addition to promoting our child's intellectual, physical, and emotional development, we are called to nurture the budding spirituality evident in young children and help them begin a lifelong faith journey. For me, this means helping children ultimately come to a saving knowledge of God through Jesus Christ.

Yet so much of our energy as parents is channeled into providing material things for our children and giving them educational opportunities and enrichment experiences, such as music lessons and participation in athletics. These worldly priorities pale, however, when compared with the importance of introducing our children to an eternal relationship with the living God, who gives meaning to every experience and hope in every circumstance. As the Scripture cautions, "What good is it for a man to gain the whole world, and yet lose or forfeit his very self?" (Luke 9:25). Fortunately, our responsibility to teach our children about spiritual matters is made easier because young children, with their unbridled imagination and magical sense of wonder, have an innate desire to know God and draw close to him.

As I recall my childhood, I am deeply indebted to my parents for their consistent model of faith and trust in God and their diligent efforts to pass their Christian beliefs to their five children. Among my most treasured childhood memories are bedtime prayers with my mother, mealtime blessings led by my father, regular church worship and attendance at Sunday school, singing in the children's choir, helping with vacation Bible school, and attending youth fellowship and church camp as a teen. Because my father was a career naval officer, our family had to move every few years. Through all the transitions and upheavals, plus the ordinary trials and traumas of growing up, God's steadfast presence in my life was a constant anchor, a moral compass, and a wellspring of strength and endurance. Naturally, when I became a parent myself, I wanted to give my children all the things I valued most in life. At the top of my list was the priceless gift of God's redemptive love through Jesus Christ.

> Fortunately, our responsibility to teach our children about spiritual matters is made easier because young children, with their unbridled imagination and magical sense of wonder, have an innate desire to know God and draw close to him.

The birth of a child always renews the mystery of creation. Parents who are firm in their faith, as well as those who may have strayed from their beliefs, often find that the awesome miracle of new life and the daunting responsibilities of parenthood motivate them to turn to God to reinforce their human inadequacies.

My first baby was born when I was barely twenty and was living in Hawaii, five thousand miles from my own parents. My sailor husband, Larry, had returned only days earlier from a six-month tour of duty aboard a navy destroyer in the West Pacific during the Vietnam War. I was a premedical student in the middle of my final semester of college, and I was carrying an extremely heavy course load, including three lab sciences. I had just received notice that I had been accepted into medical school and would begin my medical studies in the fall—provided I could finish the present semester and attend summer school in order to complete the requirements to graduate early.

Our newborn son, Peter, developed severe jaundice and required an exchange transfusion at age three and a half days. I was consumed with fear that he would die from the procedure or had already suffered brain damage as a result of his high bilirubin level. The stress Larry and I felt was further compounded by financial constraints that left us minimally prepared for our baby's care. We actually stopped at Sears on the way home from the hospital to pick up the crib we had put on layaway! Isolated and overwhelmed—with both responsibility and joy—I can't imagine taking the plunge into parenthood without the reassuring safety net of God's love, example, guidance, comfort, and strength. I am convinced there was only one set of footprints in the sand during my journey into parenthood, and my feet have scarcely touched the ground ever since!

Why Parents Should Nurture Their Child's Spirituality

Faith traditions are only one generation from extinction unless we pass them on to our children. Thus, it's been aptly said, "God has no grandchildren, only children."

Children represent our future church members and the church leaders of tomorrow. In addition to maintaining the continuity of our sacred Christian heritage, passing on our spiritual beliefs offers our children many concrete benefits that enhance their daily lives. Furthermore, most parents discover that cultivating their child's natural interest in God stimulates their own spiritual awakening and greatly enriches their parenting experience. Certainly my lifelong Christian faith has been deepened in the process of fostering the spiritual journeys of my five children and through the opportunity of being a Sunday school teacher for other youngsters.

Belief in Something Larger Than Oneself

Both children and adults are reassured by the idea of a creator God who oversees everything and has a master plan for our lives. While preschoolers cannot grasp the mysteries of a divine plan, they can understand that just as parents are the authority figures in their family, God is in charge of the whole world. As children get older, they derive great comfort from their belief that an all-powerful, all-good, and all-loving God is the one who oversees the entire universe.

As children grow up and struggle to make sense of a complex and confusing world, and when they experience disappointments or personal setbacks, we can remind them that our lives are like a giant jigsaw puzzle, of which we see only a tiny fragment. God, however, sees the whole picture, and he knows how today's events will ultimately fit into the greater story. Thus, believing in God puts our lives in perspective by offering answers to tough questions like where we came from, why we are here, and where we are going. God, who is everlasting to everlasting, represents a constant factor amid the turmoil of our lives and helps us understand our central purpose or mission. Faith in God is the ultimate source of strength and direction in this life and the source of hope for the life to come.

Unconditional Love

Among all the attempts to explain God, I believe the most simple and accurate is "God is love." I view God's unconditional love for mankind as our perfect model for parental love. Of course, a parent's love will always be flawed and imperfect, despite our best efforts. In raising my children, I took great consolation in knowing that God's love could cover my shortcomings. In God, my children would have a perfect spiritual parent, one whose incomprehensible love would never let them down. While I can't be with my children in all situations and forever, God's love is everywhere at all times. Even if our children someday stray from their relationship with God, I know his grace is so unlimited that he keeps reaching out to them in love. Not only does God promise to accept them with open arms upon their return, as Jesus made clear in the parable of the prodigal son (Luke 15:11–32), but he unfailingly pursues them and calls them into a restored relationship, as Jesus revealed in the parables of the lost sheep (Luke 15:4–7) and the lost coin (Luke 15:8–10). This unfathomable seeking love of God is even more incomprehensible than God's willingness to forgive us when we come crawling back to him in humility.

Convincing each of my five children that they are uniquely loved and cherished was one of my greatest parenting challenges, for which I turned to God's model in the personal nature of our relationship with Jesus Christ. God created each person for a one-of-a-kind, special relationship with himself. All children experience doubts about whether they are loveable and loved, especially those with physical challenges, absent fathers, or other vulnerabilities. And all children wonder whether they are valued as much as another child or valued uniquely for who they are. The psalmist proclaims the uniqueness of each person in God's eyes: "For you created my inmost being; you knit me together in my mother's womb. I praise you because I am fearfully and wonderfully made" (Ps. 139:13–14). A child experiences unconditional love in the affirmation "I am a child of God, made in his image, for a special purpose." The words in children's worship songs effectively reinforce the message of God's unconditional love. When children sing, "Jesus loves the little children, all the children of the world," they learn about the dependability of God's universal love.

Moral Development

Faith in God is a positive moral force in the social development of children. When our example falls short of the ideal, God's perfect standards provide children with an immutable moral code. The life and teachings of Jesus Christ provide a timeless set of values, morality, sense of integrity, and a meaningful way to live. The Bible is God's instruction book for our lives, containing moral absolutes and unchanging principles of right and wrong in a world of situational ethics. The Ten Commandments provide guidelines for living in right relationship with God and with one's fellow human beings. The Ten Commandments help children learn that things are considered wrong when they are disobedient to God or hurtful to others (or oneself). Although the historical setting has changed since the Bible was written, the core values and issues facing people have not changed, making the principles taught in the Bible highly relevant to our times.

Children can be taught that God gave us rules about right and wrong to make our lives better and that we should always try to do the right thing. You can use the Golden Rule to explain that we should treat others the way we ourselves would like to be treated. This behavior is a much higher standard than simply avoiding doing to others that which we would find despicable ourselves.

Preschoolers have a limited ability to reason and do not yet understand concepts of morality and the Christian faith. They consider actions to be right or wrong based on their anticipated punishment or reward by the significant people in their lives. Young children discover that some behaviors and attitudes win the approval of the adults they love and trust, while others are deemed unacceptable. As their reasoning matures, children learn to discern right from wrong and to choose to do the right thing. A Christian man I know teaches his children to do "what you ought to do, not what you want to do, whether you feel like it or not, and even when no one is watching."

Children can be taught that God sees and knows their actions and the attitudes of their heart and that he wants to help them make good choices and to learn from their mistakes. However, it is important not to create an image of God as spying to catch people doing something wrong or as punishing people for wrongdoing. Such messages about God's retribution can contribute to a negative image of God and make a child afraid to get close to him.

Comfort in Times of Stress

On countless occasions, I have observed the way spiritual beliefs offer comforting security in a world that often doesn't make sense to children. When life brings inevitable trials, sorrows, and heartache, the belief that God is intimately involved in our lives and cares deeply about our personal pain represents an enormous source of comfort, hope, and healing. Faith can help children see that pain and disappointment can work toward good, for example, by teaching us to be more patient, more compassionate toward others, and more appreciative of the blessings we enjoy.

> When life brings inevitable trials, sorrows, and heartache, the belief that God is intimately involved in our lives and cares deeply about our personal pain represents an enormous source of comfort, hope, and healing.

When our children were in their teens, my mother suffered a life-threatening aortic aneurysm. We collectively drew strength from our faith in God to help us endure a seemingly desperate situation. Miraculously, my mother survived another six years, which we came to view as God's gift of "golden time." During her final years, our anxieties about my mother's mortality only served to heighten our joys over the love we shared and the deepening relationship my children enjoyed with their grandmother. While my mother ultimately died of her illness, both she and we received the gift of learning to daily trust in God's care and love: "Because of the LORD's great love we are not consumed, for his compassions never fail. They are new every morning" (Lam. 3:22–23). As children get older and experience various losses, their belief in God can help them recognize the vast goodness in the world, convince them of God's involvement in their daily lives, offer hope in the face of death, and hold the promise that something good can come out of every adversity. Every family has many examples to show children that eventually "all things work together for good to them that love God" (Rom. 8:28 KJV).

Tradition and Community

Faith traditions and a community of believers provide parents and children with a church family that creates a sense of community and belonging. New parents are bolstered when an infant dedication or baptism is performed in the presence of a supportive community of believers who embrace the child and promise to share responsibility for her spiritual development. In a loving faith community, children benefit from the example and encouragement of others and by being accountable to a wide group of believers. Church is one place where children get exposed to people of all ages who learn together, worship together, and support one another. A church home can provide a family with surrogate grandparents, aunts, uncles, and other extended family members when the actual extended family is absent. Our investment in the church family returns dividends in the form of grandmotherly laps, grandfatherly advice, lessons in sewing or baking, parenting help, baby-sitting, assistance with a move, and shoulders to lean on or cry on. When I was a teenager, a married couple I deeply admired served as my Sunday school teachers. For over three decades, I have maintained contact with these wonderful mentors and role models, who have had a lifelong positive influence on me.

When to Begin a Child's Spiritual Development

Too many parents abdicate responsibility for teaching their children about spirituality, explaining that they want their children to choose their own religious beliefs once they are old enough. However, we don't allow our children to decide for themselves whether they will bathe, brush their teeth, eat a healthy diet, or go to school. Instead, we make value judgments about what is in our children's best interests and begin early in life to reinforce those positive values. For example, we want our children to know their close relatives, but we don't wait until they are old enough to ask about their grandparents before we introduce them to Grandma and Grandpa. Rather, we eagerly place a newborn in his grandfather's arms, even though the infant is not yet old enough to comprehend who his grandfather is. Similarly, if we value the spiritual development of our child, we should begin to foster our child's relationship with God at the earliest opportunity. Whether establishing healthy habits or ingraining faith creeds, children's early experiences profoundly shape their lives.

If we value the spiritual development of our child, we should begin to foster our child's relationship with God at the earliest opportunity.

Even if you are not affiliated with a church, you can teach your children to trust and love God. It's important that you share your beliefs with your child and help shape his perceptions of God. Children inevitably hear about God in the media, in music, in the pledge of allegiance, on our coins and currency, at other children's homes, and in phrases like "an act of God," referring to natural disasters. Many children hear the name of God spoken only in anger as an expletive. If people they trust don't tell them about God, young children will use these indirect references to formulate their own perceptions of God, which are likely to be negative. Start by sharing what you have concluded about your religious beliefs, rather than dwelling on your unanswered questions. If you and your partner differ in your beliefs, emphasize what you agree on—such as that there is one God who is good and all around us and who is involved in our lives and who has prepared an afterlife for us—rather than your differences. All believers struggle with some areas of unbelief, and I urge you to search for the truth by visiting local churches and by reading and studying the Bible. I assure you there is nothing so exhilarating as learning about God and his salvation plan for humanity.

How to Go About Instilling Spiritual Faith

Many parents who want their children to learn about God feel inadequately prepared to answer their questions. You may be unsure of your own beliefs or ambivalent about your spiritual upbringing. Many parents expect that the pastor, priest, or Sunday school teachers will instruct their children about spiritual matters for an hour or two each week. But just as we are the most influential teachers, models, counselors, and guides for our children in other life arenas, we are their most important source of spiritual direction. No one has more consistent contact with your child than you do, no one knows your child as well or better appreciates his or her uniqueness, and no one is more motivated to give your child the very best.

Spiritual beliefs are transmitted most effectively as a routine part of daily life.

Spiritual beliefs are transmitted most effectively as a routine part of daily life. That's why it's said that faith creeds are "caught more than they are taught." The following strategies will help equip you to teach young children about God and to develop a positive relationship with him. If you want to read more about the spiritual development of children and how to instill spiritual values and beliefs, visit your local Christian bookstore. I specifically recommend two helpful books: *Talking to Your Child about God* by David

Heller (New York: Perigee, 1994) and *Talking to Your Children about God* by Rick Osborne (New York: HarperSanFrancisco, 1998). I also recommend an excellent videotape, *Tell Me about God* (Brewster, Mass.: Paraclete Press, 1998).

Laying the Foundation

Contrary to popular belief, spiritual education can begin in the cradle. Developing an attitude of trust in God actually begins when a baby learns to trust in the dependability of his parents' care and love. Young children form their idea about the goodness and comfort of God from the model of their own mother and father, who are God-like to them. The trust that a child develops in the unconditional love and acceptance of his parents and other caretakers forms the basis for faith and trust in God when he is older. It is the most important foundation for learning about faith, hope, and love.

Parental Model

Whether you realize it or not, your child will first view God through your own example. As a young child's world expands, she eventually will transfer the all-powerful trait that characterizes adult caretakers to the word God. Older preschoolers have discovered that their parents aren't perfect and that other adult authority figures can also be depended upon. With this foundation, they eventually learn to put their faith in the perfect caretaker, God.

Your child also looks to your example as the model for her relationship with God. Talk to your children about your own beliefs and the ways you see God working in your life. As your children get older, don't be afraid to share your doubts as well. As you prepare to attend church, mention how you are looking forward to learning more about God and how this will help you. If you and your partner differ in the way you practice your faith, you should explain this to your child without being judgmental. Model the importance in your own life of an intimate relationship with God through daily devotions and prayer, regular worship, Bible study, and demonstrated compassion for others. Your children will take their cues from you about whether God is loving, forgiving, distant, involved, punishing, harsh, or compassionate.

An Atmosphere of Open Communication

Most children will ask questions of a spiritual nature starting in the preschool years. Your response should provide direction and guidance without being authoritarian or dogmatic. Don't be afraid to admit that you don't have all the answers. What's most important is being sensitive and emotionally available. Be careful not to criticize your child's ideas about religion, even if they are inaccurate. For example, your child might try to incorporate Santa Claus into the Christmas story or connect the Easter Bunny with the cross. Instead, gently correct any misunderstandings as you help your child learn the biblical origins of Christian holidays.

Image of God

Few things are as important to a child's spiritual development as her image of God. In addition to its profound religious significance, a child's notions of God have psychological relevance and are connected to her self-esteem and deepest aspirations. It is important that parents and Sunday school teachers help formulate for young children an intentional positive image of God—loving, caring, trustworthy, forgiving, and desiring intimacy with each of us. With young children, these messages are not communicated by teaching factual information. Rather, the essence of a loving God is conveyed through a ministry of presence and through "attitude education" that influences a child's behavior and feelings. A child's concept of God largely is conveyed through quality interactions with adults who mirror God's love and care to them. Thus, caring parents and Sunday school teachers can help young children learn to associate God's name with love and trustworthiness.

Young children still see God as a person like their mother and father, only more powerful—the ultimate adult authority. Despite a child's inability to understand God in the abstract, she can still experience a sense of God in feelings of awe and wonder over his creation and begin to use his name. Don't be surprised if your preschooler's image of God is a blend of media superheroes, your own clergy, and biblical characters. Periodically ask your child what God is like and try to discover the origin of her ideas. When asking your child about God, distinguish what she considers God's physical traits from God's personal qualities and attributes. Help her refine her image of God as she gets older.

> **A child's concept of God largely is conveyed through quality interactions with adults who mirror God's love and care to them.**

Parents have a powerful influence on the image of God their children will embrace. Many children view God as a father figure—protective, strong, and the ultimate authority. Others hold a more maternal image of God as nurturing, comforting, loving, and taking care of the world. Some see God as a benevolent grandparent—older, more powerful than their parents, and semiretired somewhere in heaven. Sadly, many children view God as an absent father—remote, distant, off in the sky, and not really interested in their lives. Often children form a mixed image of an unpredictable God who is good in some ways but who is out to get them for their sins. Other childlike images of God range from a jolly Santa-figure to a celestial killjoy, always watching to see whether a child is naughty or nice. When children form an early negative image of God, it is unlikely they will want to have a close relationship with him. I must strongly emphasize that negative concepts have no place in the religious education of young children.

> **When children form an early negative image of God, it is unlikely they will want to have a close relationship with him.**

Instead, young children can be helped to form an image of God as good and loving, trustworthy and faithful, creative and powerful, wise and understanding, righteous and moral. Children can be taught that God created people because he wants to have a personal relationship with each of us and to be intimately involved in our lives. Even preschoolers can understand basic concepts such as: "God loves me." "God made everything." "God takes care of me." "God is always with me." "God wants to help me." "God gave me a family." "I am part of God's family." "I can talk to God."

Jesus

While young children cannot grasp the concept of the Trinity or understand the meaning of "Jesus died for me," they can understand that "God sent Jesus" and "Jesus loves me." When older preschoolers learn that God sent Jesus, they can begin to appreciate that God has a special plan for the world and for them. In understanding how Jesus deeply cares for people, older preschoolers begin to love him and to want to do things to show their love toward others. Preschool children first learn about following the example of Christ when they follow the model of the loved and respected adults in their lives. As young children recognize that God and Jesus help people, they, too, can learn to accept responsibility for helping others in their own transforming way.

Prayer

Just as dialogue is the foundation for our friendships and family relationships, prayer is a powerful way to strengthen our relationship with God. For preschool children, prayer means communicating with God and recognizing his presence. When young children are being introduced to God, every effort should be made to promote a positive attitude about God. With this in mind, when we help preschoolers learn to pray, we should teach them how to praise, adore, and thank God in their prayers. If egocentric young children are taught to petition God for specific requests on their own behalf or others, they expect to get what they ask for. When an all-pow-erful God doesn't always grant their requests, a preschooler may start to con-clude that God is mean-spirited, rather than loving. For this reason, it is preferable to have young children avoid making specific prayer requests and focus on helping a child talk comfortably with God.

> **Teach your child that she can talk to God in normal conversation, in any setting, and during any activity.**

Many young children are first intro-duced to talking with God in prayer through the routine of saying a blessing before meals or reciting children's prayers as part of a bedtime routine. Saying grace at meals teaches children to acknowledge God as the creator of the plants and animals that provide our food and as the source of our daily provisions. Bedtime prayers help children establish a routine of communicating with God by praising him and giving thanks for the day's blessings. If you decide to have your child learn to recite memorized prayers, break the prayer into short phrases and make sure your child understands the meaning of words like "forgive us our trespasses" or "thy kingdom come." Your local Christian bookstore will have an excellent selection of helpful books and resources for use with preschool children.

Take care not to stifle your child's desire to pray by insist-ing that she sit perfectly still with hands clasped and by using solemn tones and formal language. Teach your child that she can talk to God in normal conversation, in any setting, and during any activity. Help her understand that nothing about our lives is too insignificant to bring to God in prayer. When teaching children about prayer, I like to use the image of having a direct telephone line to God. With our direct line, God always answers on the first ring and is eager to talk with us about anything. We will never hear a busy signal, get cut off, be placed on hold, or be interrupted by call waiting.

While memorized blessings said before meals and bedtime prayers offer comforting familiarity, even more effective than reciting a prayer by rote that can become a singsong jingle is to say brief "anytime prayers" throughout the day. Anytime prayers serve as a constant reminder that we are as close to God as a whispered word or silent thought. You can gaze at the miracle of a multicolored arc in the sky and say, "Thank you, God, for rainbows." Or event prayers can be spoken before or after a fun outing, "Thank you, God, for the good time we had at the swimming pool." Such simple prayers can help children learn to view God as the creator and source of all of life's joys.

> **Thanking God for even small things helps us remember that all things are under his control and that all blessings come from him.**

As you teach your child to pray, keep prayers short and have them reflect what is going on in your child's life—what happened that day, the remembrance of a loved one who has died, upcoming special events, the sharing of emotions, and concern for friends and relatives. Help your child understand that God is big enough to care about both the great and small concerns of the whole world and that he is interested in all the events in your child's life. Thanking God for even small things helps us remember that all things are under his control and that all blessings come from him.

To help children appreciate that prayer is a dialogue, remind them that praying involves not only talking to God but also listening for God's response and feeling his presence. Explain that God uses our prayer silence to talk to us by giving us thoughts and ideas. You might begin family meals or end bedtime prayers with a full minute of silence and teach your child to pay attention to the ways God speaks to her heart during quiet times.

You can begin praying with your children by saying prayers with them, helping them recite short prayers, involving them in deciding what to pray for, and eventually helping them form their own prayers. Preschoolers can begin to repeat prayers after us, and some will be able to offer brief prayer thoughts of their own. Later, your child can participate in "ping-pong" prayers, in which we alternate with our child in offering a prayer sentence. Eventually, children can create their own prayers while we listen, and ultimately, they will offer private prayers on their own.

Connect God to Daily Life and Nature

Try to make God relevant to your child's daily life. When a child sees God's hand in his everyday existence, God becomes meaningful and available to him. You can begin early to connect the concept of God to your child's ordinary life by helping him see how God is involved in his daily activities. During an outing at the zoo, you can say, "God made all the animals." You can prepare a special treat for your child and mention that God created everything we need and enjoy. When you tuck him in at night, remind your child that God watches over us when we play and sleep.

The beginning of faith in the Creator comes from genuine appreciation of nature—plants, animals, rocks, and rivers. Children can be helped to know about the attributes of God through the investigation and exploration of the wonders of the natural world and the appreciation of aesthetic beauty in nature. Teaching children to be good stewards of our planet is an important way to convey respect and obedience toward God.

Young children learn about God not by learning facts but by direct encounters with the environment, by touching, hearing, seeing, smelling, and tasting. You can acknowledge God's amazing design of creation whenever you and your child enjoy rain puddles, kittens, butterflies, flowers, snowflakes, and sunshine. A young child must manipulate and experience in order to learn, and joyful learning about the known lays the foundation for wanting to pursue the unknown. Because God does not have a tangible appearance, we must show our children indirect evidence of his existence. You can explain that although we can't see the wind, we can feel it on our face, hear it howling, and watch it rustle leaves or pull a kite skyward. Or you can consider God's unlimited power when gazing up at the vastness of the universe at night.

When a child sees God's hand in his everyday existence, God becomes meaningful and available to him.

Another building block of faith comes from having trust in routines and experiencing the security of God's orderliness in nature: the sun comes up each morning, and spring follows winter. Learning about daytime and nighttime, planting and growing, seasons and cycles teaches children about the orderliness and predictability of God's world and can help them begin to trust in the assurances of God.

Church Worship

Church experiences provide opportunities for children to come into contact with men and women who model the love of God and reflect Christ's character. Church is one of the few places in a community where people of all ages gather together, thus providing children a unique intergenerational opportunity. Although young children do not have the intellectual capacity to understand the central concepts of the Christian faith, they can begin to participate in its rituals. Remember that faith in the predictability of events helps little children learn to trust in God. Children naturally enjoy the predictability and familiarity of the rituals associated with worship services. Children love to imitate adults and have a strong social need to be part of what the important adults in their lives consider valuable. Young children do not understand what is said in a worship service, but they acquire attitudes by experiencing and participating in the actions of worship and ritual ceremony amid a community of faith.

Children naturally enjoy the predictability and familiarity of the rituals associated with worship services.

Preschoolers learn best when they use all their senses, and you might be surprised how a worship service incorporates different senses. Children see symbols of our faith in the cross, the altar, stained glass windows, robes, and processionals. They hear organ music, hymns, anthems, recitations, and periods of silence. They experience the welcoming touches of greeters, the handshake of the pastor, and their parents' embrace when they are cuddled on a lap. They smell floral arrangements, taste the sacramental elements, alternately stand and sit, and help pass the offering plate.

Worship services allow children to feel part of the church family and to come into contact with other caring adults who reflect God's love. It is important for preschoolers to meet and get to know the pastor. Since many young children will initially think of the church pastor as being God, or at least God-like, their relationship with God will be strengthened by having a warm, positive relationship with the pastor. Even when children attend Sunday school during the worship service, many churches welcome young children for the first ten or fifteen minutes of the service before departing for their own class. This allows the children to be present for the call to worship, the singing of a hymn, and the telling of a children's sermon.

It's a good idea to choose a church in your neighborhood, and one that has families with children the same ages as yours. This will increase the chances that your child will find friends who share similar values and beliefs.

Sunday School

In addition to traditional worship services, attending Sunday school with their peers provides an excellent opportunity for young children to learn about God through exposure to loving teachers, Bible characters and stories, Bible verses, and simple songs about Bible friends and God. A positive Sunday school experience provides quality adult relationships, an age-appropriate learning environment, structure and predictability, creative activities, and the opportunity for a child to use all her senses in the educational process. Caring teachers, who become a living commentary on the Scriptures, help young children learn to associate God's name with love and trust. When a child's Sunday school experience is enjoyable, she is more likely to remember what she has learned and to develop a positive attitude about church and the Christian life.

Caring teachers, who become a living commentary on the Scriptures, help young children learn to associate God's name with love and trust.

Help your children look forward to Sunday morning worship and Sunday school, and make the experience pleasant by not rushing to be on time and, when appropriate, by going out for a meal or snack afterward. When our children were young, we would stop at a bakery on the way to church and go out for a family brunch after worship and Sunday school. You can use this time together to talk about what your child did in class and what she learned. You can create positive attitudes about church functions by participating in fun, church-sponsored family activities, such as parties, plays, music performances, picnics, suppers, or summer camps.

Music and Singing

The use of music and singing about doctrinal concepts ("Jesus loves me, this I know, for the Bible tells me so") is a highly effective way to impress theological messages on a young child's heart. In fact, I suspect adults get more theology from the hymns they sing than the sermons they hear! Children's praise songs and choruses, with their accompanying body motions and helpful repetition ("I've got the joy, joy, joy, joy, down in my heart. Where? Down in my heart. Where? Down in my heart.") effectively teach children by the simplicity of their message and their total body involvement. Because music is so pleasurable and fun, children easily learn and remember what they sing.

Bible Stories

Children as young as two can learn to recognize the Bible and to revere it. Let them know it is called the Holy Bible. They can appreciate that the Bible has a special place in your home and, in many churches, a special lectern in the sanctuary. While young children cannot read from the Bible, they can appreciate it as a symbol of God. Give your child pictorial books of Bible stories for their very own. When you tell a Bible story to young children, it is appropriate to personalize it and "filter" out information they have no ability to understand, while still conveying the lesson of God's love and care. Of course, you will want to choose happy, joyful stories as children are learning about God and omit those with frightening aspects.

> **While young children cannot read from the Bible, they can appreciate it as a symbol of God.**

My grown children fondly remember hearing their first Bible stories from a much-loved children's Bible we still have in our home. Eventually they progressed through a series of Bibles, each geared to their comprehension and reading level. Show your child how important the Bible is by giving him his very own Bible. When children get old enough to read, you can let them help select their own Bible. Choose a modern language translation and an appropriate reading level and appealing artwork. You can augment Bible reading with other educational tools, including entertaining and informative videotapes of animated Bible stories, puzzles, coloring books, and children's songs. You may want to rent a movie, such as *The Ten Commandments* or *Exodus,* to watch with your older children or read them stories with religious themes, like C. S. Lewis' *Chronicles of Narnia.* Helping children to memorize and understand key Bible verses can be a valuable exercise.

Your own attitude about the Bible will strongly influence your children's eventual Bible-study habits. If your dust-covered Bible sits undisturbed on the bookshelf, your children are unlikely to use their own. On the other hand, if your children see you daily referring to your Bible and using it as a practical guidebook for life, chances are that they, too, will value it as God's book of wisdom and make a regular habit of studying its truths.

Reflecting God's Love to Others

An important aspect of spiritual faith is the belief that just as God loves and cares about us, we are to extend care and kindness to others. Remember that positive self-regard is the foundation for joyful service to others. You can explain to your child that God uses those who love him and know him to share his love with other people. When we are generous, compassionate, and kind toward others, it is God's love in us that overflows to them. As our actions reflect God's love, we become partners in God's divine plan.

Because children learn about compassion and empathy best by practicing it, you can arrange opportunities for them to assist those who are less fortunate, such as donating used clothes or toys, helping an elderly neighbor, volunteering at a nursing home or homeless shelter, or befriending a lonely child. One way I have tried to model my commitment to reflect God's love to others is by volunteering as a Sunday school teacher for much of my adult life.

How to Answer Difficult Questions Children Ask

Why Does God Let Bad Things Happen?

One of the most difficult questions facing children, parents, and philosophers is the problem of pain in people's lives. Eventually children will want to know why a good God allows bad things to happen. Your own response to adversity will dramatically shape your child's reaction. Show your child that while you can't change what has happened, God supplies the comfort and strength to enable you to cope with life's difficulties. You can help your child understand that life has many pleasures and blessings that we enjoy, as well as some sadness and

Emphasize that God shares our concerns, feels our pain, and comforts us in all our sorrows.

heartaches. Explain that bad things don't mean that God is punishing us or doesn't care about us, nor that he can't stop bad things from happening. Choose your words of comfort carefully. Well-intentioned comments like "God needed Grandpa with him in heaven" can leave young children confused about why a good God would deliberately let a loved one die. Instead, emphasize that God shares our concerns, feels our pain, and comforts us in all our sorrows.

Why Doesn't God Answer All My Prayers?

This is a difficult concept for young children, making it preferable to have preschoolers say prayers to praise and thank God. As children get older and offer prayer requests, including petitions for themselves and intercessory prayers on behalf of others, they will want to know why a loving God doesn't answer every prayer request. Teach children that God does indeed hear and answer every prayer. His answer to our prayer requests can be either "yes," "no," or "wait." As children get older, we can offer examples in which a "no" answer that was disappointing at the time turned out to be for the best in the

> **Reassure children that God takes good care of everything he creates and that his care continues after we die and leave this world.**

long run. For example, a child who prays that his family won't have to move to another city because of his father's promotion may feel disappointed when his request isn't granted. Months later, the same child can be helped to appreciate that the move brought many blessings, including new friends, closer proximity to his grandparents, and a yard that made it possible to have a puppy. God sees the big picture of our lives, while our own perspective is very limited.

What Happens After People Die?

Children can be taught that people go to be with God after they die. Explain that while we don't know exactly what heaven is like, we can be certain that we will continue to be in the loving care and protection of God. Reassure children that God takes good care of everything he creates and that his care continues after we die and leave this world. Explain that people who die also live on in our hearts and our memories. Because our loved ones touch our lives so deeply, their positive influence also lives on in us and is reflected in the way we love and the way we live. Help children accept death as a natural part of life by showing them that leaves fall from trees, flowers die, goldfish die, and eventually people die. (Young children should be reassured that Mommy and Daddy won't die for a very long time.)

Is There Only One Right Religion?

Help your child understand that there are many differing views about religion and that it is important to respect the beliefs of others. Explain your reasons for believing as you do, without putting down other faith traditions. Make sure your young child doesn't think that different religious groups compete with each other like sports teams to determine a winner. As children get older, you can help them explore the beliefs of their friends and to identify differences and common beliefs among various faiths. Explain that you read and study the Bible because you believe it holds the answers to what is true and right.

Does God Get Mad When I Do Bad Things?

Teach your child that God wants to help us learn what is right and to make good choices each day. Explain that although it makes God sad when we do wrong things, God is always ready to forgive us, not to criticize, judge, or punish us. You can teach your child the meaning of repentance—to admit our mistakes, to feel sorry for them, to ask for God's forgiveness, to make amends, and then to choose to do the right thing next time. Your own model of forgiveness is important in convincing your child about the forgiving nature of God. Help your child see God as his advocate who wants to guide him in making good choices, rather than viewing God as a wrathful judge out to punish him for his sins. The closer your child's relationship with God, the more he will want to obey God's moral laws.

Help your child see God as his advocate who wants to guide him in making good choices, rather than viewing God as a wrathful judge out to punish him for his sins.

Our Greatest Calling

Our goal in nurturing our children's spiritual life is not to have them parrot our particular faith creed. Rather, it is to help them embark on a lifelong pursuit of a meaningful relationship with the living God and to feel his intimate involvement in their daily lives. No material gift you offer, no educational opportunity you provide, no experiences you make possible for your child will ever be as significant as facilitating her lifelong personal relationship with God through Jesus Christ. My passionate desire is

Mistakes to Avoid in Teaching Young Children about Faith

Pushing too hard. A harsh approach to religious instruction can backfire, producing negative feelings about spirituality and creating an image of a critical, harsh God. Instead of promoting a child's spiritual growth, excessive parental rigidity about religion can cause a child to reject your beliefs. As your child gets older and expresses doubt or skepticism, make an effort to remain noncritical and accepting.

Misinterpretation. Because young children are preliterate, have a limited vocabulary, and think concretely, they are prone to misinterpret what they hear and recite about God. Such misinterpretations range from humorous ("Our Father who art in heaven, how did you know my name?") to anxiety-provoking ("Now I lay me down to sleep . . . If I should die before I wake") to theologically unsound ("Spirit of God" is imagined as God the friendly ghost). The intertwining of the Christmas story with Santa Claus leads some children to conclude that God lives at the North Pole. To minimize such misinterpretations, use simple language, define terms for your child when she is old enough to understand them, and routinely ask your child to explain concepts in her own words.

Difficult emotions. Certain negative emotions, such as fear, guilt, and anger, can stunt a child's faith development. For example, a child who has been taught that God is a harsh judge who punishes us for our sins may be reluctant to get very close to him. Or an emphasis on sins or mandatory religious rituals can produce excessive guilt that interferes with a child's authentic response to God. I can't overemphasize that negative concepts about God have no place in the religious education of young children. Parents who harbor angry feelings toward God for allowing something tragic to happen need to be careful not to portray to their child an image of God as an insensitive, punitive ruler. Similarly, you should not overreact if your child ever expresses angry feelings about God. Instead, explain that God understands and accepts our hard feelings. Help your child vent his emotions and reassure him that God loves him even when he is upset.

for each child to experience the comforting assurance that he or she is created and uniquely loved by God for a special purpose and is eternally under his care and protection.

The Essential Ingredients of Healthy Self-Esteem

What Is Self-Esteem?

Among the most daunting responsibilities of parenthood is the need to give our children a strong sense of self-worth. The measure of a child's composite inner picture of his worth and value is considered one of the most important yardsticks of parenting. Indeed, our children's self-evaluation will powerfully impact their happiness, academic performance, relationships, creativity, healthy risk-taking, perseverance, resilience, and problem-solving ability. When Jesus gave the command to "love your neighbor as yourself" (Luke 10:27), he was acknowledging that healthy self-love forms the basis for love of others. Taking responsibility for one's own welfare serves as the foundation for mutual regard for others and social responsibility.

To have high self-esteem, one needs to feel both loveable and capable, to have a sense of fundamental worth and importance along with the conviction that one is competent to handle the challenges of life. Without high self-esteem, a child's psychological growth will be stunted and he will not achieve his full potential. Low self-esteem makes children doubt their worthiness, lower their aspirations, and develop a self-defeating attitude. Children with a low self-evaluation are more vulnerable to a host of social ills, including school failure, unsuccessful relationships, irresponsibility, and self-destructive behavior. With a positive self-concept, a child feels loved, cherished, and competent and is filled with hope and confidence. The result is not only personal success and fulfillment but also a compassionate and caring attitude toward others.

The measure of a child's composite inner picture of his worth and value is considered one of the most important yardsticks of parenting.

Unfortunately, high self-esteem has been misinterpreted by some individuals to mean that children always should insist on feeling good about themselves, even if this means ignoring the evidence about their shortcomings. Some Christians misinterpret high self-esteem as being self-centered or selfish, of thinking too highly of oneself. I prefer to use the term *healthy* self-esteem to describe appropriate self-acceptance, self-love, and self-confidence. Healthy self-esteem involves truthful knowledge of oneself, and it is this self-acceptance that serves as the basis for self-improvement. Thus, a child with high—or healthy—self-esteem has a strong sense of individuality and belief in his own worth, as well as the willingness to take responsibility for continual self-improvement.

Parents represent a child's original source of unconditional love. It is parents who first convince children of their infinite worth and help them venture with confidence into the world beyond their family. A child's sense of self-worth begins at birth and continues to be shaped by daily life experiences. The family is the principal setting where young children develop a concept of self and draw conclusions about their identity, how they are valued by others, and whether they have something to offer. Parents and other adult caretakers have the most sig-

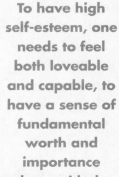

nificant influence on shaping children's self-esteem, as youngsters watch our reactions to them and hear our messages about them. Through our daily conversation, touch, countenance, and actions, we communicate to our children whether they are cherished and capable. Of course, no parent is perfect and we all make mistakes at times, but if the majority of our daily interactions convey our love, acceptance, approval, recognition, and confidence in our child, these positive messages will form the foundation for high self-esteem.

> **To have high self-esteem, one needs to feel both loveable and capable, to have a sense of fundamental worth and importance along with the conviction that one is competent to handle the challenges of life.**

The Importance of a Healthy Model of Self-Love and Respect for Others

Parents with a healthy self-image are best equipped to instill high self-esteem in their children. Parents who don't feel good about themselves find it more difficult, if not impossible, to raise children with a positive self-concept. If you suffer from low self-esteem, you owe it to yourself and your child to work on feeling better about yourself. Improving your own self-esteem will make you a more effective and happier parent. Demonstrate self-respect within your family by not making negative comments about yourself, and don't tolerate name-calling or put-downs among siblings.

The best way to teach children about their worth is to help them recognize the worth of every person created by God. When we honor the life, rights, beliefs, and property of others, when we model self-respect and demonstrate respect for others, our children naturally come to share those attitudes and, at the same time, to understand their own intrinsic value. Never use pejorative terms when referring to other people. Because lack of familiarity about people who are different from us can breed intolerance, help your child become more

> **The best way to teach children about their worth is to help them recognize the worth of every person created by God.**

knowledgeable about diverse cultures and introduce him to people of different backgrounds. Make it a habit to treat every individual as a special and unique child of God. Respect the rich diversity found among humankind and accept, without judging, people who are different from you.

How to Help Your Child Feel Valued, Loved, and Worthy

Everyone needs to feel uniquely loved and irreplaceable. The family is the first setting where a child learns that he has special significance to others and that he is born with intrinsic value. The following techniques will help you convey to your child that he is loveable and deeply loved. These strategies will help your child feel good about and comfortable with himself, which will, in turn, make him more compassionate toward others.

Provide for Your Child's Basic Needs and Physical Safety

It goes without saying that all children must feel safe and protected and have their basic needs met. A child who lives in fear of physical harm, or who lacks trust that her essential needs will be cared for, does not form a close attachment to her principal caretakers and does not draw positive conclusions about her worth. Chronic fear and anxiety lead to a heightened state of vigilance that prevents a child from feeling free to explore and learn. Her development will be impeded in all areas, including her development of a healthy sense of self. Refer to chapter 2 for strategies to help an infant develop an orientation of trust and to feel physically safe.

Communicate Your Unconditional Love

Unconditional love—love with no strings attached—is the cornerstone on which self-esteem is built. Unconditional love

Signs of Low Self-Esteem in a Child

While all children occasionally get discouraged or feel inferior, children with low self-esteem often feel unworthy and lack self-confidence. They frequently have behavior problems, are moody and fearful, display diminished coping skills, make negative remarks about themselves, and have difficulty making and keeping friends. Frequent behaviors like the following can mean your child needs help bolstering his self-image. Begin by talking with your child's teachers, other caregivers, and his physician, who can refer you to an appropriate counselor or therapist, if necessary.

A child with unhealthy self-esteem:

- Is easily frustrated and frequently misbehaves.
- Is self-critical and critical of others.
- Denies his own feelings and has trouble expressing his emotions.
- Has difficulty making and keeping friends.
- Avoids new situations and opportunities.
- Blames others for his circumstances.
- Needs constant attention and approval from others.
- Is easily swayed by peer pressure.
- Feels powerless.

means loving your child for who he is, not for what he does. It is never subject to cancellation because it is not based on any requirements about behavior, performance, or appearance. Rather, unconditional love is guaranteed and permanent; it is love come what may. When a child is absolutely convinced that his parents find him loveable and capable, he is then equipped to venture into the world and risk the acceptance of others.

Give Your Child Daily Focused Attention

The most effective way to convey unconditional love is by giving liberal one-on-one focused attention to your child. Simple interactions like reading to children, playing with them, listening to them, and expressing affection convey unconditional love and acceptance. Children are convinced that they are cherished and irreplaceable when we give them the priceless daily gift of time and undivided attention. When a parent is fully engaged with her child, she is saying, "You are more important to me than anything else right now." Focused attention is the best definition of "quality time" spent with your child. It is the reason children spell love *t-i-m-e*. To fully focus on your child, stop what you are doing and direct your attention to her, especially when your child asks for your attention. Focused attention is so precious to children that it is safe to conclude they would rather have our *presence* than our *presents*.

Unconditional love — love with no strings attached — is the cornerstone on which self-esteem is built.

In addition to spending time talking together each day, take your child on errands, ask her to help you prepare a meal, read, snuggle, and play together. Unfortunately, many parents today are too tired or preoccupied with other commitments to offer their children their full attention. If you find you are short on time, consider turning off one television program each day and using that time to be fully engaged with your children. Even twenty minutes a day of focused attention will do wonders for a child's self-esteem.

Accept Your Child the Way She Is Right Now

All parents are sometimes disappointed in their child. Because children are so eager to please, they are very perceptive about the ways they fail to fulfill our expectations of them. This deals a blow to their self-esteem and makes them feel unworthy of our love. Whether your daughter is a tomboy or dainty little lady, let her be herself without feeling judged by you. When we are able to accept our child the way she is right now—including her weaknesses and her strengths—this acceptance will go a long way in supporting her to undertake constructive change. Acceptance recognizes a child for who she is right now and leads to the desire to grow and become all she is capable of being.

On the other hand, your obvious disappointment in your child can feel self-defeating to her and effectively stifle any possibility of improvement. Continually harping, "Why can't you be more obedient, honest, kind?" will not motivate your child to adopt the desired qualities. Rather, the lack of acceptance that is conveyed when we correct, judge, moralize, command, and admonish is likely to cause our child to give up or provoke more rebellion than cooperation.

Express Your Love Openly

Every child needs daily, repeated verbal expressions of affection and frequent compliments. Children need to hear you say, "I love you," especially when we tuck them in and wake them up. Think of these daily love messages as being biodegradable, requiring constant replenishing. Give your child authentic compliments that will ring true, not generalized overstatements they won't believe. Say, "I like the way you got dressed so quickly," instead of, "You're the best little boy in the world." Your affirmations are the way you "pump your child up" each day to help buffer him against negative outside influences—teasing remarks, rebuffs, rejections, and criticisms—that poke deflating holes in his self-esteem.

While infants receive lots of touching, cuddling, and physical contact, we sometimes forget to hug and cuddle children as they move beyond the "baby stage." Preschoolers still crave physical manifestations of our affection, such as hugs, kisses, hand holding, patting, hair tousling, or putting your arm around your child. Frequent loving touches provide physical reassurance of our love and protection. I know a father who gently awakens his four-year-old each morning by lightly kissing her face.

Think of these daily love messages as being biodegradable, requiring constant replenishing.

Be aware that often these positive affirmations are most needed when a child's behavior makes him most difficult to affirm. Think of it this way: the fuel that powers good behavior is a sense of well-being, of self-esteem, of feeling capable and worthy of love. When we do not feel good about ourselves, we do not behave well. We are cranky and short-tempered and more apt to get into trouble. This is true for adults, and especially for children. When your child is misbehaving, consider whether his emotional tank has just run dry. Give him some physical affection and shower him with unearned words of love and praise for who he is (not what he does) and see if he doesn't respond with his best self.

Assume the Best in Your Child and Focus on the Positive

Let your child hear you speak positively about her and compliment her in front of others. Make a list of your child's strengths and attributes and view her as a winner. In response to undesirable behavior, say, "That's not like you to talk back to me. You're usually so respectful." Holding a positive view of your child will help her rise to meet your best expectations of her possibilities. If you view certain attributes about your child in a negative light, try reframing them more positively, the way a doting grandmother might cast them. For example, if you tend to see your child as "always into everything," try telling yourself he is "insatiably curious." Reframe your daughter's perceived "bossiness" as "leadership qualities."

Instill a Sense of Family Belonging and an Ethnic Heritage

When children are helped to take pride in their family and ethnic heritage, they acquire a sense of identity and belonging that enhances their self-esteem. Children learn to appreciate their heritage when they participate in family reunions and traditional celebrations, share ethnic foods, and listen to familiar stories about family members and ancestors. Your child's regular participation in family traditions and holiday celebrations instills a strong sense of belonging. Help your child identify famous people from the present and past who share your ethnic background.

Celebrate Your Faith Heritage

The unconditional love and acceptance a child experiences within the Christian faith heritage contributes significantly to healthy self-esteem. When children identify with Bible heroes and the great men and women of our faith, they gain a comforting sense of belonging within the family of God. Children's understanding of our faith heritage is fostered by sharing the Bible stories behind our faith traditions and celebrations, the experiences of missionaries, and the faith journey and witness of our ancestors.

Communication Techniques That Convey Worthiness and Respect

The quality of our conversations is another powerful way to convey to children their worth and value. Healthy communication helps your child feel loved, respected, and emotionally safe, and helps the two of you feel close. Two-way dialogue that enhances a child's self-esteem and strengthens the parent-child bond is very different from the one-way barrage of commands, precautions, scoldings, and orders that characterize much

Healthy communication helps your child feel loved, respected, and emotionally safe, and helps the two of you feel close.

of our daily communication with our children. Listening with empathy, and acknowledging, accepting, and validating children's feelings, helps them feel understood.

Use Body Language to Say You Desire Intimate Communication

Stop what you are doing and give your child your undivided attention. Position yourself at your child's eye level by kneeling or sitting and lean forward to show your interest, maintaining eye contact as your child speaks. I can still recall my youngest child, Mark, reaching up and taking my face in his little two-year-old hands to turn my gaze toward him to assure he had my full attention amid the clamor of four older siblings. Take your time and don't make your child feel rushed. Remember that the words *listen* and *silent* have the same letters.

Use Open-Ended Questions That Encourage Dialogue

Instead of asking, "Did you have a good time today?" inquire, "What did you enjoy most while you were at preschool this afternoon?" Let your child know that his thoughts and opinions count by soliciting his input: "What games shall we bring to Grandma's house?" or "What is your favorite ice cream flavor?"

Be an Empathetic Listener and Accept Your Child's Feelings

Listening attentively to your child when she openly communicates her feelings conveys your understanding, acceptance, and support. It's important not to refute or trivialize what your child has expressed: "That's nonsense! That's no reason to be upset." Instead, your goal is to show your child that you are listening and that you accept her feelings by reflecting what she says. Paraphrasing and validating what she is feeling helps her learn to express and handle a wide range of emotions: "I understand you're sad because Daddy didn't come today." "I can tell you're really happy to see the ducks again." "You feel left out because

I spend so much time with the baby; you wish I had more time to spend with you." By accepting your child's feelings instead of judging them, you show her that what she feels and has to say are important to you. Your willingness to openly share your own feelings can help your child become more comfortable expressing hers: "I sure am disappointed that we had to change our plans." "I'm so happy to know that Aunt Ellen isn't sick anymore."

> Listening attentively to your child when she openly communicates her feelings conveys your understanding, acceptance, and support.

Use "I" Messages Instead of "You" Messages to Discipline Your Child

When dealing with misbehavior, "you" messages tend to judge, put down, lay blame, criticize, decrease cooperation, and lower self-esteem: "Look how much water *you've* splashed in here!" "Can't *you* ever listen?" "*You've* really done it now!" In contrast, "I" messages place the focus on the behavior and your reaction to it, rather than the child: "*I* don't like to hear whining because *I* don't know what you are trying to tell me." "*I* don't like to see clothes all over the floor because it means a lot of work for me."

Avoid Giving Mixed Messages

Mixed messages result when you say something that isn't true or when your words and your body language are not congruent. For example, when you are visibly upset and exclaim, "I said I'm *not* mad!" your child receives a mixed message, which is confusing and disturbing to him. When your child rushes in and excitedly asks if you can go camping like Libby's family, it's better to give an honest response than an ambiguous message like, "Maybe someday." Mixed messages also occur when we combine words of love with criticism: "I love that little no-good brat."

Use the Connecting Word "And" Instead of "But"

This simple, one-word modification has proven invaluable in my own communications. When the word but is used to connect two ideas, it tends to negate what precedes it and to have a destructive effect on the message. A statement such as "I know you already picked up the toys, *but* there are two more trucks in the living room" tends to discount the child's effort. The constructive word *and* serves to connect two ideas of equal worth by building on what has just been said: "I know you already picked up the toys, *and* there are two more trucks in the living room."

Apologize When You Are Wrong

Don't be afraid to apologize when you have lost your temper, failed to keep a promise, let your child down, or wrongly accused him. Your sincere apology conveys respect for your child and lets him know you value his feelings. Saying "I'm sorry" is one of the most humbling and honoring gestures a parent can make toward their child. When parents honestly admit they are wrong and ask for forgiveness, children learn to appreciate that no one is perfect. In forgiving her parents when they apologize, a child finds it easier to accept her own shortcomings and to forgive herself and others. Remember that an apology, like repentance, must be coupled with a sincere effort to modify your behavior in the future. If you find yourself apologizing repeatedly, it's time to examine why your interactions with your child have not improved. You may need to seek professional help if you find yourself committing the same offenses in spite of your intentions to do better.

> Saying "I'm sorry" is one of the most humbling and honoring gestures a parent can make toward their child.

How to Help Your Child Feel Capable and Competent

High self-esteem is fostered when children are made to feel responsible and capable, in addition to feeling loved. When a child is convinced that he is good at some things, he is more eager to try new experiences and to persevere in the face of difficulties. A healthy sense of competence leads to joyful learning and helps prepare children to make good choices, handle frustration, set goals, and solve problems.

The following techniques are helpful in giving your child a "can do" attitude and building success upon success.

Use Encouragement Coupled with Praise

As parents, we become lifelong cheering squads for our children by encouraging their efforts, appreciating their interests, and showing support for all their endeavors. We delight in every milestone as if no other child ever took a step, started preschool, or rode a tricycle. No wonder our kids want to tell us first when they make a mud pie or make a friend. To acquire a sense of competence, children need both encouragement for their efforts and interests, as well as praise for their achievements.

Everyone appreciates words of praise, especially when the praise is specific and genuine. Too much praise, however, can make a child overly dependent on the approval of others. This is because praise focuses on an external evaluation of the child by another person: "I really like this picture you colored. You stayed inside the lines this time." Excessive praise can create pressure to perform and the ongoing need for compliments from others: "Do you like this picture too?" "Are you glad I ate all my beans?" Praise also tends to focus on results ("Wow, you caught the ball!") rather than process and effort ("I can see you really enjoy playing ball"). When you do give praise, be specific in your comments ("I'm really proud of the way you cleaned up without me reminding you") instead of making general statements ("You're such a good boy").

Strategies for Helping Children Feel Capable and Competent

The following techniques are helpful in giving your child a "can do" attitude and building success upon success.

- Use encouragement coupled with praise.
- Provide daily structure, routines, and limits.
- Display your child's work.
- Help your child feel responsible and independent.
- Help your child take healthy risks, learn new skills, and set goals.
- Help your child learn from mistakes.

The encouragement on which children thrive differs from praise in that encouragement rewards effort more than outcome: "You sure have been busy with those Legos. Tell me what you are making." Encouragement fosters self-approval, "You sure seem to enjoy singing!" "Yeah, I know all the words myself. I can't wait until we sing our song in church tomorrow." Encouragement promotes self-confidence and a positive attitude about a child's interests and self-effort: "Look at this picture I drew about our camping trip. I worked hard on it." Encouragement celebrates what a child may yet become. Although praise is certainly necessary and beneficial, too much

Too much praise and too little encouragement can cause a child's self-evaluation to depend upon someone else's judgment, leading to an overemphasis on pleasing others.

praise and too little encouragement can cause a child's self-evaluation to depend upon someone else's judgment, leading to an overemphasis on pleasing others.

Provide Daily Structure, Routines, and Limits

Young children gain a sense of competence and confidence when daily activities occur with some measure of predictability and when the limits of acceptable behavior are clearly defined. Simple routines, like brushing your child's teeth after breakfast, saying grace before meals, or adhering to a familiar bedtime ritual increase a child's confidence by allowing him to predict what comes next. Abiding by family rules, like buckling your seatbelt before the car starts, picking up toys after play, or rewinding a videotape after viewing it helps children fulfill their parents' expectations and feel successful.

Perhaps even more important than the predictability of daily routines is the need for a child to experience emotional predictability from parents and caregivers. A child needs to know what will make his parents laugh or be sad or become angry. If the emotional climate of the home is unpredictable—for example, when a parent is an alcoholic or suffers from mood swings—the child may become unduly anxious and apprehensive and may have difficulty taking healthy risks or trying new experiences.

Display Your Child's Work

Prominently displaying on the refrigerator or bulletin board your child's pictures and other artwork or photographs of them engaged in favorite activities serves as a frequent reminder of your pride in her accomplishments. When your child sees the cigar box she painted and decorated with macaroni sitting prominently on your desk, she is pleased with her effort. Taking the time to celebrate your child's artistic creations, listening to her tell a story or sing a song, and attending her performances are powerful ways to convey your keen interest in her achievements. Sharing the highlights of their day at the dinner table also helps build children's confidence and competence.

Help Your Child Feel Responsible and Independent

Support your child's emerging independence by letting him do things for himself that he is capable of handling, like pouring his own juice from a small pitcher or washing his hands. Willful toddlers insist, "Do it myself!" at every opportunity. Avoid making comments that sound like you lack confidence in his abilities, such as, "You're too little to do that" or "You might get hurt" or "That's very good; now let Mommy do it over." Such remarks only teach your child what he cannot do.

Allow your child to take responsibility for age-appropriate tasks, such as picking up his toys, getting dressed, or feeding a pet. And don't forget to acknowledge his efforts. Give your child your vote of confidence and strengthen your relationship at the same time by asking him to help you set the table, fold laundry, or put his books on the bookcase. Remember, however, that your child cannot accomplish any task as quickly or as well as you can. The goal of helping your child become capable and self-confident is more important than "getting the job done" or having it done "right." Resist the temptation to hold your child to adult standards of performance and be prepared to accept his imperfect efforts. Another way to promote your child's independence is to encourage his age-appropriate input in establishing family rules. Having firm limits and adhering to family rules enhances a child's sense of self-discipline and responsibility. (See chapter 5.)

Help Your Child Take Healthy Risks, Learn New Skills, and Set Goals

Your child's sense of competence is enhanced when you take the time to teach and celebrate new milestones. Compliment your child's efforts as she masters each step involved in a new skill, such as tying her shoes, riding a tricycle, or learning to put her head underwater.

Encourage your child to try new experiences, such as tasting a new food or stroking a furry pet. Your preschooler can be encouraged to greet a new playmate, attend a new classroom, or play a new game. Children need to learn that although healthy risk-taking inevitably involves some failures and discouragement, "it's better to have tried and failed, than to have failed to try."

Part of healthy risk-taking involves helping your children set and achieve realistic goals of their own, such as getting dressed on time, breaking a habit, learning to use the potty, catching a ball, or staying overnight at Grandma's house. Start by naming the goal, setting a realistic timetable, breaking the goal into smaller steps, encouraging effort, and helping your child have a "win every day."

Help Your Child Learn from Mistakes

Taking responsibility for mistakes builds self-esteem by teaching a child that her choices and actions produce consequences. Don't let inevitable disappointments spell defeat. Instead, teach your children to use their mistakes as important opportunities to learn. Examining bad decisions can be the most effective way to help children recognize the consequences of their actions and to take responsibility for their poor choices. Fortunately, small children usually make small mistakes with small consequences. Using the lessons learned from early mistakes can teach young children to solve future problems by making better decisions. Teach your child how to make amends by having her help clean up a spill, repair something she broke, apologize for rude language, or return something she took without asking.

More Than One Child: Helping Each Feel Uniquely Loved and Cherished

Every parent with more than one child soon discovers that siblings don't come from the same mold. Fostering a unique sense of self-worth in each of our children involves what I call learning to "honor the person in every child." By this, I mean identifying and celebrating our child's special attributes and conveying to each that he or she is a person of infinite worth who is irreplaceably important to us. For those of us with multiple children, learning how to convey to each child that he or she is uniquely loved and cherished can be one of the most challenging and rewarding aspects of parenting and one of the most precious gifts we can give our children.

Raising multiple children not only involves a greater commitment of physical, emotional, and financial resources; it also requires parents to apply considerable skill and insight to recognize and appreciate the innate differences in children's personalities, temperaments, talents, and interests. In addition to being shaped by their genetic makeup and our own parenting styles, children's outcome inevitably is influenced by their place in the family and the quality of their sibling relationships. Unfortunately, emotional scars can result from the painful perception that a favored sibling was deemed to be more talented, capable, bright, or attractive.

> **Learning how to convey to each child that he or she is uniquely loved and cherished can be one of the most challenging and rewarding aspects of parenting and one of the most precious gifts we can give our children.**

All parents harbor some fantasies about the ways their children will turn out and the endeavors in which they will excel. But our children are not born to fulfill a life script we have already chosen for them, as scholar, musician, athlete, model, or performer. Rather, our role is to honor our children's individuality, help them reach their maximum potential, and accept them for who they are. While living in Hawaii as a young mother, I learned to apply to family relationships the gracious spirit of Aloha: "to welcome the stranger and seek the good in him or her." Each newborn placed in our arms to join our family is indeed a stranger. Our job is to embrace this little person and allow him the freedom to express his unique potential, like a little mystery seed blossoming into his destiny.

The Influence of Birth-Order Stereotypes and Other Situations

A child's place in the family has such a powerful influence on his self-image and ultimate outcome that birth-order stereotypes are commonly observed among siblings. Often these characteristics persist into adulthood. While amusing to some degree, birth-order stereotypes, when unchecked, can place unfair expectations or limits on children. Parents who are aware of these risks can take steps to avoid implied expectations for their children and remove restrictions on their childhood experiences.

Firstborns

Typical firstborn traits are attributed to high expectations on the part of novice, anxious parents who loom as impossible role models for a small child who is eager to please. Classic firstborns tend to be highly responsible, conscientious, achievement-oriented, competitive, compliant, and perfectionistic. They often incur a disproportionate share of household duties at an early age and responsibility for younger siblings. I recall dispatching my first son to retrieve a clean diaper for his baby sister as early as twenty months of age. Years later, when my youngest son was still the diapered baby himself, I assure you he wasn't running errands! Despite how pseudomature your firstborn may appear, avoid placing excessive expectations and responsibility on him. Don't make comments like "Stop being a baby" or "You're too big for that." Let him know you love him apart from his accomplishments, and avoid forcing him to grow up too soon. Help him feel comfortable being spontaneous and playful.

Middle Children

Middle children generally are at risk for receiving less parental attention than either trailblazing firstborns or darling babies. Your middle child can always use some extra attention and one-on-one time with you. As the middle of five children myself, I know how important it is to establish a unique identity. The middle position can be extra challenging, based on a child's gender. For example, an only boy sandwiched between two sisters probably has a more comfortable placement in the family than a middle son with an older brother and baby sister. Because middles are closer in age to all their siblings than the oldest and youngest are to one another, they usually acquire more experience getting along with others. As a result, they often have highly developed social skills and make friends easily. Because the middle position offers great preparation for the real world of lowered expectations and compromise, middles tend to be excellent mediators and negotiators. Middle children may follow in the footsteps of an older sibling in terms of interests and abilities, or they may break the original mold and carve out their own identity, whether favorable or unfavorable.

Babies

By the time the youngest is born, parents usually are more relaxed and have lowered expectations. As a result, the baby typically is delightfully affectionate, adorable, and charming. However, the youngest may feel he is living in the shadow of his older siblings and worry whether he will ever be "big enough" or measure up. With doting older siblings to protect, defend, and cover for him, he often is more dependent or less responsible than the firstborn. Instead of expecting him to remain cute, cuddly, and lovable, help your youngest to set and achieve personal goals and to take appropriate responsibility.

Only Children

More parents today decide to have one child only—for personal, financial, medical, lifestyle, or other reasons. They may hear about "lonely onlies" and wonder whether their child is missing out by not having siblings. Only children tend to have typical firstborn traits and to be comfortable in the presence of adults. Parents need to assure that they provide only children with plenty of opportunities to play and interact with their age-mates, since they are often in adult company. While onlies don't have to worry about sibling comparisons or whom their parents love the most, they can be the recipient of excess parental pressure and expectation. They also may miss out on some of the lessons in negotiation and compromise that come from having siblings. If you have an only child, resist the temptation to expect too much from her and make sure you give her plenty of peer experiences to balance her exposure to adults.

Multiple Births

The birth of multiples is more common today, mainly due to new interventions for infertility. Despite the glamour and excitement of having multiples, helping children establish a unique identity is even more difficult with twins and other multiples. Our society's fascination with twins promotes the tendency to focus on their sameness, rather than their individuality. Well-meaning friends and relatives often insist they can't tell the twins apart or will refer to them as a unit, rather than as individual children. To combat the tendency to treat twins as a set, be sure to spend one-on-one time with each child. Avoid making comparisons or assumptions about similarities among multiples and help each cultivate their own interests and unique identity. Also avoid typecasting them, as a way to give each a unique identity: "She's so easygoing." "He's the anxious one." Even referring to one twin as "the older one" is a form of stereotyping. Such labeling only limits a child's sense of possibility.

Vulnerable Children

A child may be profoundly affected by her own or a sibling's exceptional gifts or disabilities. A child with a handicapping condition may be made to feel like an unwanted intruder who interrupts everyone's normal routines. Or so much attention may be given to a "special needs" child that the low-maintenance, healthy sibling is left to conclude, "I'm not special." When one child is a world-class athlete, a celebrity actress, or a musical prodigy, the other siblings may feel eclipsed by such stardom and grow up feeling jealous or inadequate. Conversely, exceptional children may feel intense performance pressure and worry whether they are loved unconditionally or only for their talents. Parents of children with special needs or special abilities have a difficult challenge giving individual time and cultivating a sense of infinite worth in each child.

The Importance of a Unique Love Relationship with Each Child

The arrival of a sibling forces a firstborn to relinquish the exclusive love of his parents. Most children assume that the love and attention showered on a sibling means less parental affection available to them. This powerful undercurrent of sibling competition fuels the hurtful tattling, name-calling, and other rivalries so common among siblings, who continually jockey for a favored position in our imaginary hierarchy of love.

Loving the Most

If he can't have all his parents' love, a child will seek confirmation that he is loved *the most*. For example, if his sibling has just misbehaved, a child may sweetly ask, "I'm not naughty like Evan, am I?" Don't succumb to the temptation to privately hint that you prefer one child to another. No matter how much children vie for such confirmation, the truth is that feeling loved the most at a given moment in time is not very reassuring to a child, since a sudden upset might send a better-behaved or higher-achieving sibling into the coveted first position. This possibility makes parental love feel tenuous, conditional, and easily subject to change, rather than permanent and unqualified. As much as your children seem to want to hear you say it, never admit or even secretly hint that you love one of them the most.

Loving Equally

While children worry about who is loved the most, parents often focus their energies on being fair and equal in distributing their material gifts, time, and attention. Be warned, however, that your noble efforts to love your children *equally* will never feel truly equal to them, and their scorecards will never match your own perception of equality. A child is apt to count the number of sprinkles on his ice-cream cone just to prove you weren't completely fair! "She got more than I did!" and "No fair!" are all too familiar refrains. Loving equally also isn't practical because children's needs and circumstances aren't equal. As the mother of five children, I soon learned that a preoccupation with being fair can't equalize our children's happiness or serve their differing needs.

Loving Uniquely

Siblings eventually accept the painful reality that they cannot garner all their parents' love, or even most of it. Sharing their parents' love equally with a sibling is not as comforting to a child as securing a unique love relationship of their own. Stop trying to love each of your children the most or the same. Instead, look to God's model of a unique personal relationship with each individual through Jesus Christ. Then concentrate on cultivating a separate, distinct

Sharing their parents' love equally with a sibling is not as comforting to a child as securing a unique love relationship of their own.

love bond with each of your children. Each son or daughter wants the assurance that you have reserved a special place in your heart for him or her and that no other boy or girl can ever replace their significance in your life: "You're my one and only Alexander, and I don't know what I would do without you. Nobody could ever take your place." The knowledge that a child is loved unconditionally for being the unique and special individual that they are can compensate for the reality that their parents' love must be shared with one or more siblings.

Children delight in the discovery of God's endless creativity. His love for the unique sets the example for us. Use picture books and television nature programs to raise the question of why God would create so many strange and wonderful creatures. Take the time to look at leaves or clouds and notice that no two are alike. Then use these opportunities to express your awe and joy for the unique way God has created your child. Let him know that there is a place in your heart, and in God's, that is exactly his shape and reserved only for him, and that no one else will ever fill it.

How to Foster a Unique Love Relationship with Each Child

The following strategies will help give each of your children a healthy, unique identity and convince each that they are one of a kind and irreplaceable.

Spend Individual Time with Each Child

The most important way to develop a unique relationship with each of your children is to spend individual, one-on-one time with them on a regular basis. Parents who are overly concerned with being fair and equal may resist spending individual time with one child when the others can't be present: "No, we're not going for ice cream today. Let's wait until tomorrow when Calvin can come too." Spending individual time with each child helps combat the development of restricting stereotypes. Your youngest is more likely to be viewed as "the baby" when all three children are present than when he's on an outing with you alone. And fewer comparisons among children arise when only one is present. Spend some one-on-one time with each of your children every day, listening with interest to what they have to say, playing a game, making a puzzle, preparing a meal, or working in the garden. Invite one of your children to join you when you run an errand in the car.

Avoid Comparisons

Most of us venture to have a second child because of the rewards and our perceived success parenting our firstborn. We automatically compare our children and search for similarities and contrasts between them. Harmless as it seems, comparison is at the root of all feelings of inadequacy because comparisons always imply a more favorable and a less favorable outcome. Even when one child comes out on top in a comparison, she is left feeling insecure about the very real possibility of faring less well in the next round. Comparisons inevitably create pressure on children and undermine their unique identity. Trying to fill the shoes of an older sibling can be a heavy burden for a child: "Bobby could sing all four verses at your age."

Comparisons inevitably create pressure on children and undermine their unique identity.

Comparisons also convey the message that specific conditions exist for parental love and acceptance: "Why can't you use the potty like Marcia does?" While parents readily appreciate the harmful effects of negative comparisons, many don't realize that even the comparisons they incorporate in the compliments they give can pit their children against one another: "Boy, you got your pajamas on faster than Roland did." Make a concerted effort to minimize all comparisons in your communications with your children. Practice emphasizing the positive attributes of one child without making reference to his brother: "Thanks for putting your toys away without being reminded." "I appreciate you looking at your books so quietly."

Avoid Typecasting or Labeling

When parents have more than one child, a strong tendency exists to typecast their attributes: "Charlie's the athlete; Sally's the artist." "Brady's fearless, but Tina's timid." However, such typecasting represents a double-edged sword. While children enjoy having a unique identity, labeling children can restrict their sense of possibility and narrow the expectations for them.

Labeling a child as shy, stubborn, brainy, or finicky limits a child's view of himself and may cause him to restrict his experiences. For example, a child with less musical talent than his brother might not be encouraged to play an instrument even if he wants to, and a less coordinated child may be steered away from sports activities she might well enjoy. Casting siblings as personality types can restrict their emotional expression: "Susie never complains about anything. She's my get-along, go-along child." Or "Jason can't say a nice thing about anyone." All parents have both positive and negative feelings about their children. Occasionally, these ambivalent emotions get expressed abnormally, when a parent projects only negative feelings onto one child while attributing only positive attributes to another. This "good boy–bad boy" distinction can leave the child labeled as naughty feeling defeated and create a self-fulfilling prophecy.

Avoid Gender Expectations

Whether spoken or not, many parents have gender preferences and expectations surrounding the birth of a new sibling. The couple with two girls often secretly or openly expresses the desire for a boy. When the third daughter is born, she may initially be viewed as "not-a-boy," rather than a precious, baby girl. Well-meaning friends and relatives may fuel inappropriate gender expectations with ill-timed comments: "Oh, maybe you'll get your little boy this time." Many perceptive children soon figure out that their gender represents a major disappointment to their parents, and they begin life with an apology for an unalterable aspect of their identity. Whatever your honest feelings about the preferred sex of each of your children, I urge you to try hard to relinquish potentially damaging gender expectations and honor the person in every child.

Avoid Sex Role Stereotypes

While many parents guard against overt sexism in their child rearing, subtle sex role stereotyping remains widespread and continues to limit children's experiences. Too many parents still tell their sons that "big boys don't cry" or their daughters that "nice girls don't get angry." Don't assume that your daughter doesn't want to learn to throw a football, play with race cars, or take karate lessons. And don't necessarily expect her to want to be a flight attendant rather than a pilot. Don't balk if your son wants to play house, help cook dinner, or learn ballet. Instead, give your sons and daughters a breadth of experiences and a future sense of unlimited possibility.

Allow Your Children to Express Their Feelings

An important way to help children feel uniquely valued and appreciated is to acknowledge the intensity of their feelings about their siblings without making judgments. When we trivialize a child's feelings ("Of course you don't want to give the baby back. Don't you ever say such a thing again!"), our child feels angry and misunderstood. When we paraphrase and reflect children's expressed feelings, we validate and legitimize their emotions, which convinces children that they really matter to us: "It makes you furious when she borrows your things

> *Simply acknowledging and accepting a child's intense feelings is a highly effective way to honor their individuality.*

without asking." "Sometimes you resent having your little brother tag along." Simply acknowledging and accepting a child's intense feelings is a highly effective way to honor their individuality.

Discipline Appropriately

When sibling disputes arise, many parents mistakenly assume that their older child must be to blame. Without knowing all the facts, they automatically come to the defense of the younger child and bring accusations against the firstborn: "You're older than she is. You ought to know better." Frequently responding in this way can thrust children into bully and victim roles in response to your expectations of them. Sometimes a younger child will deliberately provoke an older sibling, expecting you to play rescuer. This can leave an older sibling feeling like a scapegoat and make a younger sibling dependent on you to resolve her disagreements. When dealing with sibling disputes, don't be too quick to blame one child over another. Instead, focus on mutual consequences for problem behavior (both children go to time-out for physical aggression) and mutual resolution of disagreements (turn the TV off until both children can agree on what to watch). (See chapter 5.)

How to Help Children Adjust to a New Sibling

Adjusting to the arrival of a baby brother or sister can be a challenging experience for a young child. No matter how much she says she wants a new baby, your preschooler has no way of knowing how her life will change with the addition of a sibling. The little brother she once eagerly anticipated may feel like an unwelcome intruder who has become the focus of attention and the reason Mommy is so tired. You have probably heard the often-repeated story told from an adult's perspective to remind us how a child might feel when a new baby is brought home. In the story, the husband of a happily married woman proudly announces that he is bringing home a second wife. But instead of sharing his obvious joy, the first wife reacts with disappointment, anger, and self-doubt, while privately thinking, "Why wasn't I enough?" The puzzled husband innocently responds, "You've been such a wonderful wife to me that I couldn't wait to get another one. Besides, I thought you'd like a companion and helper around the house. I figured you two could be great friends and do things together." When adults hear this familiar scenario, they readily appreciate how a child might feel threatened and displaced by the addition of a new family member. When we think of the resentment we would harbor against a second wife in our home, we are amazed how smoothly most children adjust to the arrival of a sibling and manage to turn a potential competitor into a lifelong friend and ally.

The following suggestions will help prepare your child for the addition of a baby brother or sister, without dealing a blow to her self-esteem.

• *Give ample notice.* Be sure the news of your pregnancy comes from you. Don't assume your toddler can't tell something is going on. Even young children with limited verbal skills can appreciate the mother's body changes and sense the air of anticipation in the home. Explain in terms that your child can understand that a new baby is growing inside Mommy, in a place called the uterus. Let your older child feel the baby move.

• *Explain what a baby will be like.* Give your child a doll and show him how you will need to tenderly care for, nurse, diaper, and rock a baby. Let him practice these nurturing behaviors. Help your older child understand that his new brother won't arrive ready to play cars with him. Visit friends' babies to help your child get a realistic view of what a baby is like. Get out your photo albums and review your older child's babyhood with him. Explain that he was your very first newborn baby.

• *Explain your absence.* Make sure your child knows who will care for her while you are in the hospital. Take her to the hospital to see where you will be and let her know she will be able to visit you and the baby there. It's a good idea to enroll her in a sibling-preparation class in conjunction with your childbirth education classes.

• *Involve your child in preparations for the baby.* The baby's arrival creates an exciting sense of expectation. Let your older child help prepare the nursery and discuss baby names. Some parents have their older child draw a picture for home-made birth announcements. Tell your child what a thoughtful big brother he is. Do not give anything that your older child identifies as his own to the baby, such as his stroller. Instead, put it away for several months before getting it out to use with the baby.

• *Accept your child's feelings.* Even the most well-adjusted child will inevitably feel some jealousy toward a new baby and some anger toward you for creating this enormous disruption in her life. If she makes negative remarks about the baby, such as wishing he could go back to the hospital, don't judge her feelings. Simply paraphrase what she has said: "You wish babies didn't take so much time." Let her know that you can handle her hostile feelings and that you love her very much. While it is acceptable for your older child to voice her dissatisfaction with the new baby, you must make it clear that harming the baby in any way is never acceptable. Do not allow even a remote chance of this happening by leaving a young child alone with a baby.

• *Expect regression.* Young children often regress when a baby comes into the house. After all, from the older child's perspective, parents sure seem to like babyish behavior. Don't be surprised if your child resumes sucking his thumb, wets his pants, wakes up at night, or asks to be carried. Don't admonish your child to "act like a big boy, not a baby." Instead, lavish extra love and affection on your child. In fact, offer opportunities for your child to be babyish so he won't have to ask. Say, "Would you like me to cover you with a baby blanket?" or "I'm going to rock and cuddle my big baby now." Then at other times, remind him of some of the perks of being older: "This ice cream sure is good. Babies are too little to eat ice cream."

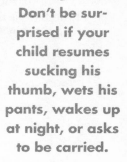

Don't be surprised if your child resumes sucking his thumb, wets his pants, wakes up at night, or asks to be carried.

• *Offer a gift from the baby.* Purchase something your child is sure to like and bring it wrapped to the hospital. When your child first meets her new sister, present her gift from "baby." This initial peace offering will go a long way toward fostering positive feelings about the baby.

• *Balance the attention of well-wishers.* After the baby's arrival, your older child will be exposed to a parade of adoring friends and neighbors who come to admire the new family member. The gush of attention being showered on the baby may leave your older child feeling invisible. Be prepared to compliment and praise him within his hearing. Let him be the official opener of the baby's gifts. He will enjoy unwrapping them, and many baby items won't seem very appealing to him anyway. However, keep a stash of small wrapped presents just for him.

• *Spend extra one-on-one time with your older child.* The physical demands of a new baby naturally mean your older child will receive less of your undivided attention. To convince her that you still love her, make a point of spending some individual time with her each day. In addition to things like reading a story to your older child while nursing your newborn, don't forget to carve out some one-on-one moments together when the baby isn't present. You can play a game or share a snack together while the baby naps.

• *Convince your child that the baby adores him.* One thing that takes the sting out of sharing their parents' love with a new sibling is that babies quickly become infatuated with their big brother or sister. It's hard to resent someone who loves you so much. You can promote positive feelings on the part of your older child toward the baby by helping him see how special he is in the baby's life. Tell him, "Look how she smiles whenever she sees you." "She gets so excited when you come in the room."

Common Errors That Erode Self-Esteem

As our child's parents, we create a window through which she views herself and her world. Through our actions and reactions, our emotions and words, we convey to her whether she is competent, valuable, and loveable. We tell her whether the world is a place of joy or fear, whether it is full of opportunities or obstacles, whether she should expect success or anticipate failure.

No parent deliberately undermines their child's self-esteem. Yet many parents unintentionally chip away at their youngster's self-worth by committing the following common errors. Poor modeling by our own parents, coupled with periodic exhaustion, role overload, and frustration, contribute to these self-esteem faux pas. If you recognize yourself in these examples, work on extinguishing one or two errors at a time.

Frequent Criticism

Unfortunately, some parents have not learned appropriate ways to discipline their children and resort to emotionally harmful verbal lashings to vent their anger and frustration over misbehavior. Their little ones get subjected to a daily barrage of criticisms and put-downs: "I've had it with you." "You're a very bad girl." "Can't you do anything right?" It takes many compliments to negate the emotional damage of a single zinger or verbal barb. While parents may forget their critical remarks shortly after uttering them, children often take such comments literally. The result is a negative self-image and feelings of

It takes many compliments to negate the emotional damage of a single zinger or verbal barb.

worthlessness. See chapter 5 for appropriate ways to promote desired behavior and deal with misbehavior that won't damage your child's self esteem.

Negating a Child's Feelings

Parents usually do a masterful job of interpreting, validating, legitimizing, and meeting the needs of small infants. Adults hover over a bassinet that cradles a crying baby and pick her up to comfort her, proclaiming, "Poor baby, what's wrong? Let's check your diaper. Could it be a bubble? There, that's a good burp. Now I bet you feel better." We jump up to meet every infant expression of distress and lavish the baby with cuddling, rocking, massaging, and socializing. Then a few short years later, the same well-meaning parent may stop validating and start negating their toddler's feelings as they blurt out, "Stop that crying or I'll give you something to cry about!" or "Quit pouting!" "How dare you say you hate your sister." Negating a child's emotions makes him feel unimportant and unworthy. Worse yet, children whose feelings are not affirmed have trouble appreciating what other people are feeling and may not fully develop the critical emotion of empathy for others. (See "Self-Esteem and Violence Prevention" later in this chapter.)

Expecting Too Much

Unrealistic expectations of a child lead to excessive pressure and feelings of inadequacy, as parents' disappointment in their child eventually causes the child to be disappointed in himself. Parents who expect too much forget to compliment and reinforce positive behavior and focus instead on what's wrong: "You haven't put your other shoe on." "You left some blocks in the living room." "You didn't wipe your face." The repeated message "you can do better" gets translated as "not good enough." Consider your child's age and abilities and ask whether you are expecting too much of him. Praise your child for what he does right, instead of focusing on what could be better.

Name-Calling, Belittling, Dwelling on the Negative

Timeless advice like "If you can't say anything nice, don't say anything at all" has survived through the ages because it contains such wisdom. There's no place in child rearing for derogatory nicknames that can become self-fulfilling prophesies, like clumsy, klutzo, troublemaker, crybaby, fatso, dumbo, or slowpoke. If you use nicknames, choose positive ones that clearly show affection and build self-esteem: honey, sweetheart, pal, ace, precious, princess, darling, or champ. Even when used with an affectionate tone, negative labels have a damaging effect. We sometimes think our children react only to the tone of our voice and not our actual words, like a dog who wags its emotional tail even when we say, "You're a very bad doggie," so long as we are smiling and scratching his ears. However, children, in their insatiable search for learning and meaning, listen and incorporate into their worldview our every word and opinion. The parent who makes a habit of affectionately saying, "You're my darling little fat boy," is actually eroding her child's self-esteem.

Overprotecting a Child and Engendering Fear

Don't be too quick to take over a task that is frustrating for your child. Comments like "Here, let me do that" or "You might spill it" tend to foster dependence and erode confidence and self-esteem. Instead, encourage your child to do things for herself, with necessary guidance from you. Whether trying to tie their own shoes or make their own bed, children need to be convinced that you have confidence in their abilities. Similarly, by overreacting to your child's expressed fears about spiders, monsters, or dogs, you may inadvertently convey the message that you doubt your child's abilities to handle life's challenges.

> Whether trying to tie their own shoes or make their own bed, children need to be convinced that you have confidence in their abilities.

Tying a Child's Character and Personal Worth to Performance or Behavior

"Look at this mess. Shame on you. I'm so disappointed in you." Verbal blasts like these are in direct opposition to the concept of unconditional love. Such comments convey that our approval is subject to cancellation when the child's behavior doesn't measure up. Focus on the problem behavior instead of criticizing your child: "This spilled soda has made a big mess. Here, let's tackle this clean-up job together." Even if the problem behavior is angry and defiant, parents should keep the focus on the behavior: "I understand you are upset, and knocking over your milk is not an acceptable way to express your feelings."

Self-Esteem and Violence Prevention

In recent years, our nation has been rocked by a wave of youth violence that has included a child perpetrator as young as six years of age. In addition to worries about our children's safety from perpetrators, many parents are understandably concerned about curbing the aggressive tendencies their children display. Violent behavior is linked to complex societal issues, such as poverty, alcohol and drug abuse, absent fathers, direct exposure to domestic and community violence, access to handguns, and widespread media violence. In addition, individual factors, such as self-image, anger management, impulse control, and empathy for others play a key role in determining whether our child will be a bully, victim, or peacemaker.

Children with low self-esteem are more prone to violence.

Why have I included a discussion of violence prevention in a chapter on self-esteem for preschoolers? It's because a positive self-concept helps assure healthy relationships, promotes emotional awareness, improves problem-solving skills, and reduces the likelihood of violent behavior. On the other hand, children with low self-esteem are more prone to violence because they have difficulty handling their emotions, are less empathic, adopt a blaming mentality, and are more susceptible to peer pressure, easily frustrated, and more impulsive. In addition, bullies typically target as their victims children who are passive and lack confidence.

The preschool years are the ideal time to begin implementing essential violence reduction measures. Violence prevention begins in the family by raising children in a safe and loving home and by imparting specific skills and attitudes which are surprisingly similar to the strategies that boost a child's self-esteem.

Promote Closeness in Your Family

Our national epidemic of youth violence has been linked to a growing lack of meaningful relationships between parents and children in American society. The best defense against violence is the family and extended family—including the church family—bolstered by support within the community. A strong, loving parental bond helps a child feel safe and secure and lays the foundation for reducing violence in a child's life. Make it clear that your child can always talk with you, even when things aren't going well. Children who lack parental love and support often vent their pain and hurt through anger directed at others. The close bonds that are forged within church families whose members share a mutual faith and worship together also buffer children against violence by helping them feel loved and secure and connected.

Model Appropriate Behavior

Both our good and bad behavior and attitudes are reflected in our children, proving that actions do speak louder than words. Children often learn violent or aggressive behavior very early in life from the adult models they observe. Learning to curb your own short fuse and volatile outbursts is the first step in promoting tranquility in your child's life. Make your home a safe, calm sanctuary for your child, where each family member is treated with respect.

Consider Alternatives to Spanking Your Children

You will want to carefully examine your view of corporal punishment and its possible link to aggressive behavior in children. Spanking children may convey the message that it is okay to hit others, while the use of nonphysical methods of discipline, such as time-outs, offers children alternative ways to settle differences. The controversial topic of corporal punishment is discussed in depth in chapter 5.

Provide Adequate Supervision

Unsupervised children have more behavior problems and are more prone to violence. Children require structure and adult guidance as they learn to make good choices. Close monitoring of children's behavior allows parents to intervene when aggression is being displayed. Children are constantly learning about the world, as new experiences give shape and meaning to their lives. Consequently, they require ongoing parental supervision, guidance, and modeling. Children are not equipped to raise themselves, peers cannot define appropriate behavior, and television can neither supervise nor be a guardian.

Promote Emotional Awareness in Your Child

We would never expect a child alone to find his way through some unknown physical setting, like a forest or a shopping mall. Neither should we expect that he would easily navigate the emotional landscape of his life without our help. A child's parents should be prepared to travel alongside as guides and interpreters, giving names to the feelings encountered along the way, helping over the rough spots, pointing out the quicksand, and generally making the unknown safe and familiar.

Many violent people are unable to recognize a range of feelings such as discouragement, sadness, and fear. Their bottled up emotions get expressed as angry outbursts. The first step

> **Many violent people are unable to recognize a range of feelings such as discouragement, sadness, and fear. Their bottled up emotions get expressed as angry outbursts.**

toward handling powerful emotions is to identify and share feelings within a supportive family network in which each member is nurtured emotionally. The ability to recognize an emotional response ("I'm really feeling angry right now") greatly increases our chances of exercising self-control and developing coping mechanisms for handling the particular emotion.

In your daily interactions with your child, describe what you see, and name the feelings she expresses: "I see you punching the sofa cushion and looking angry. Do you want to talk about what's upsetting you?" By validating and empathizing with your child's intense feelings, you affirm and legitimize his emotions: "I can certainly understand why you feel that way." "That must have been difficult for you." Self-awareness not only equips children to better handle their emotions but also enhances their social skills by helping them recognize and empathize with the emotions of others.

Allow Appropriate Expressions of Anger

Violence results from the inappropriate expression of anger, but contrary to what many people believe, anger is not a negative emotion to be eliminated from our feeling repertoire. Anger is a normal, healthy feeling. It is only natural to feel angry when one is disappointed, frustrated, or being treated unfairly. Teach children that it is okay to be angry or to feel any other emotion. It is the way we express anger that can be either harmful or positive. If a child is angry because his sister took a toy he was playing with, he can make things worse by calling her names, punching her, or confiscating something of hers. Or he can use his anger to make his needs known by saying, "I was playing with that car. I want you to give it back to me. You can ask me if you want to play with my things." Because inappropriate expressions of anger, like name-calling or hitting, may appear to a child to be effective, a parent needs to be ready to intervene to create consequences when anger is not being expressed constructively.

Here are some strategies to help your child learn appropriate ways to deal with anger.

- *Build a feeling vocabulary, beginning in toddlerhood, that allows your child to express her anger and frustration.* When your toddler erupts in a temper tantrum, give her the words to name what she is feeling, "You're mad ... upset ... angry ... disappointed ... sad. When you've calmed down, we can talk about it." A parent might create a drama game to explore emotions by their facial expressions and demeanor. You can say, "This is how my face and body look when I am happy. How does yours look?"

- *Interrupt aggressive behavior without stifling your child's feelings.* When your preschooler bites or hits in anger, immediately curb the behavior and help him express his feelings in an appropriate manner: "No hitting! Hitting hurts people. I know you're upset that Aaron has the blocks right now. Tell him you want to play too, and maybe he'll share." Remain calm, but firm. Give an unequivocal message that hurting others is not acceptable. (See chapter 5.)

- *Offer age-appropriate outlets for anger, in addition to talking things out.* Show your child that she can pound a peg board, squeeze clay, bang a drum, or hit a punching bag or pillow to let off steam. Let her know it is *not* okay to hurt others or to damage property. However,

Self-awareness not only equips children to better handle their emotions but also enhances their social skills by helping them recognize and empathize with the emotions of others.

talking about feelings is more helpful than venting them through physical outlets.

Foster Empathy

An awareness of one's feelings is necessary for empathy, or an understanding of how others may feel. Empathy—the ability to assume someone else's point of view and imagine how they would feel—is the emotional foundation of human morality. It is the driving force behind acts of kindness and is a societal buffer against cruelty. Empathy helps build connections between people and helps children take responsibility for the effects of their behavior on others. It is essential to the understanding and application of the Golden Rule.

Empathy comes naturally for most children, but the emotion must be nurtured or it will diminish. Even toddlers are capable of an emotional reaction toward others and will try to comfort another child in distress. By school age, most children can learn to appreciate another person's point of view or perspective.

When children's feelings are not recognized and validated by their parents and others, children not only stop expressing those feelings, but they lose the ability to recognize them in themselves or others.

We begin instilling the critical emotion of empathy from the moment of birth when we promptly respond to a baby's needs. Babies who are cuddled, loved, and cared for—whose emotional needs are consistently met—readily demonstrate caring behavior later, while toddlers who have been abused are more likely to hit a crying playmate. When reading a story to your child, pause and ask, "How do you think the new boy in the class is feeling? What might make him feel better?" Another way to increase your child's awareness of others' feelings is to practice conveying different emotions to your child and have him notice the words, tone of voice, body language, and facial expressions that accompany the emotion. When children's feelings are not recognized and validated by their parents and others, children not only stop expressing those feelings, but they lose the ability to recognize them in themselves or others.

Sibling relationships provide some of the earliest opportunities for children to express empathy. When sibling relationships are warm and affectionate, children get a head start on understanding the emotional states of others and learning about a wide range of human relations.

Teach Impulse Control

Your parental model of self-control is your child's most powerful example as he is learning to curb impulsive behavior. Teach your child not to act on his angry impulses when he doesn't get what he wants. Lashing out in anger or saying the first thing that comes to mind is hurtful to others and can place a child at risk for retaliation. Show him techniques for calming down, such as walking away or counting to ten, taking deep breaths, blowing bubbles, or talking things out. Praise your child for showing self-restraint when he is obviously frustrated. Encourage him to identify and talk about the difficult feelings he is experiencing.

Teach Children to Collaborate and Compromise

Nonviolence is promoted when children are taught to work together for a common goal, such as planning a Mother's Day surprise, playing on a soccer team, or building a sandcastle. Such teamwork helps children recognize and appreciate the contribution of others. When children share and take turns in play ("I get to be the princess next time"), they are learning to balance their own needs and wants with those of others. Praise your children when you see them working or playing together cooperatively.

Teach Conflict Resolution

Just as anger is a normal emotion, conflict is a normal human experience. Children need to learn that people can have different opinions about things, like where they want to eat or what they want to play. We can disagree with someone and still respect their point of view. Children who choose violent options tend to see things in black and white ("He bumped into me on purpose. I'm going to bump him back."), while nonviolent children are able to consider a variety of possible motives for other people's actions ("Maybe he wasn't looking where he was going. Maybe he tripped and bumped me."). Regular family meetings represent ideal opportunities for children to hear differing points of view and gain practice brainstorming possible solutions to dilemmas, with their parents' guidance. Whether the challenge involves making a joint decision about a family vacation, the acquisition of a pet, or the resolution of a conflict among family members, your child can gain practice hearing others' opinions and coming to a mutually agreeable solution.

Promote Problem-Solving

Learning to solve problems is a critical part of growing up and becoming more self-sufficient. Teaching children to solve problems gives them an essential foundation of information and experiences from which to draw as they creatively tackle life's challenges. Children without effective problem-solving skills are less able to cope with everyday challenges and are more prone to frustration and violence. They often make poor life choices because they have difficulty identifying a variety of available options to resolve a dilemma. Those who are adept at problem-solving are able to choose a suitable course of action from a wide repertoire of possibilities. When teaching your child to problem-solve, avoid labeling options as right or wrong. Instead, let

> **Children without effective problem-solving skills are less able to cope with everyday challenges and are more prone to frustration and violence.**

your child suggest the possible consequences and outcomes of the various alternatives under consideration before choosing the best solution. For example, if two siblings are fighting over a toy, options for handling the conflict might include setting a timer and allowing each child to play with the toy for a specified period; allowing the owner to play without sharing; putting the toy away for the rest of the day; or giving the toy to charity to prevent future fights.

We can help our children learn to be problem-solvers by guiding them through the problem-solving process in our own lives. Because of our vast experience in solving daily dilemmas, we do most of the "calculations" in our heads and move from step to step without much thought and with even less discussion. Slowing down the process and talking through the steps can be a great help to a child as she learns to solve her own problems. "Let's see, we have to be at the church picnic at 1:00 P.M. What are the things we have to do to be ready to go? What should we do first?"

Limit Media Exposure to Violence

The average child in America watches over twenty hours of television each week, viewing 12,000 acts of violence on television each year, or 200,000 violent acts by age eighteen. In addition, children are exposed to violence in movies, magazines, video and computer games, popular music, the internet, and other entertainment. More than 1,000 studies confirm a link between heavy television viewing and aggressive behavior, crime, and other forms of societal violence.[1] A steady diet of television violence can cause a child to become callused and desensitized to violence and to view aggression as the normal and expected way to resolve differences. Most violence portrayed on TV has no consequences and perpetrators usually go unpunished. The violence shown in cartoons is the most frequent and least consequential violence on television and teaches that violence is funny. Television violence is especially

> **A steady diet of television violence can cause a child to become callused and desensitized to violence and to view aggression as the normal and expected way to resolve differences.**

damaging to children under eight years because they have trouble distinguishing the difference between fantasy and reality. Furthermore, TV violence does not teach children about alternatives in handling conflict and anger. Also consider that we need to limit our child's exposure to violence on television news reports, which can be terrifying to children.

Parents should limit television to two hours a day of educational programming and monitor their children's media viewing habits. (Television is not recommended for children under two years.) When possible, watch programs with your children and discuss what they see. Help children distinguish between fantasy and real life. Ask them questions like, "What would really happen if someone did that?" Do not have a TV in your child's bedroom or in other locations that prevent you from monitoring what she is watching.

Shield Your Child from Witnessing Violence

Even when children are not directly targeted by violence, they can be emotionally and physically harmed when they are witnesses to violence. At least 3.3 million American children each year witness violence between their parents.[2] Inner-city children, in particular, are witnessing community and domestic violence at younger ages. Early involvement in aggression and violence in the preschool years can set the stage for later violence and criminal activity. Children who witness violence—including hostile verbal arguments—not only suffer psychological trauma, but they may be more likely to resort to violence as a way to handle stress, settle disputes, or protect themselves. At an early age, a child may conclude that unless he is a predator, he is destined to be a victim.

Protect Your Child from Guns

The presence of firearms in a child's home is a serious threat. Americans own over 200,000,000 handguns, and many are kept loaded and ready for use.[3] Countless latchkey children have access to guns when they come home from school. Every day, guns kill eleven American children, and many more are wounded. A gun in the home is forty-three times more likely to be used to kill a family member or a friend than to kill in self-defense.[4] The risk of domestic violence increases dramatically if there is a gun in the house. It's not enough to tell children to stay away from guns. We must keep guns away from children. The safest choice is not to have a gun in your home, especially not a handgun.

If, despite this admonition, guns are in your home, they should be stored unloaded and locked up, with ammunition locked in a different location. Find out whether guns are present in the homes of your child's friends. If so, urge the parents to empty guns and lock them up. Teach children to stay away from guns they may encounter outside the home. Insist that your children never touch a gun!

Despite the extensive media coverage about youth violence, parents need not be overwhelmed or discouraged about this complex problem. Instead, you can take heart in knowing that the kinds of everyday interactions that promote healthy self-esteem can go a long way in confronting the antecedents of aggressive behavior and laying the foundation for peace, mutual respect, and nonviolence.

I have tried to make the case for the essential need to give our children a clear sense of identity, competence, and worth. A child with healthy self-esteem feels deserving of happiness and success and capable of handling life's challenges. Not only is self-acceptance the basis for self-improvement, but self-love is the foundation for compassion toward others. A preschooler's self-esteem is primarily influenced by the quality of her daily interactions with her parents and other significant adult caretakers. A healthy self-image is promoted by the positive messages we convey to our child when we give her our unconditional love and focused attention, accept and reflect her feelings, offer encouragement, teach new skills, promote responsibility, and help her learn from her mistakes. Helping children feel loved and cherished is a priceless gift. The next chapter will equip you to promote desired behavior and handle inevitable misbehavior in your child without undermining her self-esteem or your parent-child bond.

If you would like to read more about fostering your child's self-esteem, I highly recommend the following resources:

Dorothy Corkille Briggs, *Your Child's Self-Esteem* (New York: Doubleday, 1970).

Ross Campbell, *How to Really Love Your Child* (S. P. Publications, Inc., 1992).

Bettie B. Youngs, *How to Develop Self-Esteem in Your Child: 6 Vital Ingredients* (New York: Ballantine Books, 1993).

Chapter 5

The Essentials of Discipline: Love and Limits

What Is Discipline?

Few aspects of parenting provoke as much trepidation as managing children's behavior. Yet God teaches us that discipline is a labor of love: "My son, do not despise the LORD's discipline and do not resent his rebuke, because the LORD disciplines those he loves, as a father the son he delights in" (Prov. 3:11–12). Effective discipline "produces a harvest of righteousness and peace for those who have been trained by it" (Heb. 12:11).

Sadly, many parents make discipline a dirty word that implies the use of punishments and negative consequences to get their children to mind them. Actually, to discipline means to teach. Effective discipline involves guiding, modeling, and providing essential structure in your child's life, with the ultimate goal of promoting lifelong self-discipline, responsibility, and self-control. Unfortunately, inappropriate discipline methods often leave parents feeling frustrated and children feeling misunderstood, resulting in damage to the parent-child relationship. But this doesn't have to be the case. This chapter will teach you how to make effective discipline a positive learning experience that helps your child handle tough feelings, learn right from wrong, make good decisions, solve problems, and develop a measure of orderliness. Are you up for the challenge?

Discipline Does Not Equal Punishment

Too many parents hold the mistaken belief that discipline means punishing children when they break the rules. They think of discipline as yelling, giving a time-out, taking away a privilege, or spanking. In truth, giving punishments, penalties, and negative reinforcement to correct misbehavior should make up only a small part of parental discipline. Although coercion and harsh punishments may produce desired behavior through intimidation, these techniques do not help your child develop self-discipline. Furthermore, excessive use of punishment can damage the parent-child bond, leave children feeling discouraged, and cause them to be fearful and angry. Instead, the most important way to promote appropriate behavior in your child is through the use of positive teaching methods, including your personal example, explanations, and frequent encouragement and praise.

Styles of Parenting

Three parenting categories are most commonly used by experts to describe typical approaches to parenting. No one really uses one parenting style in all situations, but most people have a dominant approach. In addition to reflecting on your parenting style, you will also find it helpful to identify the style or styles used by your parents. If you are dissatisfied with the way you were disciplined in childhood, you will need to make a conscious effort to avoid repeating your parents' mistakes. We are strongly influenced by our experience and have a natural tendency to revert to the familiar when we are under stress. However, with God's help and a firm commitment to doing things differently, it is possible to create a new and better family legacy for our children.

Authoritarian or Autocratic

One extreme in parenting styles is represented by those parents who attempt to control their children's behavior through intimidation, fear, and frequent use of harsh punishments. Such parents bark orders like "Don't ask questions. Just do what I say!" Their explanations consist of "Because I said so!" Some parents who use this authoritarian, or autocratic, approach to parenting have good intentions but are misinformed. Others choose the authoritarian model because they view their children as subordinates to be manipulated and intimidated. Unfortunately, this overly rigid approach to parenting creates an adversarial relationship between parent and child, tends to foster feelings of resentment and rejection, and undermines a child's self-esteem. Furthermore, excessive control can provoke rebellion, not only toward the parents but also against other authority figures.

Permissive or Laissez-Faire

At the opposite extreme are the parents who overindulge their children and establish few limits, which are inconsistently enforced. Often, overly permissive parents are simply unwilling or unable to expend the effort to enforce limits consistently. Others mistakenly believe they have their child's best interests at heart when they rescue their children from unpleasant consequences in a misguided attempt to give them a frustration-free childhood. This permissive, or laissez-faire, parenting style produces self-centered, spoiled, inconsiderate, and demanding children who don't learn to respect the rights of others or to take responsibility for their actions. The unrealistic expectation that they will always get their way makes it difficult for children raised without firm limits to develop satisfying relationships.

> Often, overly permissive parents are simply unwilling or unable to expend the effort to enforce limits consistently.

Democratic or Authoritative

Between these two extremes is the democratic, or authoritative, approach to parenting, which combines both love and limits. Clear and reasonable limits are established and enforced consistently, with an attitude of empathy for the child, mutual respect, and equal worth (if not equal vote). As you can probably guess, the authoritative discipline style is by far the most effective approach. With this method, firm limits are enforced with love and positive example, while maintaining respect for the individuality of the child and his increasing independence.

Why Children Misbehave

Young children naturally want to please their parents and to experience a sense of belonging. Most misbehavior is not deliberate defiance that must be squelched but is simply an appeal for love by a child who doesn't know another way to gain recognition and approval. Or a little one's unacceptable behavior can be explained by the circumstances involved. Not uncommonly, lack of experience and ignorance about early child development causes frustrated parents to misinterpret normal, age-appropriate behavior in preschoolers as "naughty."

Before you jump to conclusions about your child's behavior, step back from the situation, examine the circumstances, put yourself in your child's shoes and view the behavior from his perspective. Ask yourself the following questions.

Is the Behavior the Result of a Misguided Goal?

A child's misbehavior may be motivated by misguided goals, including the desire for attention, control, revenge, or to avoid feelings of inadequacy. For example, a child who is not getting enough positive attention (see chapter 4) may conclude that the negative attention he receives for misbehaving is preferable to feeling ignored. Or another child may feel he has no control over the events in his life, such as the separation of his parents, a move, or the birth of a new sibling. In a misguided attempt to gain a greater sense of control in his life, he may try to manipulate his mother by engaging in a power struggle and "pushing her buttons."

Children who believe that they have been punished unjustly or too harshly may misbehave, sometimes in a clandestine manner, "to even the score." For example, a child banished to his room for accidentally spilling his milk might feel justified if he decides to color on the walls while secluded there. Finally, the child of overly critical parents may despair of ever pleasing them and decide that the best way to avoid criticism is to plead incompetence: "I can't get ready." "I don't know how." By exaggerating her helplessness, she gets others to pity her ("You poor thing; let me do it for you"), but the result is self-pity and depression.

Is the Behavior Explained by Circumstances?

Misbehavior in preschoolers often is due to a child being tired, bored, clumsy, cranky, or hungry. A common example is the two- or three-year-old who has accompanied her busy mom while she runs essential errands all afternoon. When the exhausted and exasperated youngster finally throws a tantrum over a seemingly minor event, her emotional meltdown should not be viewed as misbehavior. Instead, it should be recognized as the inevitable result of skipping a snack, missing a nap, and being unable to play. As a frequent flyer, I sometimes must cope with the delayed departure of an aircraft that already has been boarded. After a critical period of time, a constrained, confused, hot, tired, and hungry toddler predictably begins to wail. When this happens, I smile and think, "That's just what I feel like doing, but can't. Thanks for expressing my frustration for me."

Misbehavior in preschoolers often is due to a child being tired, bored, clumsy, cranky, or hungry.

Are My Expectations for My Child's Behavior Realistic?

Parents who expect too much from their children often misinterpret age-appropriate behavior as being unacceptable. For example, the normal self-centeredness of toddlers makes it difficult, if not impossible, for them to share willingly. I've heard a toddler's conclusions about possessions described something like this:

> "If I like it, it must be mine."
> "If I had it a while ago, it's still mine."
> "If you put it down, it immediately becomes mine."
> "If I'm playing with some of the pieces, all of the pieces are mine."
> "If it's broken, it's yours."

When your toddler is less than enthusiastic about sharing his favorite toy at his weekly play group, he's not being naughty; he's being normal. You may need to purchase two of the most popular toys and be prepared to distract your child when a dispute arises and praise even his most limited attempts at sharing.

I recall an exuberant two-year-old whose mother joined me at a restaurant one morning for breakfast. Little Madi was thrilled to find an attractive display of packaged jams at our table. As she curiously opened a packet and eagerly licked the strawberry jam from her finger, she beamed with delight and graciously offered me a glob of jelly. She then opened several more packages and poked at them to discover whether they, too, contained a sugary treat. As Madi investigated the treasures at our table, her wise and understanding mother did not sternly admonish her to "wipe her fingers and stop playing with the jam," as some parents would have done. Instead, she recognized that Madi was not misbehaving; she was happily exercising her two-year-old drive to explore and learn.

Strategies for Preventing Misbehavior

Before I discuss specific techniques for handling misbehavior, I want to emphasize that there is much you can do to promote desired behavior in young children. Positive behavior is fostered and misbehavior is minimized when clear limits are established and enforced consistently in an atmosphere of love and affection, with respect for the individual child and her emerging independence. The following simple guidelines can encourage and reinforce positive behaviors and minimize misbehavior in your child.

Create a Warm, Loving Parent-Child Bond

A warm, affectionate bond and a positive emotional tone in the home convince a child that he and his parents are on the same team and promote a spirit of cooperation and understanding. All children crave their parents' unconditional love and need their daily guidance and support and consistent care to promote learning. The best way to convey your unconditional love is to spend "special time" or "focused attention" or "time-in" with each child daily for at least fifteen to twenty minutes. (See chapter 4 for techniques to build your child's self-esteem.) Help your child feel respected by treating him like company, speaking to him politely, and assuming the best in your child.

A warm, affectionate bond and a positive emotional tone in the home convince a child that he and his parents are on the same team and promote a spirit of cooperation and understanding.

Provide Consistency and Structure

Young children gain a sense of security and essential structure when certain activities, like mealtimes, bedtime, and play, occur with reassuring regularity. Simple familiar routines, like bedtime rituals or having a snack after awakening from a nap, give children a comforting sense of expectation and control. Establishing regular routines and predictable order in your child's life helps her know what to expect from you, thus reducing misbehavior, uncertainty, and anxiety. Many young children need assistance making the transition from one activity to another. You can help them shift gears by giving ample notice: "In a few minutes, it will be time to stop playing and get ready for your bath." "After this program is over, we'll need to leave for the store."

Set Clear Limits

Young children require developmentally appropriate boundaries to keep them safe, define the limits of acceptable behavior, and help them learn self-control. Having too few limits gives children an inflated sense of their own power and spurs them to provoke power struggles and test the limits even harder to get their parents to assert their authority. Although children may not like the rules, they deserve to receive explanations for limits and expected consequences for breaking the rules. If your children are old enough, you'll find that giving them a voice in setting the rules will increase their motivation to adhere to the limits.

Use short, simple, specific comments ("Remember, sand stays in the sandbox") rather than generalizations ("Play nicely"). Present rules in a positive and impersonal manner ("The family rule is, we eat politely"), rather than using negative or emotional terms ("I said, don't throw food!"). Generally, children understand more clearly what we expect when we state the rule in the positive: "Food is to be eaten only in the kitchen or the den." When a child hears a negative command like "No running on the furniture," the mental image she creates is running on the furniture, instead of the acceptable alternatives. If you do state a rule in the negative, like "Don't hit," couple it with the appropriate behavior: "We use words to tell people we are angry."

Enforce Rules Consistently

Even when you are physically or emotionally depleted, it is important to enforce the rules in a consistent manner. When parents are inconsistent in their expectations, children are left confused about where the boundaries really lie. The resulting mixed message only provokes more testing of the rules as the child seeks reassurance that you are in control.

While it is harder in the short-term to discipline in a consistent manner, having the fortitude to enforce rules, even when you don't feel like it, ultimately reduces misbehavior and makes discipline easier in the long run.

Having the fortitude to enforce rules, even when you don't feel like it, ultimately reduces misbehavior and makes discipline easier in the long run.

Have Realistic Expectations

Make certain your expectations for your child's behavior match her age and developmental abilities. (See chapter 2.) I recall a harried working mother who told her dawdling four-year-old daughter to just eat half of her cereal so they could get out the door on time. "What's a half?" the puzzled youngster asked.

Overcontrolling parents often make the mistake of having too many rules or setting unrealistic expectations for their child. A child's genuine inability to comply with the rules can make her appear uncooperative. For example, yelling at your three-year-old to clean her room when she doesn't know how will be an exercise in futility and will make your child appear to be noncompliant. Instead, be prepared to show your preschooler what you want her to do, then help her by guiding her as she practices the skill. Only when she has demonstrated that she is capable of performing the task herself can you expect her to do it alone. Help your child build on her successes by praising her for making a good effort or even partially completing a task. Emphasize what she has done well, rather than what could be improved.

Use Positive Communication Techniques

The most important key to effective discipline is an enduring, supportive parent-child relationship based on trust, mutual respect, and positive communication.

The Value of Rules and Limits

Rules and limits provide the framework around which children organize their learning. Having boundaries helps children understand what behavior is expected of them and what will happen if they don't comply. Age-appropriate rules that are consistently enforced offer children the following benefits.

- Firm limits reassure children that the adults in their world are in control. No matter how much your preschooler acts like she wants to be in charge, having too much power is frightening to a child. Kids intuitively know they need their parents to be in control and to place limits on their behavior.
- Rules prepare children for successful living in a complex world. Learning to obey simple family rules, like "no name-calling" and "put your toys away after you play," helps equip children to follow society's legal and moral laws of conduct.
- Rules help children learn about appropriate social interactions. Having rules of etiquette and teaching basic manners, like apologizing for hurting someone's feelings or not taking something that belongs to another without asking, teach children how to live in harmony with others and to show mutual respect in their interactions.
- Rules and limits provide essential structure. Rules help provide a sense of order and predictability by letting children know what will come next ("Wash your hands before we eat") or anticipate what will happen when a limit is broken ("You're going to time-out if you push Jamal again"). Simple rules, like "Say 'excuse me' if you must interrupt," help a child learn appropriate ways to get what he wants.

- Rules teach children to obey authority figures. Children who learn to cooperate with parental expectations are more likely to respect other authority figures, like classroom teachers, coaches, Scout leaders, and employers, ultimately preparing them to become law-abiding citizens.
- Rules help children behave appropriately and to feel competent. Children who know what is required of them are better able to comply with parental expectations and gain the sense of belonging and approval they crave.
- Gradually expanding a child's limits builds his confidence and sense of responsibility. Just as society gives children increasing responsibility as they mature, parents appropriately expand the limits placed on their child. Children take pride in achieving milestones like no longer needing a nap or having a later bedtime.
- Rules and limits help assure the physical safety of children. Just as traffic speed limits are designed to protect people from harm, many parental rules are meant to ensure our child's safety: "The car won't go until your seat belt is buckled" or "Don't talk to strangers."

Acknowledge and Accept Tough Feelings

Misbehavior often results when a child has trouble handling hard feelings. Make an effort to acknowledge and accept your child's feelings, especially difficult ones like anger and sadness. (See chapter 4.) Say, "I know you are disappointed that we have to leave now. You wish you could play longer." You don't have to actually change your decision and let your child keep playing; just let her know that you recognize her feelings and that they are legitimate. Practice active listening by reflecting what she has said, without judging: "So you think that Carol should help clean up because she played too." You can validate her feelings by saying something like, "I can understand how frustrating that must be." You can even help her take appropriate action: "Why don't you ask Carol to put some of the cars away?"

Separate Your Child from His Behavior

When dealing with misbehavior, it is essential that you separate your child's character from his actions by labeling the behavior, not the child. Never blast your child with judgments like "Bad boy," "Shame on you," "I'm so disappointed in you," or "You're so clumsy." Your child needs to know that you love him even when you don't like his actions or words. Keep your focus on the behavior by saying, "No hitting," "Stop teasing," or "Use your indoor voice."

Your child needs to know that you love him even when you don't like his actions or words.

Use "I" Messages Instead of "You" Messages

"I" messages are less emotionally charged because they communicate the effect of your child's behavior on you. On the other hand, "you" messages tend to criticize, nag, or blame your child. Say, "I don't like to hear fighting because it makes me think someone is getting hurt," instead of exclaiming, "Stop that fighting, you two! Can't you ever get along?" (See chapter 4.)

Show Your Appreciation for Your Child

Another way to build your child's sense of self-worth and promote positive behavior is by thanking him for his contributions and making him aware of his significance to others. Name the specific behavior and tell your child how it makes you feel: "Thanks for sharing with your sister. It makes me proud and happy to see how kind you are to her." Your child feels valued and respected when you humble yourself by apologizing to him when you have behaved inappropriately: "I'm sorry I yelled at you for spilling your lemonade. I realize it was an accident. Will you forgive me?"

Be a Good Role Model

Let your own healthy model and frequent praise for positive behavior motivate and instruct your child. Just as God gave us a human example of the perfect way to live in the person of Jesus Christ, parents represent a positive role model (albeit imperfect) for our children. Your parental model of cooperation, sharing, handling disagreements, displaying good manners, and showing respect for others will powerfully shape your child's behavior, since young children naturally mimic adults. Actions do speak louder than words, and children would rather see our living sermon than hear us preach to them. Because children despise hypocrisy, you won't be able to shape the behavior you want by screaming at your child for talking back at you, slapping her for hitting her brother, belittling her for teasing, or whining at her about her whining. You should also consider the other role models who may influence your child's behavior by monitoring what she watches on television and helping her choose playmates who set a good example.

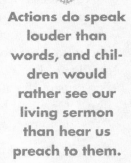

Actions do speak louder than words, and children would rather see our living sermon than hear us preach to them.

Give Your Child Appropriate Choices

Young children often feel they have little control in their lives. After all, no one asks their input about Daddy's departure, Mommy's work schedule, or their new child-care arrangements. A child's need to feel a greater sense of control can provoke power struggles with his parents. Allowing young children to make simple daily choices about what to wear, what to eat, or which story to read can reduce misbehavior by giving them an appropriate sense of control. In addition, offering choices teaches children about making decisions, honors your child's individuality, and makes your rules more acceptable.

Keep choices simple, however—two are adequate for preschoolers—so you don't overwhelm your child. Also, never offer a choice when none exists. For example, don't ask, "Do you want to fasten your seat belt?" Instead, you could offer, "Do you want me to tell you a 'knock-knock' joke while I buckle you up?"

Avoid the Overuse of No

Consider the number of times your preschooler hears you say no to his requests in a single day. Excessively telling your child no can increase his feelings of powerlessness. Think about whether you can give a qualified yes instead of always saying no. For example, when your youngster petitions, "Can I go outside?" you can answer, "Yes, you may, right after your nap." Or when he asks, "Can I watch TV?" you can reply, "Yes, of course, as soon as we finish picking up the toys."

Unhook from Power Struggles

Even with the best of intentions, some parent-child conflicts inevitably will arise. Refuse to fall for the common trap of needing to prove your power over your child whenever she provokes you. Instead, when you find yourself in an emotional tug-of-war, just drop your end of the rope and withdraw from the conflict, not from your child. Don't take your preschooler's outbursts personally, become emotional, or allow conflicts to escalate. Instead, keep your anger under control, and watch her anger quickly fizzle. Don't succumb to the temptation to argue back when your child protests, stomps, calls you names or says she hates you. Instead, acknowledge her hard feelings, and let her know that you still love her, even though you disapprove of her behavior. When you defuse a

When you find yourself in an emotional tug-of-war, just drop your end of the rope and withdraw from the conflict, not from your child.

volatile situation by leaving the battlefield, you are showing your child that the power of love can overcome a power struggle.

Reinforce Desired Behavior

One of the most important principles of effective discipline is to never take positive behavior for granted. Many parents make the mistake of trying to foster positive behavior by punishing wrongdoing. Yet the best way to promote more of the behavior you want is to reinforce your child for getting things right. For example, praising a child for sharing will help increase his generosity, whereas scolding or coercing him to share will only make him resentful and more possessive.

The best secret to shaping positive behavior in your child is to "catch him being good" and give immediate positive reinforcement. Positive reinforcement, or the use of rewards, encourages desired behavior by providing attention (smiling, touching, patting, compliments, praise) and tangible rewards (treats, stickers, tokens, toys, activities) for behaving well. Positive reinforcement is most effective when given immediately, rather than delayed. Reward even small steps toward the desired behavior, such as completing a single task in his bedtime routine. Acknowledge any improvement you observe: "You made pee-pee in the potty this time. That's great!" By three or four years of age, when children can understand delayed gratification, you can use token rewards for positive behavior (stars or stickers accumulated on a chart) that can be collected and redeemed for special gifts, treats, or favorite activities with Mom or Dad.

When you praise your child, be specific and let her know exactly what she did correctly. Instead of saying, "You've been such a good girl," explain, "I like the way you helped me pick up all the play dough," "Thank you for putting your own dish in the sink," or "I appreciate how gently you are petting the cat."

Generally, the effectiveness of positive reinforcement is based on its timing. An incentive given simultaneously with the desirable behavior is the most effective. When you stop folding the laundry to lean over and give three-year-old Rachel a hug, saying, "I like to see you turning the pages of your book so carefully," you encourage more of the desired behavior.

> **The best secret to shaping positive behavior in your child is to "catch him being good" and give immediate positive reinforcement.**

Rewards are promised incentives to be given after a specific behavior has occurred. A reward is something your child can work toward and feel proud about earning: "Taylor, if you stay in your seat while we are at the restaurant, I'll take you to the playground afterward." The younger the child, the closer the reward needs to be to the desired behavior: "Devon, Grandma's ready to read you a story, as soon as you get your other shoe on." Be careful not to overuse rewards or your child may come to regularly expect payment for positive behavior: "What will you give me if I pick up all my toys?"

A bribe is an advance payoff given either to produce desired behavior or to stop undesired behavior, "I'll buy you the pack of gum if you promise not to ask for anything else." "I'll listen to what you want to say if you promise not to interrupt me again during my telephone call." The crucial difference is that a bribe is given *before* the desired behavior and is always less effective than positive reinforcement or rewards given in close proximity to the behavior. In fact, all too often, a bribe produces a result opposite of what you had hoped.

Effective Consequences for Misbehavior

Although the preceding strategies will go a long way toward decreasing problem behavior, even the most cooperative children sometimes will misbehave. When they do, parents are responsible for consistently enforcing the limits and redirecting misbehavior.

Do you ever feel you lack the creativity to manage problem behavior? Instead of selecting an appropriate strategy from a

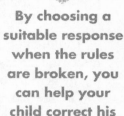

wide variety of available, effective discipline techniques, many parents overuse a limited repertoire of punishments: yelling, time-out, threatening, or spanking. By choosing a suitable response when the rules are broken, you can help your child correct his behavior without dealing a blow to his self-esteem or your relationship. Depending on the individual child and his age, the circumstances, and the particular misdeed, you may decide to do nothing, impose a penalty, call a time-out, ask your child to be part of the solution, or take other action. Because every family is different and each child is unique, some techniques will work better for certain families and situations. Watch your child's reaction to the penalty you impose. Remember, the purpose of redirecting misbehavior is to help your child gain self-control and learn to make better choices about how to act—not to leave him discouraged and resentful. Below are some strategies to consider. Choose those that seem most effective and comfortable for you and your child.

> *By choosing a suitable response when the rules are broken, you can help your child correct his behavior without dealing a blow to his self-esteem or your relationship.*

Distractions and Environmental Modifications

You will recall from your child's infancy that discipline for babies under a year of age requires a baby-proof environment in which an infant can safely explore and your vigilant supervision. When a baby ventures toward an unacceptable activity, such as reaching for electrical wires or dumping the trash can, we dutifully and skillfully distract him and steer him toward something else. Although we can say no as we remove them from danger, babies and toddlers cannot be expected to understand rules and consequences and, thus, need constant supervision. Distraction is still effective in many situations involving toddlers and even preschoolers. Instead of always reprimanding your child about something off-limits and overwhelming him with "no-no's," try distracting him by starting to tell a story or saying, "Oh, come look at this over here."

Ignore Minor Transgressions and Nondestructive Misbehavior

Children often misbehave when they are seeking attention, under the mistaken belief that they can gain a sense of belonging by getting their parents to focus on them. Even a scolding can be rewarding for an attention-craving child who basks in his parent's undivided attention during the reprimand. By ignoring minor, attention-getting offenses, you also avoid subjecting children to excessive negative criticism that can damage their self-esteem.

The types of behaviors that are best ignored include whining, pouting, arguing with siblings, dawdling at meals, or experimenting with swear words. Ignoring is most effective when it is coupled with plenty of focused attention for the desired behavior; for example, listening attentively when your child speaks in a normal tone of voice or giving compliments for getting ready on time. "Thank you for getting ready so quickly. Now we'll have time for a story before we go." I should warn you, however, that ignoring misbehavior might initially cause it to increase before it decreases, as your child intensifies his efforts to draw attention to the behavior.

You should also make a concerted effort to ignore the verbal resistance, high drama, and excuses ("No fair." "I don't want to go to bed." "I'm not even tired.") that your child uses to distract you from the issue at hand. Try to view such protests as harmless grumbling and simply ignore the uproar.

Warnings

Young children just learning appropriate behavior need frequent reminders about rules and consequences. A brief, well-timed warning can prevent misbehavior before it starts or cut it short. To be effective, however, threats or warnings need to be specific and carried out as promised: "Robbie, I'm warning you; if you throw food again, we're leaving the restaurant." Then add "You choose" or "You decide" to remind your child of his personal power, that the actions he chooses will dictate the consequences he experiences. Although enforcing a warning may, at times, be more inconvenient to you than to your child (for example, leaving a restaurant if your child becomes disruptive), your prompt compliance with the terms of the warning will quickly convince your child that you mean what you say, making your future warnings highly effective.

> A brief, well-timed warning can prevent misbehavior before it starts or cut it short.

Firm warnings are very different from the empty threats that children quickly learn to ignore. Many parents are in the habit of using exaggerated threats of dire consequences they have no intention of carrying out or that are so vague they are meaningless: "That's it! I'm giving all your presents away." "This is the last time I'm warning you! You're really going to get it this time!" "Do that again and you're going to regret it!" Children quickly learn to tune out this kind of chatter as harmless background noise. In the long run, you'll discover that specific, deliberate warnings that are promptly enforced are far more effective than exaggerated ultimatums or idle threats.

Scoldings and Reprimands

Often a properly administered verbal scolding is all that is needed to redirect misbehavior. However, there is a big difference between an effective scolding and a protracted tirade that erodes a child's self-esteem. Do not deliver an inappropriately long scolding or link your child's character with his misbehavior by making comments like "How could you do such a thing?" "What a troublemaker," "I'm so disappointed in you."

Don't shame your child or inflict excessive guilt with destructive remarks like "Shame on you. You're a bad boy. You ought to be ashamed of yourself."

Instead, begin by briefly expressing your command to stop the undesired behavior: "Stop throwing dirt." Offer a brief explanation for the limit: "People don't like dirt on their clothes or in their eyes." Continue the scolding by enforcing the established consequence of the misbehavior: "You know the rule. If you throw dirt again, we'll have to leave the park." An effective scolding also provides an acceptable alternative: "Dirt belongs on the ground." Be sure to end the reprimand on a positive note, by giving a compliment, hug, smile, or other affirmation: "Good listening, Joey. Thank you."

Physical Assistance

A common parental complaint is that their preschooler won't obey simple commands; for example, to wash up for dinner or put his toys away. The parent finds herself calling out the same request a dozen times, without taking any action to assure the child complies. Instead of getting her child to obey her, however, giving repeated commands only teaches a youngster to ignore and tune out parental instructions. To increase prompt compliance with a parent's commands, follow the principle of "one request only." When you tell your child to do something, stand nearby, make eye contact, and state your instructions clearly: "I expect you to get in the car now." Then if your child does not begin to carry out your request within about ten seconds, take his hand and guide him in the completion of the task. You may have to carry your child to the car or pick up most of the toys yourself, but he will get the message that compliance is expected now, not when or if he feels like it. Stay calm while shepherding your child in completing the task. Don't get angry, nag, or create a power struggle. In a matter-of-fact way, just make it clear that he will do what is requested.

Natural Consequences

Children over three years can start to grasp the concept of cause and effect and can learn from the natural consequences of their actions. Letting your child experience some natural consequences of his behavior can be particularly effective when his undesirable behavior doesn't directly affect you. Because natural consequences are impersonal and unemotional, they are especially effective modifiers of behavior. A child soon learns that if he teases the dog despite your admonitions, he might get nipped. Or a child learns that if she doesn't consider the needs and wants of others, she can't expect to keep a friend engaged in play. Or a child finds he gets hungry midafternoon if he declines to eat what was offered at lunch. A toy that has been broken through mishandling is less fun to play with than when it worked right.

Logical Consequences

As adults, most of the consequences we experience for breaking society's rules are logical. If someone gets too many traffic citations, they risk losing their driver's license, not their ski pass. If they don't make their car payments, their vehicle gets repossessed, not their furniture. Consequences for children are more instructive when they are logically related to the offense. When your four-year-old twins argue over a particular toy, put the toy away until they can work out a solution (which will probably require your input). If they fight over which television program to watch, turn the TV off until they can come to an agreement. If your five-year-old rides his bike in the street, the bike gets put away for the rest of the day. Toys that aren't picked up as required get placed in an "off limits" box the next day.

Consequences for children are more instructive when they are logically related to the offense.

Loss of a Privilege

The loss of privileges can be an effective deterrent to misbehavior. Temporarily taking away something a child values, like TV time or a favorite toy, can teach the lesson that if you break a rule, you must pay with something you like. For example, when your uncooperative dawdler takes too long getting ready for bed, he may have to forego hearing a story. Or if your child doesn't stay in his room during "quiet time," he doesn't get to watch a video later in the day. You might want to determine in advance some reasonable consequences for common offenses to avoid giving an overly harsh or inappropriate penalty during a moment of anger. For example, it's never appropriate to withhold your affection or reject your child emotionally as a punishment. I also don't advise taking away dessert if your child didn't eat his meal. Chronic eating disorders can be fostered when food is given emotional connotations.

Making Restitution

When a child's misbehavior causes another person to suffer hurt feelings, creates inconvenience, or results in property damage, it is appropriate to require your child to make restitution, which can be likened to court-ordered community service. Restitution can be as simple as asking your preschooler to apologize for her rude remark or return a sibling's toy "borrowed" without permission. Or it can involve helping rebuild her brother's tower of blocks that she knocked over, or gently patting the "owie" she caused by hitting him. Being required to help clean up after creating a spill or mess is also a form of restitution. Making amends teaches children about the rights and feelings of others, being responsible for their hurtful actions, and correcting their mistakes.

Time-Out

A particularly effective way to deal with misbehavior in young children is to briefly remove the child from activity and attention to sit or stand in a quiet, subdued location. This form of brief social isolation—known as time-out—quickly helps a frustrated or angry child cope with hard feelings and regain self-control. It is most effective when used sparingly and immediately to interrupt a few problem behaviors, especially those that infringe on the rights of others. Time-out is an excellent technique to reduce aggressive or other antisocial behavior (such as biting, hurting others, emotional outbursts) in young children and to help them gain control over their impulses.

Social isolation is especially appropriate for antisocial behavior, since it requires a child to leave her family or friends when her behavior is unacceptable and allows her to rejoin the others once she has regained her composure and can control her impulses. Taking a time-out can be very helpful when a child or parent is upset; it defuses a tense situation and gives both parties a chance to calm down and start over. During the time-out period, the child can think about her unacceptable actions, while the parent can reflect on how to better handle the behavior. If your child refuses to go to time-out, physically assist her. If she gets up, escort her back and reset a portable timer nearby for the full duration. You may have to calmly but firmly place your hands on her shoulders to remind her to stay seated. The following suggestions for using time-out will maximize its effectiveness.

> Taking a time-out can be very helpful when a child or parent is upset; it defuses a tense situation and gives both parties a chance to calm down and start over.

- Time-out is most effective when enforced immediately. Remove the child from the mainstream of activity as soon as you observe the inappropriate behavior and take her to the time-out place. Give an immediate time-out even when you are away from home, instead of threatening, "As soon as we get home, you're going to time-out."

- A good rule of thumb for time-out is one minute for each year of age. Leaving a child for longer periods does no good and may actually backfire. Young children quickly forget why they are there and become impatient and resentful, which provokes more misbehavior. Setting a timer, which is impersonal, to signal the end of time-out will decrease your involvement in monitoring the elapsed time.

- Assume that your child wants to behave in a manner she can be proud of. Treat time-out not as a punishment but as a compassionate means of helping a disruptive child control her impulses, regain her composure, and start over in her interactions. Thus, if a child announces that she has calmed down before the time-out period is up and says she is ready to come out, congratulate her on being able to compose herself so quickly and welcome her back into your midst. Then talk about her frustration or anger that triggered the inappropriate behavior and help her learn acceptable ways to cope with difficult emotions.

- Select only one or two undesirable behaviors to reduce with this discipline technique. Time-out works best to curb impulsive, aggressive, or antisocial behavior. Over-reliance on time-out for too many problem behaviors may diminish its effectiveness and lead to resistance.

1-2-3 or Counting Method

This popular technique is described in detail in Dr. Thomas Phelan's practical discipline guide, *1-2-3 Magic* (Glen Ellyn, Ill.: Child Management Inc., 1995). It is a specific warning method used to stop undesirable behavior, such as arguing, whining, or interrupting. When the offensive behavior begins, you hold up one finger and calmly announce, "That's one." If your child persists with the negative behavior after a few seconds, you hold up two fingers and simply say, "That's two."

Then if your child still doesn't stop the problem behavior, you hold up three fingers and say firmly but without getting emotional, "That's three. You're going to time-out." Maintain a matter-of-fact attitude as you count and enforce the penalty every time you reach three. After you have used the counting method a few times, your child will probably correct her behavior on the count of one or two. It's important that you count without making other remarks, as any nagging or editorializing you add will only detract from the power of your warning and encourage your child to argue and test you more. Obviously, the technique is not recommended for behavior that must be interrupted immediately, such as biting.

Use of a Timer

A timer can be useful in helping a child learn self-control; for example, being able to sit still for a short period or not interrupt while a parent is talking on the telephone. Set the timer for one to three minutes at first, while you give your child something interesting to occupy him like a puzzle or storybook. You can make it a game by inviting your child to set self-imposed limits and rewarding him for sitting still or remaining quiet for the designated length of time. You can use the timer, coupled with a reward to reinforce the desired behavior: "If you can sit quietly and color for four minutes while I finish this phone call, I'll play race cars with you."

"When . . . Then"

This concept is known as "Grandma's Rule" or "Work before Play." The technique of "When . . . then" involves offering your child a positive incentive for complying with your directive. The method works well when you want something done, like getting dressed in the morning, and are willing to wait for it to be accomplished. You make something your child wants to do conditional on something else that needs to be done first: "When you are finished getting dressed, then we can make pancakes." "When you get your pajamas on, then you can have your story." "When you get up from your nap, then we will go to the pool." It's important to say "when," which conveys the message that the job will get done, rather than "if," which implies that it may not get done at all.

Involve Your Child in Resolving the Problem

Assume that your child wants to cooperate with you and wants you to be pleased with her behavior. Choose a time when both of you are happy. Sit down together and ask for your child's input regarding the problem—bedtime battles, fighting, talking back. Explain that you don't like having daily hassles over bedtime and that you want to make your evenings happier and more peaceful for both of you. Ask your child to make suggestions for finding a mutually acceptable solution, and whenever possible, implement one or more of her suggestions.

Involving children in the resolution of sibling disputes can be helpful in reducing this common source of frustration for parents. Even preschool children can help set ground rules for disagreements and suggest consequences for breaking the rules. For example, siblings can agree that fair fighting means not to hit, call names, or break toys.

The Spanking Controversy

The subject of spanking, or corporal punishment, is highly controversial in our society. Part of the controversy stems from the wide interpretation of what constitutes corporal punishment, which can range from slapping the hand of a child about to reach for something dangerous to severe beatings and other forms of outright physical abuse. While many well-meaning parents sometimes spank their children, concerns have been raised in modern society about the negative effects of spanking on children's outcome and the risk that any use of corporal punishment could escalate into child abuse.

One consensus of thought is reflected in the 1998 American Academy of Pediatrics (AAP) policy statement "Guidance for Effective Discipline." In this document, the AAP recommended that parents should be encouraged to use methods other than spanking to manage children's misbehavior because corporal punishment has limited effectiveness compared to other discipline methods and has potentially harmful side effects.[1] Acceptable spanking was clarified as striking a child with an open hand on the buttocks or extremities in order to modify behavior without resulting physical harm. The AAP identified the following types of physical punishment as never being acceptable:[2]

Parents should be encouraged to use methods other than spanking to manage children's misbehavior because corporal punishment has limited effectiveness compared to other discipline methods and has potentially harmful side effects.

- Hitting a child with an object
- Hitting a child anywhere except on the bottom or extremities
- Leaving marks that are visible for more than a few minutes
- Pulling a child's hair or jerking a child by the arm
- Shaking a child
- Hitting a child in anger

On the other side of the spanking argument are those who insist that limited physical punishment, when accompanied by affection and explanation, is a safe and effective parenting tool for special situations, such as dangerous misbehavior and willful disobedience. For example, a swat on the bottom or slap on the hand may startle a child and abruptly stop undesired behavior. Some Christian parents may feel they have a biblical mandate to use corporal punishment to correct misbehavior. They turn to verses such as these: "Do not withhold discipline from a child. . . . Punish him with the rod and save his soul from death" (Prov. 23:13–14); and "The rod of correction imparts wisdom, but a child left to himself disgraces his mother" (Prov. 29:15). Proponents of spanking argue that just as the painful nip of a dog or the burn from a hot stove teaches a child about dangers in the physical world, the pain associated with a spanking for deliberate misbehavior teaches a child about the need to adhere to life's social boundaries.[3]

Even those who advocate corporal punishment, however, caution that its use should be infrequent, that spanking should be confined to the buttocks, and that no one should spank in anger or when out of control.[4] Obviously, even parents who occasionally spank will need to rely on the other discipline methods outlined in this chapter to correct misbehavior in their child.

With some thirty years' perspective as a parent and health professional, I have carefully examined the spanking issue for myself and come to the firm conclusion that it is preferable *not* to spank. I will outline here some of the arguments that I found most convincing in my own decision to recommend against spanking.

- Spanking offers no significant benefits and poses the risk of physical harm. The numerous discipline techniques outlined in this chapter are highly effective in shaping positive behavior, enforcing limits, and ensuring a child's physical safety. You can be a highly effective disciplinarian without resorting to hitting children, yet thousands of times each year, physical punishment escalates to outright child abuse. Even well-meaning parents can lose control and unintentionally hit too hard. The majority of parents who spank say they would rather not if they had an effective alternative discipline method. Although many parents insist they can remain calm while spanking, the truth is that parents often are angry and agitated when they resort to physical punishment.

Accidentally hitting too hard can't happen to parents who don't spank at all.

- Spanking is not a helpful model for a child. A child who has been spanked for misbehaving certainly can't smack his parent, sibling, or a playmate when he doesn't like the way they act. Instead of teaching a logical lesson, spanking is highly confusing to children when parents inappropriately use physical punishment to correct aggressive behavior, as in *(whack)* "Don't hit your brother." Repeated spanking promotes aggression as a way to handle conflict and may increase aggressive behavior in preschool and school-aged children.

- Spanking can result in emotional harm to a child and an altered parent-child relationship. This is especially true when parents combine corporal punishment with harsh criticism and disparaging remarks (yelling, shaming, ridiculing).

- Spanking in our present social context may be more dangerous than in past generations. Most adults today were spanked as children and formed an opinion about spanking based on their parents' practices, which they feel the need to justify. I often hear adults exclaim, "I was spanked, and I turned out okay." In today's society, however, it may be more difficult for parents to spank with appropriate restraint. The rise in single-parent, dual-earner, and blended families, coupled with our societal epidemic of violence and the magnitude of our national drug and alcohol problem, has increased the stress and complexity of our family lives. While you may be able to spank appropriately, many stressed parents today are likely to lose control, leaving many children at risk as long as spanking remains socially acceptable.

The fact is that spanking is losing popularity in our society, and parents who spank increasingly risk public scrutiny and even claims of child abuse. For those parents who want to keep

Common Discipline Errors

Despite our best intentions, it's easy to fall into discipline traps that can strain your parent-child relationship and leave both of you feeling frustrated. Faced with problem behavior when their defenses are down, many parents unthinkingly revert to familiar, ineffective patterns of responding to misbehavior. Beware of these common pitfalls.

- *Excessive use of punishment.* Some parents forget that punishments should be used sparingly. They find themselves giving more and harsher penalties for increasing misbehavior. But the excessive criticism and reprimands their child receives leave him too discouraged to choose more appropriate ways to feel accepted and valued. To reverse this destructive pattern, parents must break out of the punishment trap, start encouraging their children, and reshape their behavior through positive reinforcement.

  Begin by giving your child your focused, positive attention (time-in) at unexpected times throughout the day, while reducing the negative attention he receives for the problem behavior. Praise your child whenever he demonstrates the particular behavior you are trying to promote: "Thanks for coming the first time I called you." "I appreciate your cooperation." Better yet, link your verbal compliment with a small reward. You can say, "Wow, you're almost done picking up your toys. As soon as you finish, we can frost the cupcakes." Mention the things your child does well: "That was a lovely song." "You sing very well." Let your child know how much you love and accept him: "That was a great story. I sure enjoy reading to you." As your child learns that he can gain a sense of acceptance and belonging through cooperation, he will naturally respond with increased self-motivation and responsibility.

- *Waging too many battles.* Many parents dilute their discipline effectiveness by waging too many battles. If a tape were played of their daily verbal interactions with their child, they would hear an endless string of admonitions, commands, and reprimands: "Stop that!" "Just look at this mess." "Don't touch that again." "I said no!" "Eat your carrots." "Put that down; it's dirty." "Wipe your hands!" "Don't use that word again!" Subjected to an unrelenting barrage of verbal imperatives, your little one may be unable to distinguish a life-threatening safety concern from an insignificant, irritating behavior. Don't get stuck in the trap of believing you must police every move your child makes. Instead, choose your battles wisely and appreciate that in discipline, less is better.

- *Overuse of time-out.* I often hear parents complain that "I've tried time-out, but it doesn't work." Usually the explanation is that time-out is either being overused or inappropriately enforced.

  Common errors parents make in imposing time-outs include using the technique for too many problem behaviors (everything from hitting others, not picking up toys, to not eating a meal); giving a delayed, instead of an immediate, time-out ("You're going to time-out as soon as dinner is over!"); and imposing an excessively long time-out period, instead of one minute per year of age ("You're not coming out for half an hour!"). I think it's also inappropriate to treat time-out as a sentence to be served in full ("I don't care if you say you're ready to come out. You're staying there until the timer goes off!"). Because I view it as a benevolent way to help a child learn impulse control, I think we should let her rejoin our company if she has pulled herself together before the timer goes off. What's important is talking about the episode that triggered the need for time-out once everyone has calmed down. By avoiding the trap of misusing time-out, you can maximize the effectiveness of this popular discipline technique.

- *Perpetuating power struggles.* Many parents allow themselves to become entangled in destructive power struggles with their children that can damage the parent-child relationship. Instead of allowing your anger and frustration to fuel a disagreement with your child, learn to recognize your part in a power struggle and disengage from destructive conflicts before they escalate. Let your child know that the two of you are not adversaries, but that you are both on the same team. Try to identify the hard feelings she is experiencing and convey your acceptance: "I know you don't want to leave right now. You were hoping to finish watching the video." Remember to give ample notice before an enjoyable activity must end. Adhering to daily routines for meals, naptime, and playtime helps reduce power struggles by letting young children know what to expect from their parents. Similarly, giving limited choices about what to eat or do or wear helps give children appropriate power that reduces their need to wage a battle with you.

- *Withdrawing parental affection.* Although withdrawing a privilege, like restricting TV time or access to a favorite toy, can be an effective deterrent to misbehavior, parents should never withhold their affection as a form of punishment. Saying, "I wish you were never born," giving your child the cold shoulder treatment, or rebuffing his attempt to hug you or apologize to you makes your child feel terribly rejected. Such behavior damages the parent-child relationship and teaches your youngster that your love has conditions. Instead of withdrawing your affection, make it clear that you still love your child, even when his behavior is unacceptable.

spanking as part of your discipline repertoire, I offer the following guidelines.

- Do not spank a child under eighteen months of age or over six years.
- Do not spank for physically aggressive behavior.
- Use only your open hand, not a belt, switch, or paddle.
- Swat only the child's bottom or give a hand slap.
- Hit only one time and leave no marks.
- Never shake a child; shaking can cause severe brain injury!
- Never spank in anger or if you have been drinking.

How to Manage Common Problem Behavior of Preschoolers

Now let's turn our attention to the practical application of the preceding concepts. As is often the case, the transition from theory to practice can be difficult. Confronted with the behavior problems common to preschoolers, a parent can easily be distracted from the purpose of discipline. For the Christian, discipline must always be an act of love. In our exercise of discipline, we partner with God in the growing of his and our child. Whenever discipline becomes something "about us"—our pride, our control, our need for approval or to meet expectations—then we miss the mark for both our child and God. Rather, discipline must always be about giving our children the skills, attitudes, and competencies that allow them to live in a manner pleasing to God. It is about guiding their steps in his way, so that when they are old, they "will not turn from it" (Prov. 22:6).

It is impossible to overstate the need for us to approach our parenting, and especially our discipline, with prayer and the heartfelt seeking after God's wisdom, patience, and self-control.

Consequently, it is impossible to overstate the need for us to approach our parenting, and especially our discipline, with prayer and the heartfelt seeking after God's wisdom, patience, and self-control. The following section outlines specific strategies you can implement to effectively manage the common behavior problems of preschoolers. In every case, take care not to stifle your child's spirit but to encourage, nurture, and cultivate the bloom of Christlikeness in her.

Tantrums

As young children gain increasing independence, they develop clear ideas about their wants and desires. When their abilities don't measure up to their expectations or when their parents must intervene to stop dangerous behavior, toddlers and preschoolers are easily frustrated. (See chapter 2.) Because young children lack the verbal skills to talk about their frustrations and feelings of powerlessness, they resort to communicating their intense feelings with their whole body by kicking, screaming, lying on the floor, or throwing something. A tantrum outburst can result from a parental refusal of a request or a child's inability to manipulate a toy successfully. Think of a tantrum as an outward display of intense internal frustration. Once the eruption has begun, a child may be inconsolable until her emotional tirade has subsided.

Think of a tantrum as an outward display of intense internal frustration.

How to handle tantrums:

- When your child is in the throes of a tantrum, she needs you to remain calm, instead of becoming upset yourself. That way she can "borrow" some of your control to help her regain her composure. After the tantrum has subsided, talk about the hard feelings that provoked the outburst. Hold and comfort her as you explain that you understand it is hard to want to do something and not be able to.
- Do your best to model self-control when you get upset. For example, when you spill coffee all over your suit jacket as you head out the door to go to work, don't act

like it's a catastrophe. Instead, say, "It looks like I'm going to have to change into something else. I don't like being late, but there's nothing else I can do."

- Help your child learn to handle frustration in small doses and try to reduce unnecessary stress by not letting her get overly tired or hungry. Make sure her toys are age-appropriate and not too difficult for her to manipulate. Help her transition from one activity to another by giving her ample warning: "In five minutes, we'll have to start getting ready for bed." Plenty of outdoor play and physical activity will help her discharge tension.

- Support your child's budding independence and feelings of competence by allowing her to do things for herself, even if you can do them faster and better. Help her be successful in taking appropriate responsibility for self-care: for example, by putting her clothes in lower drawers, placing a child's footstool by the bathroom sink, or hanging her coat within her reach.

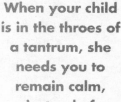

When your child is in the throes of a tantrum, she needs you to remain calm, instead of becoming upset yourself.

- If your child throws a temper tantrum to try to manipulate you or to feel powerful, ignore the outburst and leave the room if possible. Do not give in to your child's demand or comfort her afterward. Rewarding her in this way will only reinforce the tantrum behavior. You can talk about her angry feelings after she has calmed down. Allowing your child to make simple choices and providing appropriate structure and routine in her daily activities are appropriate ways to increase her sense of control.

Willful Defiance

Young children often feel powerless and vulnerable. A discouraged child may mistakenly believe that exerting power or

> A discouraged child may mistakenly believe that exerting power or control will bring her a sense of belonging and acceptance.

control will bring her a sense of belonging and acceptance. The power trip associated with refusing parental requests gives a child a sense of value, while submitting to a parent's wishes can make her feel overwhelmed and worthless. As both parent and child attempt to show the other "who's boss," an escalating war of retaliation and revenge can result. "You can't make me" is the typical battle cry of the power-hungry child, followed by the parent's retort, "Oh, yes I can!"

How to handle defiance:

- Don't allow yourself to be drawn into a destructive power struggle to prove your dominance over your child. By immediately disengaging from arguments and unhooking from power struggles, you stop fueling your child's anger and begin to defuse the situation. Resolve to demonstrate tolerance, understanding, and self-control, even when your child is emotionally volatile and demanding.

- Tell yourself that you can't make your child do anything and that cooperation has to be cultivated, not forced. Show your child through your daily interactions that you both are on the same team. Whenever possible, make requests of your child, rather than demands. Remember to praise him whenever he demonstrates cooperation and compliance.

- Specific discipline techniques that help reduce defiant behavior include giving choices about consequences and imposing logical consequences and natural consequences, which are more impersonal. Offering choices is a healthy way to give a child legitimate power through his decisions: "You can stop what you're doing when I tell you to get in the car, or you can stay home with

Daddy while I go to the store. You decide." Linking your request with something your child wants to do (using the "when ... then" technique) is another way to give your noncompliant child some appropriate personal power.

- A power struggle also can be avoided when a parent tells the child what she will do, not what the child must do. Announcing, "I will put away for the rest of the day any toys I see left on the floor after the timer goes off," is far less provocative than yelling, "I told you to pick your toys up off the floor!"

- Use the "one request only" technique to teach your child that his refusal will not be tolerated. Physically assist your child in complying with the request, such as coming to dinner, buckling his seat belt, or washing his hands. Remember not to get emotional, display anger, or become physically aggressive, however.

Anger at Parents

Young children feel things intensely and have trouble controlling their impulses. In a fit of temper or frustration, a preschooler may blurt out, "I hate you!" Do not take his outburst personally or overreact. Instead, recognize that his verbal assault results from depleted coping skills and mounting frustration and anger. Having been told to "use words" to express his hard feelings, your child is simply lashing out at the nearest target and in the best way he knows how. A preschooler has trouble understanding that it is possible to love his parents and simultaneously harbor intense negative feelings. If you retort with an angry outburst of your own, he may fear that you will permanently withdraw your love for him. As young children gain increased awareness of their emotions,

A preschooler has trouble understanding that it is possible to love his parents and simultaneously harbor intense negative feelings.

they learn that people can still love one another even when they are angry.

How to handle anger toward parents:

- Be a good role model by not engaging in name-calling or using angry put-downs. Do not retaliate when your child attacks you verbally. Appreciate that your child needs to express angry feelings, and don't take such comments personally. You can reply, "I'm sorry you feel that way right now. I understand you are upset, and I love you anyway."

- Often a child will verbally lash out when he is feeling unlovable. Be careful to always separate your child's behavior from his personal character. Never make disparaging or shameful remarks about your child, such as "I'm ashamed of you" or "You're so naughty." Help your child understand that you can be upset with his behavior without withdrawing your love for him.

- If your child shouts, "I hate you," for example, when you refuse a request, do not respond in anger. You can explain that you understand he hates your decision and let him know you accept his intense feelings of disappointment: "I know you are upset that we have to go. You were really enjoying all the animals." Then state that you expect him to tell you he is angry without being rude or disrespectful.

- Don't act sad or tell your child how much his words hurt you. Overreacting to his verbal tirade can teach your child to use emotional threats or name-calling to manipulate others and feel powerful. And don't try to control him by making him feel guilty for his remarks.

Biting and Hitting

Because young children have limited verbal skills to express their difficult feelings, they often act out aggressively to get what they want. Or they may resort to physical aggression as

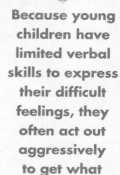

a way to gain a false sense of power when a social situation is too stressful. Since biting and hitting usually draw an immediate parental response, young children who crave attention may bite or hit in order to be the main attraction. Biting and hitting may also result from anxiety and stress surrounding the birth of a new sibling, overly harsh discipline, a move, or a change in child-care arrangements.

> **Because young children have limited verbal skills to express their difficult feelings, they often act out aggressively to get what they want.**

Often biting starts as exploratory behavior in a toddler, but when it gets a big reaction from parents, the victim, and others, it can turn into a real behavior problem. Being the parent of a young biter is extremely difficult and frustrating. When another child is the victim, the problem is embarrassing and awkward. It also can create a great inconvenience since a child-care center may refuse to accept a biter because of the risk they pose to other children.

How to handle biting and hitting:

- Always respond promptly and firmly to curb aggressive behavior. Remain calm, however, even though your child may be upset. Make it clear that hurting others is not acceptable. Say, "No biting (or hitting). Biting (hitting) hurts. We use words to say we are angry." Repeat this every time he bites or hits, or attempts to, without exception. Your consistent response will soon convince him that his behavior is not acceptable.
- Because biting and hitting occur most often as a result of frustration, give your little one a vocabulary of feeling words to help him express his tough emotions verbally. Help him learn words like angry, mad, sad, frustrated, mean, or unfair, to allow him to talk about what has upset him instead of resorting to biting or hitting. Let him know that you accept and understand his feelings, but

that biting other people is *not* okay. Say, "You were mad because T. J. took the blocks. That's why you bit. I understand how you feel, but no more biting!" Be firm, but don't get angry yourself. Encourage him to talk about what upset him: "I don't like it when you take all the blocks." "It makes me mad when Justin calls me names."

- Monitor the kinds of situations that provoke your child to bite or hit. You will need to watch your child carefully and step in whenever you think he might lose control due to mounting frustration. You may have to limit the length of play and number of companions when your child is in a playgroup and increase adult supervision during this temporary phase. Because biting can be extremely traumatic to the victim and human bites can readily become infected, it is imperative that parents and other caretakers of a known "biter" provide close supervision until the habit is curbed.

- Encourage your child to talk about what was happening before his display of aggression. Explain that you understand your child's frustration, and show him how to use words to get what he wants. Help him say, "I want you to give my blocks back to me." "You can play with some of them."

- Time-out is an ideal discipline technique for managing aggressive behavior. A brief period of social isolation helps an angry child calm down and gain control of his impulses. Make sure you give your child extra "time-in" to help him feel loved and accepted. Praise him when he manages to cope with a stressful situation without being aggressive.

Never spank or use verbal or physical intimidation to punish aggressive behavior.

- Never spank or use verbal or physical intimidation to punish aggressive behavior. Certainly, don't bite or hit your child back. Despite how often such retaliation is advised, biting back is the least effective and least desirable way of dealing with the problem.

- Require your child to make amends. He can gently pat another child's sore arm that he has hit or bitten, saying, "I'm sorry I hurt you." Focusing on the victim is especially effective for youngsters who bite in order to gain attention.
- When biting persists beyond two-and-a-half and reflects outright aggression, I recommend you seek professional help for your child.

Bedtime Battles

Most children need less sleep than parents wish they needed. Young children may resist sleep for a variety of reasons, ranging from boredom, lack of fatigue, overstimulation, loneliness, fear or anxiety, or power struggles with their parents. While we can't control the amount our children sleep, we can influence their attitude toward bedtime. In fact, trying to force sleep is a sure way to start bedtime battles you can't win, whereas establishing healthy bedtime routines may pave the way for a lifetime of restful sleep.

Although children vary in their individual sleep needs, most preschoolers sleep about eleven hours each night. Despite parents' concerns, children usually manage to get all the sleep they need. It's only as we grow older that we willfully postpone sleep or force ourselves to get up early due to outside demands and pressures. Perhaps our own chronic sleep deprivation makes us worry whether our children are getting enough sleep.

How to handle bedtime battles:

- Preschoolers enjoy ritual, and pleasantly structured bedtimes often facilitate better sleeping patterns. Preparation for bedtime actually should begin about an hour before the appointed time. Try to initiate a relaxing period of winding down from the day. Avoid roughhousing, scary

TV shows, or other forms of overstimulation. Gently give a ten or fifteen minute warning that bedtime is approaching, instead of dropping the announcement like a bombshell. Waiting until you are at the end of your rope before announcing bedtime can create a negative connotation surrounding this transition. A bedtime snack with milk may aid sleep. A warm bath is both relaxing and a form of play for preschoolers.

- One of the most effective ways to make bedtime pleasant is to associate it with parental attention and affection. Many of our fondest childhood memories of parental affection surround the familiar bedtime routines that herald sound sleep. Talk to your child about the day's events and tomorrow's upcoming activities as you help her brush her teeth and put on pajamas. Once she is ready for bed, other supportive rituals, such as reading or telling a story, will help her wind down. Regularly saying bedtime prayers together is calming, comforting, and emotionally reassuring. Tuck your child's stuffed animals in bed with her, leave a night-light on, and let her say good night to you and to favorite toys if desired. Then kiss her good night, wish her sweet dreams, and don't return to the room. It's impractical to mandate that your child fall right asleep, and it shouldn't matter whether she remains in bed or plays in her room. She will fall asleep when she is tired.

> One of the most effective ways to make bedtime pleasant is to associate it with parental attention and affection.

- Common mistakes that lead to bedtime battles include displaying excessive concern or distress if your child doesn't fall asleep right away. This often tends to make the child resist sleep even more. Avoid banishing your child to her room during the daytime as a form of punishment; this could make her resist going to her room at bedtime. A child's room should be her private sanctuary, and being there should be considered pleasant, not punitive.

- When your preschooler comes out of her room repeatedly at bedtime, she needs you to take decisive action instead of giving halfhearted warnings that carry no weight. Consistently walk her back, calmly state the limit ("You are to stay in your room after I tuck you in"). Many of the strategies described below also apply to the problem of a child coming out of her room at bedtime.

Coming into the Parents' Room at Night

Parents naturally expect their sleep to be disrupted when they have a young infant who requires nighttime feeding and care. By the time their child has reached the preschool years, however, parents usually feel entitled to a good night's sleep, except for special circumstances when a child awakens with an earache, has a nightmare, or gets frightened by a thunderstorm. Although some parents subscribe to the "family bed" parenting philosophy, others find that "three is a crowd" when it comes to restful sleep. Even when parents do not allow their child in their own bed, many go to the child's room and lie down with her until she falls asleep at bedtime and during night awakenings. Either way, chronically disrupted sleep can leave parents feeling physically depleted.

Everyone awakens several times each night as part of the normal cyclical process of sleep. Ordinarily, we are able to go right back to sleep because we immediately recognize our surroundings and know how to fall asleep on our own. Infants who have not learned to fall asleep without a set

> Although some parents subscribe to the "family bed" parenting philosophy, others find that "three is a crowd" when it comes to restful sleep.

of "props" can't go back to sleep readily when they awaken. Instead, they must summon their parents to come and re-create their familiar bedtime environment—breastfeeding, rocking, and being held. To avoid this problem, parents are advised, whenever possible, to put their infant in her crib before she is fully asleep. If her last waking memory is the crib, she will awaken under the same conditions that she has learned to fall asleep and will be able to soothe herself and return to sleep without needing her parents' help.

What begins as a legitimate infant need can soon become a rewarding habit. From a child's perspective, getting to cuddle next to Mommy and Daddy is comforting and cozy. Children who must share their parents' attention with siblings or those who spend time in child care may seek nighttime contact with their parents as a way to have Mommy and Daddy all to themselves. The habit gets perpetuated because tired parents choose the short-term solution (let the child in your bed) that allows them to go back asleep instead of mustering the reserve to solve the problem long-term. If your child's nighttime visits are leaving you feeling resentful and depleted, it is in both your best interests to require her to stay in her own bed all night.

How to handle coming into the parents' room at night:

- Explain to your child that you need a good night's sleep in order not to be cranky during the day. Tell her that you will no longer allow her in your bed and that you also won't lie down with her in her room. State that the new family rule says, "Everyone sleeps in their own bed."
- Helping your child learn to fall asleep on her own at naptime and bedtime will make it easier for her to go back to sleep when she awakens in the middle of the night. Pleasant bedtime routines and rituals, such as stories, soothing lullaby music, favorite stuffed animals, and bedtime prayers, help young children relax and induce sleep.
- If your child gets out of her bed and comes into your room, immediately walk her back to her own bed, with-

out talking or showing emotion. Be prepared to escort her back dozens of times if necessary until your child finally concludes that you mean what you say about no more sleeping in your bed. Expect your child to cry out for you and even to escalate her protests initially as she tests your resolve. Calmly repeat, "It's bedtime now. We need to go to sleep." Tuck her in, pat her reassuringly, and tell her that you will come back and check on her in five minutes. The first few nights of this plan, you can count on getting less sleep. If you remain consistent in your response, however, very soon you will be rewarded with uninterrupted sleep.

> **If your child gets out of her bed and comes into your room, immediately walk her back to her own bed, without talking or showing emotion.**

- Some parents opt for a more gradual plan. Initially, they may let their child come into their room and sleep on a mattress or sleeping bag next to their bed, without getting in the parents' bed. Gradually, the mattress can be moved further away.

- When you are feeling guilty about your child's protests, remind yourself that learning to sleep on her own is a help to your child, as well as to you. Ask your child what might help her stay in her room all night, such as a nightlight, bathroom light, flashlight, or cup of water.

- Don't get angry or upset when your child keeps testing you, as that will give her a sense of power over you. Don't shout threats or try to intimidate her. Just remain calm and keep enforcing the new sleep rules.

- Offer your child liberal praise and tangible rewards for staying in her bed all night. Initially you might present her with a small toy on mornings when she didn't wander. Then a star chart or tokens can be used to redeem a weekly reward, which is eventually discontinued.

Dawdling and Noncompliance

Busy parents have a keen sense of time, while preschoolers have little concept of time. Children often seem to operate in slow motion when we most need them to get ready quickly or to fulfill a request. Their procrastination then prompts the parent to issue incessant reminders about what needs to be done: "Emily, finish your breakfast; we have to leave." "Max, get your clothes on now, or we'll be late." Instead of cooperating by moving more quickly, however, children who are given frequent reminders only learn to tune out repeated parental requests. Young children are prone to dawdle simply because they are easily distracted and have trouble staying on task when something more interesting comes along. Some preschoolers, however, learn to use habitual noncompliance as a way of manipulating their parents and gaining attention. Children of working parents may experience excessive stress during the family's hectic morning rush to get out the door. Dragging his feet may be a child's primitive way of protesting the pressure he feels each day. Too many parents and children start their day on a bad note by getting embroiled in morning hassles over getting out the door on time.

> Young children are prone to dawdle simply because they are easily distracted and have trouble staying on task when something more interesting comes along.

How to handle dawdling:

- You can help prevent unpleasant morning battles by adhering to a predictable routine, including both events and the time frame involved. It's easier for your child to comply with your expectations when he can anticipate what should come next. Since your preschooler can't tell time, he can't guess whether you are operating at a leisurely pace or in fast motion on a given morning.

- Discontinue your habit of nagging your child and state your request once, along with a specific consequence for not complying. A logical consequence is ideal. "Lucas, I need you to get dressed now. If you aren't ready in another few minutes, I will have to assist you with putting your clothes on." Or you could even warn, "I will have to take you to preschool in your pajamas and you can get dressed there." Do not give empty threats, however. You must be fully prepared to enforce the consequence.

- If you suspect your child is dawdling as a way to manipulate you, remind him of his personal power by adding "You choose" when you state the consequence: "Aaron, if you don't come in and wash up for lunch now, you won't be allowed to play outside this afternoon. You choose."

- Help your child comply with your request more readily by allowing ample time in your morning routine without making him feel rushed. Complete as many preparations as possible the night before, including letting your child choose clothing and deciding what to bring along, to reduce the morning stress level. Get up a few minutes earlier yourself, so you aren't racing about in a frenzy that may cause your child to feel pressured.

- Help your child stay focused and show him that he can get positive attention for his compliance by praising him periodically for the progress he is making toward the goal: "Ricky, that's great! You've got your shirt and pants on. I see your shoes right next to the bed." Another way to keep things pleasant is to make a beat-the-clock game of getting ready by saying, "I'll bet you can't get dressed before the timer goes off."

- Offer your child an incentive for getting ready on time, remembering that one of the best rewards for children of employed parents is individual time with Mom or Dad. Tell him, "If you can get dressed before the timer goes off, we'll have enough time for French toast together. I

know it's your favorite." Help your child see the benefits of not dawdling: "Now that you are ready, you can
watch cartoons while I pack my briefcase."

Begging and Pleading

Young children quickly learn that they often can turn a parent's "no" response into a resigned yes by persistent begging
and bargaining. Appealing television ads and exposure to endless products in stores make children want the things they see
marketed. Since young children do not understand the concept
of money, they don't comprehend why you won't buy them
whatever they desire. And when it comes to activities,
preschoolers don't see why you can't always structure your day
around what they want to do.

How to handle begging and pleading:

- Say what you mean and mean what you say, so your child
  won't be confused about whether no really means maybe.
  To make it clear that your decision is final, you can add,
  "My answer isn't going to change, even if
  you keep asking." When you stop waver-
  ing after saying no, don't be surprised if
  your child thinks she has to beg and plead
  longer to change your mind. Be prepared
  for this reaction and don't give in. Before
  long, your consistency will convince your
  child that pleading no longer pays off.

- When you must say no to your child's
  request, you can soften the blow by
  acknowledging her legitimate disappointment. She will feel affirmed just by having
  you validate her desires. Say, "I know you
  like stuffed animals." "It would be fun to
  have a kitty." "Those slippers sure are adorable."

- Instead of voicing your outright refusal, you can offer an
  acceptable compromise when feasible: "We can't go to the

> Young children
> quickly learn
> that they often
> can turn a par-
> ent's "no"
> response into a
> resigned yes by
> persistent beg-
> ging and bar-
> gaining.

park today, but I can take you tomorrow afternoon." "No, I can't buy you a toy, but we can stop for ice cream." If she keeps pestering you for the toy, you can state, "Sounds like you have decided not to get anything." Another way to buffer your refusal is to offer to place the desired item on a wish list of possible gifts for your child's next birthday.

Teasing and Name-Calling

Hurtful name-calling is a common way children attempt to exercise power over others, to express angry feelings, or to gain their parents' attention. As preschoolers rapidly expand their verbal skills, they test the power of their words on others. A youngster quickly discovers that calling another child a derogatory name can make her stop doing something he doesn't like, reduce her to tears, and get his parent's attention. Young children often develop a fascination with a derogatory label, like stupid or dummy, and begin using it repeatedly. Keep in mind that teasing of siblings is mainly motivated by boredom or the desire for parental attention.

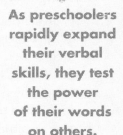

As preschoolers rapidly expand their verbal skills, they test the power of their words on others.

How to handle teasing and name-calling:

- The most effective way to curb rude language is to be a good role model and never resort to name-calling or the use of hurtful nicknames or remarks. Explain that name-calling is not acceptable because it is disrespectful and hurts people's feelings. Require your child to make restitution by apologizing for name-calling, or have your child take a time-out.
- Acknowledge your child's frustration that has led to the name-calling. Help her express what is bothering her without using a verbal attack: "I wanted to play with the farm animals, and he wouldn't let me." When your child is the

brunt of name-calling by someone else, teach her how to respond without retaliating: "I don't like that name, and I won't play with you when you call me names."

- If your child has a fascination with a derogatory word like stupid head, you can have him "wear out the word" by requiring your child to say it nonstop for one minute per year of age.
- Compliment your children when they are playing cooperatively so they won't need to resort to teasing as a way to get your attention. Instead of providing attention for teasing, give extra attention at other times.

Swearing and Other Offensive Language

As preschoolers rapidly acquire language, they often repeat the swear words they hear and experiment using taboo words for their shock value. Young children are fascinated by the power of words and experience a sense of control when they say something that gets your immediate attention. Since we tell young children to express their hard feelings with words instead of biting or hitting, they naturally choose powerful words. During and after being potty trained, children retain a strong interest in things related to using the toilet and will frequently use offensive bathroom words (poopy monster) much to the chagrin of their parents. Part of a child's achievement of bowel and bladder control includes mastering the vocabulary pertaining to these bodily functions. The more offensive you find the words, the greater their appeal to your child.

How to handle offensive language:

- Explain that bad language is disrespectful and rude. Make it a family rule that no one uses swear words, including the parents. Help children learn to express their anger and frustration by using acceptable words.
- Don't overreact when young children use bad language, since a big response from you can make the words seem even more powerful. State in a matter-of-fact way,

"Nobody likes to hear that kind of talk." You can impose a time-out as a reminder that social isolation is the penalty for behavior that is offensive to others. Or send your child to the bathroom if she wants to repeat "bathroom words" without offending you.

- Help your child make up some acceptable strong words to convey his anger and frustration. Create fun-to-say, silly expressions, like "gadzooka," "balonymaloney," or "phewypetewy," that your child can exclaim when he gets mad. Help him develop a vocabulary of feeling words to express strong emotions and to tell others when their behavior bothers him, "I don't like that."

Back Talk

Young children often learn to speak in a rude or disrespectful way after they have heard it modeled by their parents, siblings, friends, or actors on television. In addition to actual spoken words, back talk can include the tone of voice used and body language. Common examples of back talk include "You shut up," "No!" "*You're* being naughty," "You can't make me." Kids talk back as an attention-seeking ploy, to test their power, and to try to dominate their parents, peers, and others. Being able to manipulate a conversation and use words to make other people angry or sad gives children a heady sense of power. In addition to being disrespectful, back talk creates a negative atmosphere in the home and undermines the parent-child relationship.

> In addition to being disrespectful, back talk creates a negative atmosphere in the home and undermines the parent-child relationship.

How to handle back talk:

- Deal with back talk promptly, and don't let your child benefit from it. Give a clear and immediate message that back talk is unacceptable and will not be tolerated. Do not give in to your child's demands or allow her to intimidate you with words. Back talk will only escalate if using it allows your child to get her way.

- Calmly explain that the family rule says "Everyone is treated with respect." Don't make a big deal or overreact, and be sure to focus on the rude language, not on the child. Offer your child the face-saving option of starting over, and then thank him for cooperating and speaking respectfully.

- Acknowledge your child's feelings. Children often use back talk when they are angry, frustrated, disappointed, or feeling unlovable. So don't take it personally. Encourage your child to express his negative emotions in an appropriate manner, instead of lashing out verbally.

- Explain that no one likes to be disrespected and that back talk makes a person feel angry, hurt, and sad. In a calm, matter-of-fact manner, state the effect that your child's back talk has on you. For example, you can explain that his disrespectful remark hurt your feelings and made you no longer want to do something nice for him.

- Promptly impose a consequence for your child's rude, hurtful, or embarrassing language and his accompanying negative attitude. An ideal consequence is the immediate loss of a privilege, which has a logical link to the back talk: "Your mean words have upset me, and I don't feel like continuing to read this story to you. You'll have to find something else to do." The consequence you choose should be seen not as retaliation for but as a logical result of your child's disrespectful behavior. For young children, a time-out can be a suitable alternative to the loss of a specific privilege. The time-out allows everyone to calm down. Or you can choose to give a warning instead of an immediate consequence: "I don't like to be spoken to that way. If you call me that again, I won't keep playing the game with you." It's important that you don't overpunish your child, however.

- Children often use back talk to get your attention, to make you angry, and to draw you into a power struggle. Don't let this ploy hook you into modeling the disrespectful behavior you dislike in your child. Responding in anger to his verbal tirade or trying to refute your child's accusations will only make the situation worse. Instead of regressing to your child's level, say, "You seem to like to argue and complain, and I won't get involved in your mean talk."

Whining

Few things irritate parents as much as whining—a child's incessant, high-pitched pleading, asking, and cajoling. Children tend to whine more when they are tired, bored, cranky, or feel that things aren't going their way. Parents who should know better often give in to whining, only to find they have reinforced this common verbally manipulative communication.

How to handle whining:

- Resolve to turn a deaf ear to whining and grant no requests made while whining. Say, "These ears don't hear whining. When you ask me in a normal tone of voice, I'll be able to listen to you." Don't give your child too much negative attention for whining, as your strong reaction can make her feel more powerful when she whines.

Resolve to turn a deaf ear to whining and grant no requests made while whining.

- Because young, cranky children may not realize they are whining, demonstrate for your child what you consider to be whining. Then have him practice asking for what he wants several times using a normal tone of voice, and grant his request, if reasonable. Be a good role model for your child by minimizing the amount of adult whining or complaining that you do.

- You can send your child for a time-out in a "whining place," where she can cry and whine until she feels ready to talk to you in a calm voice. Consider, however, that persistent whining often means your preschooler is feeling frustrated and cranky. What she may need most is your loving attention and comfort until she feels emotionally refueled.

- In addition to ignoring your child's whining, give immediate positive attention when he speaks in a normal voice. Say, "Thank you for asking so nicely," even if you have to add that you can't grant him what he wants. By giving positive reinforcement for communicating pleasantly, eventually your child will conclude that a normal tone of voice speaks louder than whining.

Interrupting

A common form of rude communication that parents find annoying is a child's frequent interrupting of adult conversation. Young children often interrupt when their parents are talking on the phone or visiting with another adult in their home or car. Interrupting usually results from the child's need for attention and is designed to pull the parent's focus back to the child. In handling frequent interruptions, parents must balance their needs for social interaction with their child's need to be reassured of her parents' love.

How to handle interrupting:

- The best strategy is to give your child your periodic attention so she won't have to demand it. Acknowledge her presence so she won't feel like an outsider when you are engaged with someone else. When appropriate, include her in the conversation. Periodically smile and nod, offer your nonverbal approval, and see if she needs anything. Give her some stimulating toys and compliment her often: "I'm glad to see you playing nicely by yourself."

- Teach your child to say "excuse me" when she needs to interrupt your conversation for a legitimate reason. Then, reward her good manners by listening to what she has to say. If she interrupts you inappropriately, help teach her consideration for others by asking, "What do we say when someone is speaking?"

- Keep your expectations age-appropriate, and be prepared to disengage from a conversation if your child's attention span has elapsed. If you must make a lengthy conference call, consider hiring a teenager to watch your child in another room or playing her favorite video.

- Help your child learn to wait her turn by saying, "As soon as I finish serving Aunt Martha her iced tea, I'll be ready to listen to you." Then thank her for not interrupting, and by all means, keep your promise about turning your attention to her.

Lying

Young children under four years have difficulty distinguishing between fantasies and lies and may tell imaginary tales without meaning to be deceptive. By age four, children can understand that lying is wrong. However, preschoolers are so eager to please their parents and to be perceived as "good" that they will lie about something they regret doing because they wish it weren't so. Many older children lie to avoid punishment or responsibility because they believe they cannot handle the consequences of their misbehavior or the demands made on them. Children with low self-esteem often lie to make themselves look better.

How to handle lying:

- Avoid putting your child in a situation in which she is tempted to lie. When you find your preschooler with tell-tale frosting on her face, don't ask if she ate one of the cupcakes you just baked. Instead, state the obvious, "I see you ate a cupcake after I told you not to touch them."

- When caught in a lie, ask your child to practice telling the truth to see how it sounds. Help your child feel good about herself so she won't feel she has to lie to avoid your displeasure or tell exaggerated tales to attract your attention. Teach her the difference between make-believe tales and deceit.

- When your child answers honestly about something she has done wrong, praise her truthfulness and reduce her punishment for the infraction. If your child is caught in a lie, try to stay calm. Your overreaction may only provoke more adroit and more frequent lying in order to avoid your fury. And don't label your child as a liar. Not only will such a negative label deal a blow to her self-esteem, but she also may feel compelled to fulfill your expectation of her. Instead, forgive your child, and have the courage to trust again.

- When dealing with problem behavior, don't focus on placing blame: "Who spilled pop in the living room?" This only encourages children to lie about their culpability. Instead, spotlight the inappropriate behavior that caused the problem and focus on solutions: "My carpet is soiled because you broke the family rule about not bringing food into the living room. Please get some paper towels and help me clean up."

- Our model of truthfulness, even in seemingly small things, is the best way to teach children to be truthful. When our children hear us tell lies of convenience, like making

> Our model of truthfulness, even in seemingly small things, is the best way to teach children to be truthful.

up an excuse to decline an unwanted invitation, we send a message that devalues honesty. Although partial truths are sometimes necessary to shield a child from the harsh realities of life, try to minimize the use of deception. For example, if you arrive late and miss part of your child's performance, it's best to admit the truth than to risk getting caught in a lie by pretending you saw the whole show.

Stealing

Parents are naturally upset when they discover their child has taken something that doesn't belong to him, such as an item from a store or another child's toy. To make matters worse, when confronted about the origin of the item, children often lie about how they acquired it. Many parents overreact to stealing and conjure up images of a life of crime for their child. Preschool children are still learning about right and wrong and feel they are entitled to anything they want. They do not know that taking things they want is not acceptable unless we teach them. We must be their conscience until they develop one of their own. Some children steal as a way to feel powerful or to get their parents' attention by wrongdoing.

How to handle stealing:

- Be a good role model by respecting what belongs to others. Teach your child to always ask whether he can take something. For example, show him how to ask a friend if he can play with a toy that he likes. Or tell him he must ask you if you will buy a candy bar for him. Explain the difference between borrowing and stealing. When shopping, help him understand that the items in your cart don't belong to you until you pay for them.
- If your child steals something, don't overreact or give your child a lengthy lecture. Instead of encouraging him

to lie about the theft by asking where he got the item, confront him with the facts. Then explain in a matter-of-fact tone that it is not okay to take something that belongs to someone else without asking or paying for it. Let your child know that people don't like it when you take something that isn't yours. However, don't label your child as a thief, and don't keep bringing up the incident.

- Have your child make restitution by apologizing and returning the stolen item to its rightful owner. If an item like partially eaten candy must be paid for and your child has no money, have him do something for you to "work off" the cost of the item. Or have him temporarily relinquish the use of a toy.

- Compliment your child for asking for things instead of taking them. When possible, reward him by making the purchase. If you can't always comply with his request, say, "I'm glad you asked me. Maybe we can get it tomorrow or for your birthday."

Sibling Fighting

One of the most frustrating discipline problems for parents with more than one child is the frequent fighting, teasing, and bickering that inevitably occurs among siblings. Mediating sibling disputes can leave parents feeling emotionally depleted. Since sibling squabbles often result from competition for parental love, helping each child feel uniquely loved and special (see chapter 4) will reduce sibling rivalry and strengthen family bonds.

How to handle sibling fighting:

- Encourage love and affection between siblings. Compliment your children several times each day for cooperating, playing together amicably, helping and sharing, expressing empathy, or showing special consideration. Help them remember each other's birthdays and special occasions with cards and gifts. Foster positive feelings among siblings with remarks like "See how easily you can make Juanita laugh"; "Amy says you showed her how to play the game and now she really understands it." Encourage your children to become lifetime companions and best friends.

- Clarify the ground rules. Establish and enforce consistent rules for treating family members, including no physical aggression or name-calling and no taking possessions without asking permission. Use objectivity when enforcing these limits by announcing, "The family rule says ..." Maintain zero tolerance for physical or verbal assaults.

- Model positive behavior. Treat your spouse, your siblings, in-laws, and others with mutual respect and consideration. The behavior you model in your daily interactions will speak louder than your verbal admonitions to be nice.

- Help young children settle disputes. Toddlers and preschoolers who are fighting can't be expected to negotiate solutions on their own. Instead, they need direct intervention to settle a disagreement. You will need to supervise the sharing of possessions, taking turns, equitably dividing toys and art supplies, and distracting young children. As your children get older, you can gradually avoid interceding too quickly as mediator, referee, or judge. Instead, you can begin encouraging them to work out their differences on their own and find solutions to minor squabbles. Don't focus on how the disagreement started; focus instead on what needs to happen to resolve the conflict.

- Have mutual consequences for sibling disagreements. Regardless how a

Don't focus on how the disagreement started; focus instead on what needs to happen to resolve the conflict.

fight started, you can usually assume both children are partially responsible. Don't automatically assume your older child is to blame or that your younger child needs to be rescued. Whoever is participating should go for a cooling-off period in time-out. Then ask each child to acknowledge the way in which they contributed to the conflict and to apologize for their part. Encourage the children to come up with a mutually agreeable solution (such as how to share an item) to avoid mutual consequences (putting the disputed possession away for the rest of the day). Congratulate children on their resourcefulness in achieving a peaceful solution to their problem.

- Arrange separate play areas or storage areas for sibling's toys. When conflicts are triggered by age differences (a younger child grabbing at a sibling's elaborate construction project), let the older child play in a room of his own, safe from the toddler's menacing reach. Give the older child a toy box, cabinet, or upper shelf to store his toys.

- Ignore tattling. Most tattling is done to make the tattletale look better in her parents' eyes. Frequent tattling can pit siblings against one another, especially when parents feel they must act on all reports of misbehavior: "Tell your sister I said to start picking those toys up now!" Instead of rewarding tattling, say, "I don't want to hear about it." Emphasize that each child is responsible for her own behavior. The exception is any behavior that could be harmful to oneself or another person, which must always be reported promptly to the parents to assure each family member's safety.

- Help children learn appropriate ways to deal with angry feelings. Teach children acceptable ways to cool off when they are angry and how to curb impulsive behavior. Help them express their angry feelings in words and find creative and nondestructive outlets for anger. (See chapter

4.) Congratulate your children when they are able to handle hard feelings in a constructive manner.

Effective discipline begins with an enduring, supportive parent-child relationship that sets the tone for cooperation and learning. Remember that your own healthy model and frequent positive reinforcement powerfully shape desired behavior. Misbehavior is minimized if clear limits are enforced consistently in an atmosphere of love and affection. When rules are broken, consider your child's misguided motives for misbehavior and choose an appropriate response from a variety of effective discipline techniques to help her regain self-control and learn to make better choices. If you want to do more reading about effective discipline for young children or how to manage specific problem behaviors, I recommend the following excellent resources, from which I have drawn many of the suggestions offered in this chapter.

Don Dinkmeyer Sr., et al., *Parenting Young Children: Systematic Training for Effective Parenting (STEP) of Children under Six* (Circle Pines, Minn.: American Guidance Service, Inc., 1997).

Rudolf Dreikurs with Vicki Soltz, *Children: The Challenge* (New York: Plume, 1992).

Jane Nelson, *Positive Discipline* (New York: Ballantine, 1996).

Charles E. Schaefer and Theresa Foy DiGeronimo, *Teach Your Child to Behave: Disciplining with Love from 2 to 8 Years* (New York: Plume, 1991).

Jerry Wyckoff and Barbara C. Unell, *Discipline without Shouting or Spanking: Practical Solutions to the Most Common Preschool Behavior Problems* (New York: Meadowbrook Press, 1984).

Jerri Wolfe, *I'm Three Years Old!* (New York: Pocket Books, 1998).

To learn more about handling sleep problems in children and promoting sound sleep habits, I suggest you read *Solve Your Child's Sleep Problems* by Richard Ferber (New York: Fireside, 1985) and *Guide to Your Child's Sleep*, a new publication of the American Academy of Pediatrics, George J. Cohen, ed. (New York: Villard, 1999).

Chapter 6

Those Essential Others: Alternate Caretakers

Few parenting choices are weightier than the decision to work outside the home and delegate partial responsibility for your children's welfare to an alternate caretaker. I know this all too well, because I struggled with my own career-family dilemma, beginning with the birth of my first child. The decision whether to be a full-time parent or to involve alternate caretakers in your child-rearing plan is a highly personal one, and each family must discern the will of God for their lives concerning this matter. I, like so many other parents, have wrestled with guilt, anxiety, and uncertainty when my precious and priceless children were temporarily entrusted to the care of another. However, this chapter is not a discussion of the pros and cons of working outside the home. Rather, it is written for parents who have thoughtfully considered the matter and have already decided to seek some type of substitute care for their preschool child. There can be no greater priority than to ensure that your children are physically safe, emotionally secure, and intellectually stimulated during your absence. The information in this chapter will help you navigate the maze of child-care

215

options and equip you to recognize and choose quality care that will give you peace of mind about your decision and your child's welfare.

The Importance of Quality Child Care

The majority of children under age six receive care and education by a nonparent. For many families, this decision is based on the choice or need for the parent or parents to work outside the home. In fact, 75 percent of women with children under five are employed,[1] and more than 25 million Americans require care for their preschool children while at work. Other parents of young children enroll their child part-time in a preschool to provide opportunities for socialization and intellectual stimulation. Still other parents occasionally leave their young children in the care of others to allow them periodic breaks from the incredible demands of being home full-time with preschoolers.

When you recall that most of your child's brain development occurs in the first years of life, it becomes evident that this process goes on whether your child is with you or under the care of someone else. The care your child receives today will help shape the kind of adult he will become. However, even when parents know the importance of high-quality care, few manage to find affordable, accessible, quality options. The present status of child care in America remains a hodgepodge of inconsistent quality services and settings. Often the care is mediocre, and in some instances, young children are cared for in situations that fail to meet their basic health and safety needs.

> The care your child receives today will help shape the kind of adult he will become.

During a span of twelve years, Larry and I used no less than sixteen different child-care arrangements to piece together care for our five children. We used child-care homes, child-care centers, in-home care, neighbors, and care by a relative. Sometimes we used multiple care settings at once to meet our children's differing needs. At times, we were overwhelmed with worry about the adequacy and availability of care. We made some good choices, as well as a few unfortunate ones. Today, while many more child-care choices exist, vulnerable and inexperienced parents, like I once was, still must sort through highly diverse options, trying to reconcile sometimes competing priorities such as affordability and convenience with high-quality, loving care. Parents not only worry about the affection, education, and stimulation their preschoolers receive in their absence, but they are concerned about the convenience and financial burden of child care. A wide gap still exists between what is sought and what is settled for.

Knowing that a child's most accelerated learning occurs in the first six years of life, parents of preschoolers need to know how to find a child-care setting that will help optimize their child's development. Quality child care is much more than baby-sitting. High-quality child care promotes the social, emotional, intellectual, language, and physical development of children in an emotionally nurturing and physically safe environment. Numerous studies have shown that high-quality early care and education results in significant, lasting, positive effects on later school achievement, high school graduation rates, and social outcomes.[2]

Conversely, lack of early stimulation has been linked with lower academic performance and various social ills. Thus, quality child care has been called "essential brain food." Yet many child-care settings do not adequately stimulate the development of young children. I suspect that parents who use these inadequate options are either uninformed about quality care or have not opened their eyes to the deficiencies. In fact, many parents do

> High-quality child care promotes the social, emotional, intellectual, language, and physical development of children in an emotionally nurturing and physically safe environment.

not recognize poor quality care and give high marks to the center they use, whether deserved or not. Although in many respects, you get what you pay for in the child-care market, price is not always a good indicator of quality care. Strict national licensing standards for child-care providers and accreditation for child-care centers are necessary to assure children receive quality care. Until uniformly high-quality care is available, parents need to become quality-conscious consumers on their child's behalf. Parents who know about the importance of quality care for their child's development should settle for nothing less than care that promotes their child's growth and learning. When more parents demand high-quality care for their young children, improvements in both public and private child-care programs will inevitably follow to meet this demand.

> In fact, many parents do not recognize poor quality care and give high marks to the center they use, whether deserved or not.

Types of Child Care to Consider

The type of care you choose may depend on many factors, including convenience, proximity to your home or work, affordability, flexibility, and other practical considerations. Unfortunately, too few parents accurately assess the quality of care in making their determination. The main types of child-care options include in-home care (your own or a child-care family home) and center-based care. An estimated 30 percent of parents use more than one child-care arrangement to patch together care that fits their schedule.

In-Home Care

Having someone come to your home and match their work hours to your schedule can be very convenient for you and your child. If you must leave for work early, your child does not have to be up, dressed, and ready to head out the door on time. Instead, he can remain in familiar surroundings and maintain his usual routine. Your child will probably get more attention and be exposed to fewer infectious diseases if he remains in his own home. You can decide whether to ask the person to do some light housework as part of their responsibilities, and you get to set the hours and the pay rate. This type of arrangement is especially attractive for an infant or toddler who can form a strong attachment to a single caretaker.

Finding skilled care can be a challenge, however, as no standards exist for in-home care, and trained, experienced providers are in short supply. In some parts of the country, the majority of in-home care providers are recent immigrants for whom English is a second language. The language barrier can pose a challenge to effective communication with your provider.

With in-home care, you will need to have backup plans for times when the provider is ill, has an emergency, or goes on vacation. Because there are no other adults present to monitor what goes on, you may not know whether your provider actually gives quality care while you are gone or whether she watches TV, invades your privacy, or even mistreats your child. In addition, your child may lack opportunities to socialize with other children and may spend too much time watching TV.

Having someone come to your home and match their work hours to your schedule can be very convenient for you and your child.

You will want to check references thoroughly and do a background check before hiring someone to come to your home. You should require a period of in-home observation of the provider's interactions with your child before leaving him in her care. You should also drop by at unexpected times to check on things. The convenience and flexibility you get with in-home care can be relatively expensive. If you use an in-home provider, you must pay Social Security, other taxes, and possibly even health insurance.

Nannies and Au Pairs

Some parents employ a nanny or young caregiver from abroad, known as an *au pair*. Many nannies are highly trained and most have prior experience caring for children. Au pairs are usually college-age girls who reside in the United States under an exchange program. They care for children up to forty-five hours a week in exchange for a modest salary, plus room and board.

Spousal Care

Many two-earner families arrange their work hours so that the children are always left in the care of a parent. While this arrangement avoids child-care expenses and can give parents enormous peace of mind about the quality of care their children receive, the marital relationship may suffer. Finding time alone together when both partners are rested and able to focus exclusively on one another can be a challenge.

Cooperative Arrangements

Some parents are able to work part-time and develop a cooperative child-care arrangement with one or more other part-time working parents. Participating families can save money by exchanging child-care services. One downside to this arrangement is that you are unable to give your child your undivided attention on the days you do not work and must care for the other employees' children.

Family Child-Care Homes

Under this arrangement, groups of multi-aged children are cared for in the provider's own home. Often the caregiver has small children of her own. Some children may come only before and after school, while others remain all day. A family child-care home can be small (usually six or fewer children including the provider's own preschoolers) or large (seven to twelve children, including the provider's own preschoolers).

Generally, child-care homes should not have more than six children per adult caregiver, and even fewer if infants and toddlers are present.

When selecting a family child-care home, you get to choose the specific provider who will care for your child. Because family child-care homes usually are located near the child's own home, providers often have a closer personal relationship with families than caregivers at child-care centers. The group size, which is usually smaller than center-based care, may be more suitable for some children's personalities, and siblings can be cared for together. The caregiver may offer flexible hours to accommodate your schedule and the cost is usually more economical than care in your home or center care.

Despite the advantages, a family child-care home can have potential drawbacks. The caregivers often have less training and qualifications than staff at a day-care center. Although a child-development or preschool curriculum may be offered, a family child-care home probably will have fewer educational materials and activities than larger child-care centers. While some do offer stimulating enrichment programs, others provide little more than "custodial" care. In the worst cases, children are inadequately supervised, making the situation unsafe. If only one adult is present, backup care must be immediately accessible in case of an emergency.

If you choose a family child-care home, make sure you select a home with licensed or registered providers. Ask when the home was last checked by an inspector. Licensure requirements include training hours, knowledge of first aid and CPR, as well as annual continuing education.

Because family child-care homes usually are located near the child's own home, providers often have a closer personal relationship with families than caregivers at child-care centers.

Care by a Relative

More than half of family child-care providers are relatives, who may or may not be paid. While a close relative often makes an ideal caretaker, many relatives provide care only as a favor to the family, not because they really want to be a caregiver. On the positive side, relatives who care for children may already have a warm, loving relationship with your family, and the child can be cared for in a familiar setting. Relatives often have a great emotional investment in your child and may share similar values and philosophies of child rearing. On the other hand, you may feel less comfortable telling a close relative the things you would like them to do differently, especially if they are charging you less than you would pay someone else. Occasionally, care by a controlling relative can leave you feeling overly dependent on them.

Center-Based Care

Child-care centers are licensed facilities that provide care for groups of children in a nonresidential setting designed for young children. They include nursery schools, preschools, and learning centers that care for children from infancy through the elementary school years. Centers can be independently owned or part of a chain. They may be affiliated with a church, community group, school or university, or sponsored by social services or Head Start. Some centers may espouse a certain philosophy of education, such as the Montessori method, which uses a multisensory classroom environment to promote "learning by doing" at a child's own pace. Christian preschools include religious education as part of the learning experience. The escalating demand for center care has led to the appearance of deluxe facilities in affluent communities, where tuition is comparable to many public universities.

Center-based care is a very popular arrangement for children age three to five, who enjoy the socialization with their peer group. Hours of operation may be part of a day, a full day, or even extended hours. The center may have several class-rooms, with children grouped by age. Look for a facility that has two caregivers per room and a window or glass door to permit visibility within. Some employees are fortunate enough to have a child-care center at their place of work, allowing them to have contact with their child during the workday, if desired.

Because you are contracting with an organization, rather than an individual, you are less likely to need a contingency plan because a provider has called in sick. You can expect a child-care center to offer an educational program and to provide a stimulating environment that promotes your child's intellectual and social development. In addition, the program staff is likely to have specialized

Center-based care is a very popular arrangement for children age three to five, who enjoy the socialization with their peer group.

training in child development and early childhood education. Child-care centers are licensed by the state and inspected regularly for health, safety, cleanliness, staffing, and program content. Your city, county, or state department of social services can provide information about local regulations for child-care centers.

On the other hand, you can expect to pay more for center-based care than care in a family day-care home. In addition, your child may have greater exposure to infectious diseases, especially in larger centers and those that care for diapered children. Adjusting to a larger group size, a non-home-like atmosphere, and multiple caregivers may be difficult for some children. The quality of the caregivers and the educational programming can be highly variable, with some centers having inadequate numbers of caregivers, unqualified staff, and high staff turnover.

Health Implications of Child Care

While the child-care experience poses unique health concerns for young children cared for in groups, it's also true that a quality child-care program offers significant health opportunities that can improve a child's well-being. Child-care providers can serve as a resource for families whose children do not have a "medical home" by offering a list of local pediatric health professionals. Many provide information on child-passenger safety issues or give reminders about annual vision and hearing screening. Some child-care settings administer medications, provided parents complete a medication authorization form. While this can be a great convenience to parents, you should keep in mind that in a large center, numerous medications may be dispensed in a single room each day, increasing the risk of a medication error.

Infectious Diseases

It should come as no surprise that placing children together in group care increases the spread of infectious diseases, since children share germs when they share toys and activities. Diarrhea and respiratory infections are among the most common illnesses known to be easily spread in child-care facilities. Respiratory-tract infections, including ear infections, are more common in children who attend a child-care program. The risk of diarrhea illness and outbreaks of hepatitis A are increased in settings in which diapered children are present. While hepatitis A infection may cause no apparent symptoms among children attending day care, the illness causes more severe symptoms in the adult staff and adult members of the children's families. Other infections, like cytomegalovirus, may not produce obvious illness in children and child-care staff, but it can have serious consequences for the fetus of pregnant contacts or individuals with compromised immunity. Head lice is common in child-care settings and is easily spread through direct contact or casual contact with clothing, bedding, and hairbrushes. Chickenpox also occurs frequently among children in child care if they are not immunized against this common childhood illness.

The spread of infections in child-care facilities can be limited by 1) proper education of staff regarding standards of hygiene, such as frequent handwashing; 2) teaching children to wash their hands after using the bathroom; 3) disinfecting surfaces that are prone to contamination; and 4) separating diaper-changing and toileting areas from food preparation areas. Up-to-date immunization of all children also reduces the spread of infectious diseases.

Injury

Not only are children less likely to be injured at a child-care site than at home, but patterns of accidents differ between the home and the child-care setting. Most injuries in a child-care setting occur on the playground, and fortunately, the majority are minor scrapes and bruises, requiring only first-aid treatment. Many injuries are due to tripping and falling by young children with still-developing motor skills and a high activity level. The most serious injuries are associated with falls from playground equipment onto hard surfaces. These can be prevented by the use of impact-absorbing materials under playground equipment and providing close supervision of children. Being bitten by another child is a common day-care injury that can be prevented by increased supervision of children. (See chapter 5.)

Health Promotion

A quality child-care program can be the source of many positive health messages and services to families. Many children learn a great deal about healthy nutrition, dental hygiene, injury prevention, physical fitness, and positive mental health through their participation in a child-care program. These health and safety messages—ranging from the importance of hand washing to

A quality child-care program can be the source of many positive health messages and services to families.

what to do in case of a fire—can be incorporated into the daily routine and will help lay the foundation for good health habits. Vaccination rates for children in licensed child-care programs are higher than the general population. Trained staff are qualified to make relevant observations about a child's physical development, language and social skills, hearing and vision, or behavior.

Many child-care facilities have a physician consultant who plays an important role in the training of child-care staff and who can provide guidance and assistance with various issues affecting the health and safety of the children. In addition, program staff may offer regular parenting-education classes and various forms of family support. Regular meetings with the caregivers can be a valuable source of information about your child's adjustment, development, and behavior.

Finding Quality Child Care

Most communities have child-care resource and referral agencies with trained referral specialists who can help you find local child-care services and learn how to choose quality child care. Many businesses form partnerships with child-care resource and referral agencies to provide their employees with information on child-care programs.

Providers also can be found through personal networking, ads in local papers or homeowner's newsletters, local family child-care associations, employment agencies, yellow pages, or nanny schools. Many pediatric health-care providers take a keen interest in the issues and concerns of children in child care and can provide a list of reputable child-care centers or family child-care homes. After you have obtained three to five recommendations from various sources, make an appointment to visit the settings or meet with potential in-home providers. Your firsthand impression is the single most important guide to selecting quality care.

Visit Several Settings

Visit the best center, even if you don't think you can afford it or your child won't get in. It still can serve as a helpful model of quality care, the gold standard by which you rate other programs. Ask if you are welcome to visit sites anytime during operating hours and if you are allowed to see all areas. I suggest you look elsewhere if you are ever prohibited from dropping by.

Inquire how long the program has been in operation, and ask to talk with parents of children currently enrolled. Before making a final decision to go with a particular program, visit it several times, at different times of the day. Observe the children on site and notice whether they are stimulated or bored, nurtured or neglected. Do the children in attendance represent your community's diversity? Notice the quality of the interaction between the children and the care providers.

> When you visit a family day-care home, ask yourself whether the provider really seems to enjoy her work.

When you visit a family day-care home, ask yourself whether the provider really seems to enjoy her work. Ask to see all areas of the home where children spend time. The provider's license should be current and posted where it can be easily seen. Find out when the center was last inspected.

The Interview

Interview an in-home caregiver at least two times. Use your intuition and trust your instincts about the person. Inquire about the training, education, and experience of the applicant. You should also ask about her philosophies concerning discipline, nutrition, and toilet training. If they are not consistent with your own, you should know that it may be very difficult, if not impossible, for her to reflect your values in your absence. Create "what if" scenarios by asking the applicant what she would do in a variety of circumstances ranging from misbehavior to medical emergencies. If you decide to hire an applicant, begin with a two-week to one-month trial period before deciding to continue the arrangement.

References

No matter what type of child-care arrangement you choose, always check all references! Ask for a list of families who currently use the caregiver or child-care center and families who no longer have children in the program. Even if you have a letter of recommendation, *follow up with a telephone call*. You should also check all references even if you hire someone through an agency that has screened the applicant. You can check with your local authorities about the availability of background checks on potential employees.

No matter what type of child-care arrangement you choose, always check all references!

Caregiver Staff

In general, child-care programs with better-educated, better-paid staff and higher staff-to-child ratios provide higher-quality, safer, and healthier care. Use the accompanying chart to tell whether the child-to-staff ratios and the group size meet or exceed recommended standards. Although effective caregivers for young children need training related to child development and early childhood education, many child-care providers have no such preparation. Ask whether the program director and the staff have formal training and experience in child growth and development and whether they participate in continuing education programs.

Adequacy of teacher wages is another key factor in determining quality care. Most child-care providers could earn higher wages working in a fast-food restaurant, and few receive benefits or paid leave. Low pay leads to high teacher

Recommended Staffing Ratios

Age of Children	Child to Staff Ratio	Maximum Group Size
25–30 months	4:1	8
31–35 months	5:1	10
3 year olds	7:1	14
4–5 year olds	8:1	16

American Academy of Pediatrics, "Part 2: Basic Caregiving," in Caring for Our Children, National Health and Safety Performance Standards: Guidelines for Out-of-Home Child Care Programs, Video Series Handout Masters (1995), 11.

turnover rates, which is hard on little ones who need stable relationships to feel safe and secure. The loss of a primary caregiver causes a grief reaction that can inhibit learning.

You will want to closely observe the providers' interactions with children, since the most important component of quality care is the relationship between the child and the caregiver. Ask yourself whether the program staff are warm and caring and clearly like and enjoy children. The caregivers' conversations with children should be positive and encouraging, not harsh and critical. Do they treat each child like an individual and call each child by name? Ask for a description of other children in the child-care program and listen to the way the staff talk about the youngsters. Find out if there will be one principal caregiver responsible for your child. Try to elicit the providers' commitment to their work. Do they see child care as a mission, just baby-sitting, or drudgery?

Find out what arrangements are made if a caregiver calls in sick or must leave the premises. Verify that children are supervised at all times! Ask how behavior problems are handled. Give some examples, such as biting or hitting, and listen to the caregiver's response.

Environment

The child-care environment not only must be physically safe; it must also provide an atmosphere for learning. The child-care center or family child-care home should be well ventilated, bright, cheerful, and appealing to a child. The room setup should be comfortable and inviting, with child-sized furniture. The facility should have adequate indoor space, including a sleeping or quiet area. The equipment should be safe, clean, and properly maintained. Each child should have a designated cubby or special place for her belongings, personalized with her name and photograph. The outside area should be fenced, safe, and free of hazards, with age-appropriate, well-maintained play equipment. Both indoor and outdoor climbing equipment should have impact-absorbing materials, such as wood chips, beneath them.

> The child-care environment not only must be physically safe; it must also provide an atmosphere for learning.

Find out if smoking is banned from the child-care facility. Ask if smoke detectors and fire extinguishers are present. Check to see if emergency phone numbers are posted, along with an emergency route. Are practice emergency drills performed periodically? Ask a family child-care provider who is available to assist her in case of an emergency. Make sure cleaning supplies are locked away from children and safety plugs are installed on all unused electrical outlets. Ask to see a copy of the facility's health and safety policies and procedure manual.

Food and Hygiene

Food served to your child at the child-care site should be nutritious, age-appropriate, properly prepared, and appealing to children. Meals should be served family style, with the care-givers sitting, eating, and interacting with the children in a leisurely manner and teaching age-appropriate table manners. Menus should consider the developmental, cultural, and emotional needs of children. Foods that pose a choking hazard should not be served to children under four years (whole grapes, hard candy, nuts, popcorn, raw carrots and celery, hot dogs, chunks of meat). Children should be given opportunities to help prepare healthy foods as a group activity. No coercive measures should be used to influence a child's eating, and food should not be used as a reward or withheld as punishment. (See chapter 7.) Inquire how children's food allergies and special nutritional needs are accommodated.

Separate sinks should be used for food preparation and hand washing. If diapered children are present, there should be a clean diaper-changing area with a nearby sink. Toilets and sinks should be clean and child-sized with soap, towels, and toilet paper within a child's reach. Notice whether child-care providers wash their hands after changing a diaper, wiping a nose, or helping a child use the bathroom. Do they require children to wash their hands before eating and after using the toilet or playing outside?

Learning Opportunities

Children should have many age-appropriate toys. The classroom should have child-sized tables and chairs, as well as multiple activity centers, such as an art area, library corner, housekeeping area, and science-nature area. Do the children appear to be happy and are they encouraged to talk with each other? Are they

Preschoolers need a balance of quiet and active play, group play, individual time, and quiet time.

involved in varied activities? Are there sufficient materials and resources for each child? Ask to see a written plan for daily routines, including play and learning activities, nap or rest time, snacks and meals.

Preschoolers need a balance of quiet and active play, group play, individual time, and quiet time. They need a variety of learning experiences involving colors, shapes, numbers, and role playing. Inquire whether both inside play and outside play are a part of each day. In addition to structured time, young children need some "free play" that allows them to make choices about who to play with and what to do. They also need opportunities for "creative play" making arts and crafts and for "imaginative play" that involves pretending.

Too many parents push a sick child to attend child care when he is not well enough to participate in routine activities and when his presence unnecessarily exposes other children to illness.

Find out how much time children spend watching TV and which programs are viewed. Television should be limited to one or two hours a day. Ask whether field trips are scheduled periodically and how transportation is handled.

Care of Sick Children

Of course you will need to make sure you can be reached at all times, in case your child gets sick while being cared for by someone else. You will need to know what criteria are used for excluding sick children from the child-care setting (such as fever, rash, cough) and what arrangements are made for children who become ill at the facility, while they wait for a parent to arrive. Too many parents push a sick child to attend child care when he is not well enough to participate in routine activities and when his presence unnecessarily exposes other children to illness. You should have several contingency plans for those inevitable days when you awaken to the dreaded words, "Mommy, I don't feel good." By having a backup plan—one parent takes the day off or Grandma is available to watch your sick child—routine childhood illnesses don't have to become a scheduling crisis. A child who is too sick to attend regular day care definitely creates stress for his employed parents. However, you should also consider the stress on your sick child of adjusting to alternative arrangements at a time when he most needs the attentive love and care of a parent.

Ask whether the staff will give medication to your child (you'll need one bottle at home and one for the child-care facility). All medications must have the prescription label, and records must be maintained of all medications given. If your child has a special medical problem, find out if someone is qualified to administer an asthma treatment, deal with an allergic reaction or an epileptic seizure, test a diabetic child's blood sugar or give an insulin injection. Find out if there is a pediatrician or other medical consultant available to program staff. Inquire whether the staff is trained in first aid, injury prevention, management of choking, and child CPR.

Licensure and Accreditation

To help identify a quality program, parents need to know the difference between licensure and accreditation. Licensure helps reduce risks to children by assuring compliance with basic health, safety, cleanliness, and staffing standards. Licensed providers have met specific training requirements and passed a criminal background check. Find out if the child-care facility is licensed or registered with the local government and ask to see a current document. Although using an unlicensed

Accreditation is an excellent way to assure not only that a program has met basic health and safety requirements but also that it is designed to optimize your child's social, emotional, and intellectual development.

provider may increase the risk to your child's safety, health, and development, a licensed facility does not necessarily guarantee quality.

Accreditation by an agency such as the National Association for the Education of Young Children (NAEYC) or the National Association for Family Child Care (NAFCC) is a higher standard of quality than licensure. A distinct difference exists between safe supervision of children in care and optimizing children's growth and development in the child-care setting by meeting the critical developmental needs of each child. Accreditation is an excellent way to assure not only that a program has met basic health and safety requirements but also that it is designed to optimize your child's social, emotional, and intellectual development. Voluntary accreditation assures that a program meets rigorous national standards in staff qualifications and development, curriculum and activities, staff-child and staff-parent interaction, staffing ratios, physical environment, health and safety, nutrition and food service, and administration. Although some very reputable facilities may not have sought accreditation, due to the lengthy process involved, national accreditation provides excellent assurance that you are dealing with a quality program.

Cost

Many companies offer flexible work schedules, flexible work sites, on-site child-care services, enhanced resource and referral service, or direct assistance in paying for child care. Many employers have learned that it is good business to help their workers with their child-care needs. Check with your company's human resources or personnel office to see what kinds of child-care assistance may be available. For example, many employers offer dependent-care spending accounts, direct payment through cafeteria plan benefits, voucher programs or company benefits. In addition, your local child-care resource and referral agency may have information about the availability of subsidized child-care services for low income families.

The Agreement

When you hire someone to provide in-home care, it is always best to have a written agreement that spells out the expectations on both sides. Clarify policies for sick leave, pay raises, vacations, and health insurance. You can get sample forms from referral agencies. Consider paying an in-home provider for periodic training sessions to increase her knowledge of early child development. Even a few hours of training can greatly improve the care a provider gives. Include in your agreement your expectations about driving your child somewhere. Be explicit about how you want the caregiver to handle misbehavior, tantrums, toilet-training accidents, and so on. Be emphatic that she *never* has your permission to hit your child.

Ask a family child-care provider or child-care center for a written statement of policies dealing with such things as fees, discipline, sick children, transportation, and the dispensing of medication. Find out what days the site is closed and whether alternative care is available. Provide written instructions to your caregiver about any special dietary, health, or other needs.

> Even a few hours of training can greatly improve the care a provider gives.

Your Ongoing Relationship with Your Child-Care Provider

While incompetent, immoral, and outright dangerous caretakers do exist, many thousands of highly competent, extremely diligent, and deeply caring men and women possess the rare capacity to genuinely love someone else's children and to share meaningfully in their upbringing. Should you have the good fortune to find such a person, allow your child the privilege of loving her reciprocally without feeling threatened or jealous. I promise your child won't forget who his mother is!

Quality child care can strengthen families and improve children's health and development. Staff who invest in your child's well-being can serve as extended family members whose interactions can teach and model healthy behaviors. Treat your caregiver with consideration and respect for the important work she does. Make it clear that your provider is more than a baby-sitter. Pay what you owe on time, and honor the terms of your agreement. Don't abuse your caregiver by leaving a sick child or arriving late.

> Treat your caregiver with consideration and respect for the important work she does.

A positive relationship between parents and caregivers—an important component of quality care—is built on two-way dialogue and parent participation. It requires a sense of mutual respect, investment, and effort. Family child-care providers with limited staff especially appreciate parent volunteers who can participate in celebrations, field trips, and other special events.

Deal with issues when they come up, and don't let problems fester. Remember that you are the employer and that your expectations are legitimate. You should talk with your caregiver on a daily basis and receive information about both positive and negative experiences affecting your child. Many caregivers provide parents with a daily written report of their child's activities and special accomplishments, a collaborative ritual that provides obvious cooperation and mutual pleasure.

Drop by at unscheduled times or pick your child up earlier than usual to monitor the quality of care when your presence is not expected. If you have concerns about practices you observe, contact your state agency that handles child-care centers. Formal complaints can be filed without your name being revealed to the caregiver.

Your Child's Adjustment to Child Care

To help your child feel comfortable with your child-care arrangements, visit the program with your little one before you enroll him. Show by your body language, words, and tone of voice that you like the caregiver. Begin in-home care by leaving your child with the caregiver for a short time only.

Separation Anxiety

The reluctance of a young child to be separated from his mother or father is known as separation anxiety. (See chapter 7.) Even when a child likes to go to preschool or his family day-care home, separation will be difficult for him until he is confident that you will return. Although some children say good-bye at the door with ease and never look back, others are wary about their new surroundings and cry, protest, and cling to their parent. Your child's healthy, strong attachment to you makes it developmentally appropriate for him not to want to be away from you. Eventually a child learns that his parents regularly come and go and that they can be trusted to return when promised. Children who generally have more trouble adjusting to new situations usually have more manifestations of separation anxiety. Storybooks that deal with separation and games like hide-and-seek can help prepare a young child for absences and reassure him about reunions. If your child is anxious about your departure, showing his distress by crying is preferable to becoming withdrawn.

Even when a child likes to go to preschool or his family day-care home, separation will be difficult for him until he is confident that you will return.

Parents also experience varying degrees of anxiety when they must be separated from their young children. Many working mothers are ambivalent about daily leaving their youngsters in the care of others. If parents don't learn to handle their own ambivalent feelings about separation, they can unwittingly make departures more difficult for their child.

The following strategies will help your child make the transition to his child-care setting each day.

- Start the day on a pleasant note, not a mad rush. Allow some extra time each morning for a few relaxed moments of cuddling or play before leaving the house. (See "dawdling" in chapter 5.)
- When you arrive at the day-care home or preschool, adhere to a predictable routine. For example, take off your child's outer clothing and give her a hug before telling her that you are leaving. State the time you will return, such as after her nap or lunch, and always keep your commitment! Explain to your child that her teacher or caregiver will take good care of her until you return.
- Convey your confidence in her substitute caretaker by remarking about their upcoming day together. If your child starts to cry or protest, calmly explain that you are sure she will be fine shortly after you are gone. Once you have said good-bye, leave without lingering.

Young children are amazingly perceptive and intuitive, accurately taking their emotional and behavioral cues during potentially stressful situations from our tone of voice, non-verbal communication, and body language. Thus, our facial expression, eye contact, body posture, and general affect are more influential than the words we speak. If your expression conveys, "Poor honey, you must be so upset," no words of reassurance will ever sound convincing. If you prolong your departure because of your child's protests, your hesitancy will unmistakably transmit your anxiety. The effect will be to increase your child's anxiety and cause her protests to escalate. Upon your return, remind your child that you came back just as you promised earlier.

View the Setting from Your Child's Perspective

An ideal provider genuinely cares about your child, gives your child liberal attention, diligently protects and safeguards your child, and regularly communicates with you about your child's development. Ask yourself whether your child looks forward to going to her child-care setting. Does she feel safe, welcomed, and cared for? Does she have friends to play with and lots of varied learning activities? Does she talk in a positive manner about her caregiver? Are there any aspects of the arrangement that cause you concern? Does the program honor your values and cultural background?

Changing Your Child-Care Provider

Even after you have selected and begun using a particular child-care arrangement, the need to critically evaluate the setting does not stop. Too many parents continue to use subpar care because of the daunting obstacles involved in making a change. Although consistency in your child-care arrangements is important to your child's sense of security, it is inevitable that you will need to change your child-care situation from time to time, based on your child's needs or your circumstances. While in-home care may have been ideal when your child was an infant, your preschooler may now prefer to be with his peers in a learning center. Your family child-care provider may move to a new city. Your child may be overwhelmed in a large center and be more comfortable switching to a small child-care home.

> **Too many parents continue to use subpar care because of the daunting obstacles involved in making a change.**

Whenever a change occurs, whether by choice or out of necessity, it's important to recognize the impact on your child. Remember that a change in caregiver represents a significant loss to him. Talk to him about the upcoming change to give him time to accept the idea but not so far in advance that he dwells on it. Explain why the change is necessary. Let your child express his feelings about the change. Commemorating the event with a party or making a scrapbook of memories about his caregiver and friends can help him with the transition.

Occasionally, an immediate change becomes necessary when you have evidence or your intuition tells you that your child's safety and welfare are in jeopardy. Observe your child for any changes in behavior that suggest he is not thriving emotionally under the present circumstances. Fortunately, preschoolers, unlike infants, have the verbal skills to tell a parent about physical, verbal, or sexual abuse. Too many parents make the mistake of continuing to use an arrangement that has proven to be suboptimal. Making arrangements in the first place is usually so difficult that many parents are reluctant to change, even when a change is in their child's best interests.

It's essential that you maintain an atmosphere of open communication with your child, giving him ample time to talk about his day. Convey your acceptance of his comments so he will feel free telling you anything. While it's important to have a positive relationship with your child's caregiver, make it clear to your child that he can tell you something negative about the provider without incurring your criticism. If your child ever tells you something to make you believe he is in danger in his child-care setting, consider it an emergency. You must *not* take your child back to the situation. Show him that you will protect him from any kind of harm by refusing to return him to a potentially risky setting. If you suspect there are problems at your child's facility, call your state agency that governs child-care centers and discuss your concerns.

Working Mothers' Guilt

If you work outside the home, make the most of the available time you do have with your child. By making a concerted effort, many employed mothers actually spend as much or more time directly interacting with their children than at-home mothers. Prominently display a photo of your child and your spouse at work to help you keep them in your thoughts throughout the day. Bring your child to your place of work so she can picture where you are while she is at child care. Seeing her photo will

reassure your child that you are thinking of her at work. Explain the nature of your responsibilities and how the work you do benefits others. Convey a positive attitude about your job and model for your child a healthy work ethic.

Look for meaningful ways to reconnect with your child at the end of the workday. Giving her your undivided attention for even fifteen to twenty minutes as she tells you about her day can convince your child that she is a blessing to you and not a bother amid your many competing priorities. The first few minutes after you pick up your child or arrive home often sets the tone for the rest of the day or evening. No matter how rushed or stressed you are, resolve to make your first critical minutes together have a positive impact on your family.

> **Bring your child to your place of work so she can picture where you are while she is at child care.**

If, having read this chapter, you find yourself struggling with guilt and unease, review your reasons for your choice to work outside the home and honestly assess your job satisfaction and rewards. Use the guidelines outlined in these pages to ask yourself whether you have found a child-care option that promotes your youngster's optimal development and assures her physical safety and emotional security. Then evaluate whether you have sufficient family support to enable you to juggle all your commitments and still nurture your child optimally when you are at home. If you come to the painful conclusion that you are using substandard care or need to enlist more help, modify your work hours, or change jobs, don't despair. Every working parent must periodically reevaluate their situation and decide when a change is warranted. Instead of allowing guilt to weigh you down like a heavy anchor, use the information provided here to empower you to take appropriate action and to feel better about your choices.

Fortunately, many employed parents make the happy discovery that their child's ultimate outcome is actually enhanced by the fact that they work outside the home, provided that they manage to find high-quality child care, that they enjoy their job and receive enhanced self-esteem from their work, and that they have adequate sources of support.

If you want to read more about finding quality child care or choosing an optimal preschool educational program for your child, I recommend *Child Care: A Parent's Guide* by Sonja Cooper (New York: Checkmark Books, 1999) and *Smart Start: The Parent's Complete Guide to Preschool Education* by Marian Edelman Borden (New York: Facts on File, 1997).

Chapter 7

Essential Answers for Common Concerns

Preschoolers display a variety of common yet perplexing behaviors that often cause parental anxiety. Whether the concern is over a toilet-training glitch, picky eating, irrational fears, embarrassing habits, or imaginary friends, parents may be unsure how best to handle it. This chapter provides practical help and reassurance to enable you to emotionally support your child in dealing effectively with such common concerns. You will learn to distinguish normal from problematic behavior, accomplish toilet training with minimal stress for your child or yourself, avoid destructive power struggles over food, and work in partnership with your little one as you guide her through the emotional and psychological milestones of the preschool years. The information and suggestions provided here should help demystify many of the developmental behaviors in preschoolers, build your confidence, calm your fears, and strengthen your parent-child relationship.

Toilet Training

Few child-rearing topics evoke more parental anxiety than the prospect of toilet training. Yet there is no valid reason for parents

Brief History of Toilet Training in the United States

In the early 1900s, toilet training was begun inappropriately early, often before twelve months of age. The principal motive was convenience — to save mothers the drudgery of washing diapers. In addition, the acquisition of toilet skills was viewed as a major developmental milestone, and competitive parents pressured their babies to perform in this arena. Children who were trained so early certainly did not walk to the potty-chair without prompting and use the potty with minimal supervision. Rather, it was the mother who was "trained" to interpret the signs of an impending bowel movement or anticipate the probability of a full bladder after a nap. She painstakingly held the child over the potty, hoping for a response that would spare her a diaper change. Meanwhile, the child usually understood little of the whole process.

In recent decades, disposable diapers have made babies so comfortable and diaper changes so easy that many parents postponed toilet training until the child actually could carry out each step herself. Parents began to take a laissez-faire approach to toilet training, bolstered by the conviction that all normal children in every society eventually learn accepted toilet practices, along with the evidence that coercive training could be emotionally harmful for children.

Now, with the growing number of working mothers and children in child-care, some families are feeling increased pressure to train their children. With the recent awareness that diapered children contribute to the spread of disease in day-care centers, toilet training has become a public health issue.

Many day-care centers will not accept children until they are trained because of epidemics of diarrhea and hepatitis A that occur mainly in centers that care for children in diapers.

to approach this routine child-development issue with trepidation. Toilet training is not a competition; it is a necessary social skill that all normal children acquire at their own pace. With a relaxed attitude and a child-oriented approach, most children will have achieved daytime dryness by thirty-six months of age and nighttime training by forty-eight months.[1] The process need not be a source of conflict or frustration. Rather, when approached with confidence in the child's ability to learn at the right time, toilet teaching and toilet learning have the potential to forge a stronger parent-child relationship and to enhance a child's self-esteem.

Signs of Toilet-Training Readiness

Medical experts in the United States generally recommend delaying formal toilet teaching until your child displays certain signs of readiness. Although toilet-training readiness varies widely among children, most youngsters are ready to begin training around eighteen to twenty-four months and are successfully trained by two and a half or three years of age. The appearance of readiness signs is similar for boys and girls, but girls tend to complete training sooner than boys. Rushing things offers no advantage. Generally, the earlier you start, the longer it takes. For example, I began training my first child when he turned a year old, but he was well past two before

Although toilet-training readiness varies widely among children, most youngsters are ready to begin training around eighteen to twenty-four months and are successfully trained by two and a half or three years of age.

he was really able to use the potty himself. By the time my fifth child was born, I was much more relaxed and didn't start training until he was about two and a half years old. With the example of four older siblings and other children in child care, it was only a matter of weeks until he grasped the concept of using the potty. What's important is that the process is child-oriented and reasonably paced.

The following signs of physiologic and behavioral maturation will help you recognize the "window of opportunity" when your child is most receptive to toilet training.

- A child's nervous system needs to have matured enough to allow him to control the muscles that regulate urination and stooling. A child needs to be sufficiently aware of his bladder and bowel sensations and to demonstrate that a bowel movement or urination is imminent by changing his facial expression, pausing in play, posturing, straining, grunting, squatting, or grabbing his crotch. You can help your toddler interpret these telltale signs by saying, "Bobby is trying to make doo-doo. Let's go sit on the potty." In addition, your child should wake up from a nap with a dry diaper, and urinate large volumes at a time.

- A child needs to understand the relationship between using the potty and staying clean and dry and must also be willing to cooperate with his parents. He should be able to indicate that he wants his soiled diaper changed and to obey simple commands like "Put the book down" or "Bring me the cup." If he is too negative, stubborn, or protests too much, it is best to wait until he is more cooperative and willing to please. Generally, children call attention to wet and soiled diapers between eighteen and twenty-four months. By two years they can announce that they are about to wet, and by two and a half to three years, they can hold back their urine in time to get to the potty.

- A child needs to have adequate language skills to tell you when he needs to use the potty. He must also grasp the distinction between "wet pants" and "dry pants" and know specific words for urine and feces.
- A child's motor skills need to be sufficiently developed to allow him to sit on the potty unaided. He also needs to be able to walk to and from the potty and to pull his pants down and up again.
- A child needs to show an interest in toilet training by following his parents into the bathroom and desiring to mimic them. A child who begins putting things where they belong is usually ready to begin learning where urine and feces should go.

Even if your child displays these signs of readiness, your attempts to toilet train could be thwarted in the presence of major life events that place your child under stress. It is usually preferable to postpone toilet training until your child has adjusted to a significant event, such as a move to a new home, the birth of a sibling, separation of the parents, a change in child-care arrangements, or a major illness in the family.

Choose Your Words

You will want to think carefully about what words you will teach your child for body parts, urine, and bowel movements. Not only will you hear these words yourself each day for the next several years, you can be sure your child will repeat them freely to relatives, baby-sitters, neighbors, and bystanders.

To foster a healthy body image, I recommend you use anatomically correct names for all body parts, including the genitals. When a nose is a nose, but a penis or vagina has a code name, like weenie or pee-pee, children may wonder why this part of their body can't be called by its real name. You should also avoid using offensive terms like yucky, nasty, messy, or stinky to describe bowel movements because these can unintentionally create shame in a child about a normal bodily function.

While terms like urine and feces aren't realistic for young children, suitable words include wee-wee, pee-pee, wet, or tinkle for urination, and poo-poo, doo-doo, BM, or poop for bowel movements. For the sake of consistency, consider using the same terms that are used at his child-care setting. The phrase "going potty" can be confusing because it doesn't distinguish urination from defecation.

Equipment

Once you decide your child is ready to begin toilet learning, you will need a few supplies.

• *A child's potty-chair.* When you begin training, your child will probably prefer using his own small potty-chair. Later, he can graduate to using a child's attachment for the toilet. The potty-chair should have a sturdy base to prevent it from tipping over. Urine deflectors may sound like an attractive feature on a child's potty-chair, but children are easily injured by a urine deflector when getting off a potty. If you pass on the deflector, teach your little boy to lean forward to aim his stream into the pot. Built-in handlebars give a youngster something to push against when having a bowel movement. If you decide to get a toilet attachment instead of a child's potty, make sure it has a footrest that allows your child to sit with his feet firmly planted for pushing.

• *Cloth diapers and training pants.* If your child usually wears disposable diapers, you might consider switching to cloth to make it easier for her to feel when she is wet. Your child needs to perceive being wet as soon as she urinates in order to learn to distinguish between "wet pants" and "dry pants." You will also want to purchase eight to twelve pairs of training pants large enough so your child easily can pull them down and up. Take your child with you to select attractive underpants that will increase her incentive for staying dry.

During potty training, your child will prefer to wear simple, loose clothing, such as shorts or pants that are easy to pull up and down. Avoid overalls and clothing with buttons, snaps, or zippers that will be cumbersome for her. When you are at home, it is best to dress your child only in underpants and a short shirt.

• *Rewards*. Conflicting advice exists about giving rewards for using the potty. Some experts advocate stocking up on your child's favorite treats (candy, sugared cereal, chips, crackers) and rewarding him for using the potty. Others counter that the comfort of remaining clean and dry, abundant parental praise and approval, and the sense of accomplishment that comes with mastering a grown-up skill is reward enough. I suggest initially offering treats, in addition to social rewards, to help foster a cooperative attitude in your child. As soon as possible, taper the treats while continuing your verbal praise and hugs.

• *Learning aids*. Your child will probably enjoy having you read him a story about potty training or watching a video during the training process. Frequent repetition of the steps involved in using the potty helps him understand what is expected. Many excellent resources are available that have proven popular with children. Imitation with a doll can also be useful in helping a child understand the steps involved in using the toilet. You can buy your child a doll that wets and dress her in training pants. Fill the doll with several ounces of water, then let your child "teach" the doll how to use the potty by removing the training pants, sitting her on the potty, making her wet, and praising her for being a "big girl."

> It is usually preferable to postpone toilet training until your child has adjusted to a significant event, such as a move to a new home, the birth of a sibling, separation of the parents, a change in childcare arrangements, or a major illness in the family.

Getting Started: Preparing Your Child

Preparation for toilet training should be a low-key experience aimed at introducing your child to the potty and helping him become comfortable sitting on it. During this time, your child will probably still wear diapers as he gains practice interpreting his body signals and making "pee-pee" and "poo-poo" in the potty, with your guidance.

• Begin explaining diaper changes by saying, "If Tommy goes pee-pee in the potty, he won't have to feel all wet." When you see your child grunting or urinating, explain what is happening with his body. It may take a while for him to understand the distinction between "has wet," "is wetting," and "will wet." Then he has to learn how to hold the urge until he gets to the potty.

> **It may take a while for him to understand the distinction between "has wet," "is wetting," and "will wet."**

• After your child has become comfortable sitting on the potty, have him sit undressed and ask him to try to go pee-pee (or poo-poo) in the potty. Do this at a time when he is likely to urinate (right after a nap or about forty minutes after drinking fluids) or to have a bowel movement (shortly after breakfast). Encourage imitation by having your child sit on his potty chair when you sit on the toilet. Be sure to offer praise, even if he sits only briefly and nothing happens. Say, "Robbie is sitting quietly, just like Mommy does." Never attempt to coerce your child in any way. If he starts to protest, just back off.

• After your child has used the potty successfully, encourage him to tell you when he thinks he will make pee-pee or poo-poo, so you can help him go to the potty. If your child tells you he needs to use the potty or displays familiar signs that he is about to eliminate, take him to the potty and explain that the pee-pee or poo-poo wants to come out. It is preferable not to talk too much or distract him, so he can relax and concentrate. You might read a story or give him a small toy to manipulate to encourage him to remain seated.

• Don't be surprised if your child says he needs to use the potty after he has already wet or soiled. Remember that "has gone" is the first step in achieving awareness of bowel and bladder activity. You can ask your child to sit on the potty-chair with the soiled diaper for a minute. Then remove the diaper and place it in the potty so your child will know where pee-pee and poo-poo should go. Try to be more alert to his body signals that suggest elimination is imminent. Then you can coordinate practice runs to the potty chair at opportune times.

> **Don't be surprised if your child says he needs to use the potty after he has already wet or soiled.**

Not uncommonly, a parent will ask whether their child needs to make pee-pee, only to find that he has already wet by the time he gets to the potty-chair. This happens because your word cue triggers a response before your child can get to the potty. Or a child may sit compliantly on the potty, then promptly wet after getting up. Be patient. With practice, he will improve his timing and learn to hold back until he reaches the potty and to stay seated long enough to release urine or a bowel movement.

• When your child does urinate or have a bowel movement in the potty, immediately show your approval and lavish him with praise. Be demonstrative and excitedly praise your child, hug him, and even clap your hands. To make it clear why he is receiving your approval, say, "Jeremy made poo-poo in the potty. He's a big boy." Because children typically learn to recognize the need to pass a stool earlier than they perceive the need to urinate, most will learn to have a bowel movement in the potty before they achieve bladder control. On the other hand, urination occurs more often, giving children more practice.

Building on Success to Accelerate Learning

Your child will need to practice his new skill, probably for months, before achieving consistent control. Gradually, you will decrease your direct involvement and physical help as your child slowly gains increased mastery over the steps involved in using the potty. He will continue to need your ongoing emotional support and encouragement throughout this period.

• Once your child has successfully used the potty several times or asks to stop wearing diapers, you can introduce "big boy" training pants or pull-ups. Toddlers love to wear training pants because they are more comfortable and make a child feel more grown up. Help your child learn to pull his pants down and up by himself. This will be easier if he places one hand in front and one in back of the waistband, instead of on either side.

• You will still need to remind your child to sit on the potty every couple of hours or whenever you notice body signals that suggest he needs to urinate or have a bowel movement. While gentle reminders will be necessary to build on your child's early success, excessive nagging will only provoke resistance. To minimize power struggles, do not ask a direct question that could be answered no, such as "Do you want to go pee-pee now?" Instead, simply state, "It's time to go sit on the potty." You can help your child feel more in control by offering a choice whenever possible: "Do you want to look at a book or play with a toy while you sit on the potty?" Or you can use the "when . . . then" technique to offer an incentive by saying, "When you're done using the potty, then we'll go outside."

After your child has achieved a measure of success with each step in toileting, you can suggest he use the potty on his own, while you remain nearby in case your help is needed. If he stops cooperating and starts resisting the training process by throwing tantrums or becoming negative, immediately back off and stop all efforts for a week or two.

• Verbal rehearsal is a valuable technique for helping your child better understand that he is expected to make pee-pee or poo-poo in the potty and not in his diaper. Use frequent statements and questions to let your child verbally practice what he needs to do. Say something like "Daddy goes pee-pee in the potty." Then ask, "Where are you going to make pee-pee?" Or state, "Babies wear diapers," and then ask, "Do big boys wear underpants?" Help your child rehearse what he should do by asking, "What will you say when you have to go pee-pee?"

• There's no set time when boys should start urinating in a standing position. Eventually the desire to imitate their father or older brother usually is the motivating factor. A little boy will need a footstool to allow him to reach over the rim of the toilet.

• In general, young children should stay in diapers at night until they start waking up dry with some regularity. Most little ones will prefer to wear a diaper at night than to wet the bed. If your child asks to wear training pants to bed, you can put rubber pants over them to protect the sheets or have her wear pull-ups.

The Importance of Consistency

Consistent expectations are important, both among different caretakers in the home and in different settings outside the home.

• With so many mothers of small children in the workforce, countless youngsters spend part of their day with a substitute caretaker. Sometimes training is started in one location but is not reinforced in the other. A baby-sitter might initiate toilet teaching, only to find that exhausted parents—who may lack the commitment to pursue consistency in the evenings and weekends—do not reinforce her efforts. Or parents may begin toilet training, only to find the child-care provider keeps the child in diapers all day. Unless all caretakers consistently reinforce toilet training, a child may view toilet learning as a game to be played off and on, rather than a new, more grown-up way of life. Ask your baby-sitter to use the same words your child hears at home and provide her with a potty-chair like the one you use, as well as training pants, books, and treats. Make it clear that she is *never* to punish your child in connection with toilet training.

• Once your child is wearing underpants, you should not put her back in diapers, even when you venture out of the home. In the first place, it is confusing to the child to figure what is expected of her based on whether she is wearing diapers or training pants. Furthermore, your child may figure that you lack confidence in her if you switch back to diapers for an outing. Make it a family policy that everyone uses the toilet before leaving home. Many parents keep a spare potty-chair in the car trunk or bring along a portable potty attachment to place over a public toilet. Families with minivans may choose to keep a spare potty in the vehicle so young children can use it in the privacy of the van.

> **Take your child into public restrooms so that you can point out that bathrooms are everywhere and they look different from the ones at home.**

• Prepare your child well in advance for the day he will need to use a public restroom. Without proper instruction, young children can be frightened and overwhelmed when asked to urinate in an unfamiliar restroom. Take your child into public restrooms so that you can point out that bathrooms are everywhere and they look different from the ones at home.

• Explain that sometimes, when no bathroom is available, a person might have to make pee-pee or poo-poo outdoors. Let your child practice this before the need arises. Help little girls remove their underwear and squat, preferably over grass or sand to prevent splashing. While practicing for an emergency will prove valuable someday, try not to make toileting outdoors into a game.

Be Patient and Never Punish

Perhaps more than anything, successful potty training depends on a relaxed, positive attitude and an atmosphere free of anxiety.

• Remember to show your approval for every small step your child makes toward learning to toilet himself. At first, you will need to show your pleasure and delight for his wearing training pants or simply walking toward the potty. Later, you can show approval when your child has completed a part of the process correctly, such as pulling his pants down or sitting on the potty. Eventually, you will reserve your praise and rewards for urinating or having a bowel movement in the potty. Finally, you will focus your approval on having dry pants.

> Always remember that there is no place in the toilet training process for criticism, coercion, shaming, or punishment of any kind.

• Strive to show optimism and never show impatience. If you ever need to gently guide your child through a motion, use a very light touch. Toilet training should be a cooperative experience in which your child receives abundant adult praise and a gratifying sense of accomplishment at mastering a new level of independence. Always be patient with your child and remain positive, taking care to communicate your approval and acceptance.

• Recognize that any change in routine or a stressful event can affect a child's progress. Training may need to be temporarily interrupted if a child is less cooperative due to houseguests, visitors, illness in a parent or child, or a new child-care arrangement. Your child usually is the best indicator of the need to relax training for a day or so. I recall a compliant little boy who had used the potty successfully for several days when he surprised his mother by announcing one morning, "I don't want to be a big boy today." Apparently, the pressure to perform was emotionally exhausting, and the little guy needed a break.

• Always remember that there is no place in the toilet training process for criticism, coercion, shaming, or punishment of any kind. The last thing you want to provoke is a battle of wills by your excessive nagging and reminders or by forcing your child to sit on the potty for long periods. The more you pressure, the more a child is likely to resist. Even well-intentioned parents may find themselves getting frustrated when their capable child doesn't seem to be cooperating. Regrettably, some parents resort to physical punishment when they simply don't know what else to do. More child abuse occurs during toilet training than any other developmental step. Don't let this happen to you! Doing nothing at all is far better than doing the wrong thing. Coercion never improves cooperation.

> Sometimes children who are competent to use the potty become defiant and refuse to do so, waging a battle of wills.

• If your child is resisting, it is best to back off and turn all responsibility for toileting over to the child. Sometimes children who are competent to use the potty become defiant and refuse to do so, waging a battle of wills. Do not allow yourself to get into a toilet-training conflict with your child! Instead, unhook from the power struggle by telling your child that he is capable of using the potty on his own and doesn't need any reminders from you. Reward him for successes and be silent about accidents.

• Sometimes a child will deliberately withhold bowel movements if he perceives excessive pressure concerning toilet training. Withholding can result in hard stools that are painful and difficult to pass. This can make a child fearful of having a bowel movement, leading to a vicious cycle of chronic constipation. If you notice your child's stools have become less regular or if your child seems uncomfortable when passing a movement, contact his doctor. (See "Soiling" later in this chapter.)

Expect Accidents

Potty-training accidents are inevitable, and they usually are as upsetting for your child as they are for you. Even children who have been trained a long time can suffer occasional lapses when engrossed in play, overly tired, excited about a trip, or in new surroundings. Intermittent accidents are an inevitable part of the toilet-training process.

• A child may not feel the urge to urinate until his bladder is completely full. Thus, he may wet himself a few minutes after insisting he didn't have to go, which makes his parents furious. An all too common scenario goes like this: Your four-year-old says he doesn't need to use the potty as you get him ready for an outing. Upon arriving at the mall, he announces that he has to go real bad. You tell him he'll have to "hold it" until you can find a bathroom, but he wets himself before you can get him there. You are very upset and keep asking, "Why didn't you tell me sooner?" The truth is that he didn't feel the urge until he got out of the car. While an adult knows to empty her bladder before a long car ride or other outing, young children need to be reminded to use the potty before leaving the house, going to bed at night, or going to a movie—even if they don't think they need to.

Even children who have been trained a long time can suffer occasional lapses when engrossed in play, overly tired, excited about a trip, or in new surroundings.

• Keep an extra set of underpants and a change of clothing in the car, at the child-care setting, and in your "supply bag" that you bring on outings. It's completely inappropriate to leave a child in soiled clothing as a training method. Having an accident is distressing enough to your child without the additional discomfort of not being clean and dry or the embarrassment of wearing stained clothing.

Toileting Hygiene

Teaching proper hygiene is an essential part of toilet training. Children need to learn how to wipe themselves and to wash their hands after using the toilet.

- Teach your child how to wipe after a bowel movement and show girls how to wipe themselves from front to back to prevent bacteria from being introduced into the vagina or urinary opening. Many children still need help with wiping until about four or five years of age.
- All children should be taught to wash their hands after using the bathroom and before meals. A child's stepping stool in the bathroom will enable little ones to reach the sink. Colorful soaps, soap pumps, and paper towels will make washing more attractive to young children.
- Let your child flush the toilet after the potty contents have been emptied. The sound and sight of a flushing toilet, with its swirling water, is distressing to some children. Others feel possessive about their bowel movements and resent seeing them flushed away. Some children like to say good-bye to their bowel movements. It is best to familiarize your child with flushing before you attempt to flush contents of their potty bowl.
- Do your best not to overreact if you find your toddler playing with his bowel movement. Horrifying as this is to parents, it is quite normal among naturally curious young children. Few children learn the social skill of toileting without at least one incident of smearing or smooshing their feces. Try to remain calm and neutral as you clean your

> child and state matter-of-factly, "We don't play with our poo-poo." Such "messy" exploratory behavior may be minimized by offering your child supervised opportunities to handle play dough, finger-paint, and play in the dirt.

- Provide your child with constructive instruction to help prevent future accidents. You can explain, "You wet your pants because you didn't stop playing to go to the potty. Next time, go quickly to the potty."
- Never scold, nag, belittle, tease, or otherwise punish your child for a toilet-training accident. Instead, reassure him by saying, "You're doing just fine. Soon you won't have any accidents. You'll go pee-pee in the potty every time."
- Don't be oversolicitous after an accident. You will need to supervise cleaning up after a bowel movement, but your child should help. Have your child step out of his wet or soiled underpants, carry them to the soiled-pants location, and then bring clean pants and put them on. This will remind him why it is preferable to remain clean and dry. Keep the emphasis on encouraging your child about his progress by praising successes and downplaying accidents.

Bedwetting

Although many children begin to achieve nighttime dryness by age three, approximately 30 percent of four-year-olds and 20 percent of five-year-olds still wet the bed occasionally, as do about 10 percent of first graders and 3 percent of twelve-year-olds. The spontaneous cure rate is about 15 percent per year after the age of five.[2] Bedwetting, also known as enuresis, affects boys two to three times as often as girls. There is a strong family predisposition toward bedwetting, often with one or both parents of an enuretic child having been a bed-wetter themselves. Bedwetting should not even be considered a problem until age five in girls or age six in boys, or until it starts to interfere with the child's social life.

Primary bedwetting, in which the child has never achieved nighttime dryness, occurs most commonly. Secondary enuresis, or the occurrence of bedwetting after a dry period of many months, may follow a stressful episode, such as the birth of a sibling, a move to a new neighborhood, a family crisis, or serious illness.

Bedwetting should not even be considered a problem until age five in girls or age six in boys, or until it starts to interfere with the child's social life.

The cause of bedwetting is not clear, although many theories have been proposed. Coercive or inappropriately early toilet training has been associated with subsequent bedwetting. However, the vast majority of bedwetters have no underlying psychological or medical problem. Rather, they simply appear to have a developmental delay in the physiological maturation of bladder-control mechanisms. In many instances, the child who wets the bed has a smaller bladder capacity than normal and urinates often during the daytime. Some bedwetters seem to be deep sleepers who don't awaken at the sensation of a full bladder.

In approximately 3 percent of bedwetters, an underlying medical problem exists to cause enuresis. A medical problem is more likely when there is daytime enuresis, enuresis that starts after a child was once dry, dribbling urine, or associated problems having bowel movements. Before attributing enuresis to a simple maturational delay, a child should be examined by his pediatrician and have a urine sample cultured and tested.

Fortunately, nearly all bedwetters outgrow the problem without any specific intervention. On the other hand, an inappropriate parental response to bedwetting can certainly prolong enuresis and undermine a child's self-esteem. Scolding, ridiculing, shaming, or punishing should never be used. Parents should not display disgust at an odorous bed or at having to wash the sheets. You should not urge your child to "try harder" or promise lavish rewards for consecutive dry nights. Making a child anxious, ashamed, or discouraged only compounds the problem and prolongs bedwetting. Although some children respond well to positive rewards for being dry, such as a star chart, praise, or small gifts, giving rewards for being dry—or "good"—may imply that wetting is purposeful or "bad." The truth is that children have no control over bedwetting.

No specific intervention is indicated for a preschool child who wets the bed, as this is considered entirely normal. In school-age children who want help with the problem, several treatments have been used with variable success, and each has pros and cons. You should discuss such options with your child's doctor. In the majority of cases, the most effective treatment for enuresis is an optimistic and matter-of-fact explanation to the child that 1) his problem is common (even though other children don't talk about it); 2) one of his parents also had the problem and outgrew it (if this is the case); 3) he is physically normal; 4) he is not to blame; and 5) he will be consistently dry someday.

No specific intervention is indicated for a preschool child who wets the bed, as this is considered entirely normal.

You can make sure your child urinates completely before going to bed, have him wear thick underpants, and spend a few peaceful moments tucking him in and quietly talking together so that he approaches sleep relaxed and secure. Some parents choose to awaken their child to urinate before they retire. Protect your child's mattress with a plastic mattress cover, and place a flannel-lined rubber mat over the bottom sheet. As your child gets older, he may prefer to take responsibility when he awakens wet in the middle of the night, so a big deal isn't made of it. He can change into clean pajamas kept nearby and place a towel over the wet spot.

Soiling

Some children begin soiling again after becoming potty trained. Chronic fecal soiling in children four years and older is known as encopresis. The problem usually results from a combination of physiologic, developmental, environmental, and parental response factors. Most often, encopresis is related to chronic constipation, which may or may not be obvious to the parents. The soiling results when liquid feces leak around a large impacted stool. Children usually are unaware of their accidents and are unable to control them. Boys are affected more often than girls.

Many things can predispose a child to constipation, including a low-fiber diet, illness, inactivity, changes in environment, psychological stress, gastrointestinal problems, too little fluid intake, and family bowel habits. Sometimes passing a large, hard bowel movement will cause a painful tear in the anus. A young child who has experienced discomfort during defecation may understandably be apprehensive about having another painful bowel movement. However, holding back the bowel movement only causes more stool to build up and dry out in the rectum, thus producing a larger, harder movement that is even more difficult to pass. This often leads to a vicious cycle of pain-retention-pain, and eventually involuntary encopresis can result. Habitual stool withholding causes the rectum to stretch and diminishes its ability to normally expel a bowel movement, thus aggravating the situation. I recall a case where a preschool youngster developed severe constipation while on a family camping trip because he was afraid to use the unfamiliar campsite toilet facilities. His voluntary withholding of stool eventually resulted in encopresis.

A child with encopresis should be evaluated by his pediatrician to determine the cause of the problem and begin therapy. Constipation usually is present, and treatment is aimed at decreasing its severity, which then eliminates the overflow leakage of stool. An initial period of bowel cleansing may be necessary to remove any impacted stool. Maintenance therapy with laxatives and stool softeners helps assure adequate stool frequency, avoids the passage of large stools, and prevents further withholding of stool. The child's diet should be modified to increase the amount of fiber intake and the consumption of water. Fruits, vegetables, bran cereals, and wheat bread are good sources of fiber, which is a natural laxative that produces bulkier, softer stools that are passed more rapidly and easily. Because excessive intakes of milk and cheese can be constipating, they should be consumed in moderation. Bowel-habit retraining is also necessary to reestablish normal bowel movements. The child should be encouraged to sit on the toilet and attempt to pass a stool for five to ten minutes once or twice a day, preferably after meals.

> **There is no place for ridicule, shame, or blame in the treatment of encopresis.**

Never punish a child who has encopresis for his soiling accidents. There is no place for ridicule, shame, or blame in the treatment of encopresis! Instead, you should maintain a neutral attitude and have your child help you with cleaning up. Praise your child liberally for any successes. After several months of normal stooling patterns, medications to treat constipation can be tapered and ultimately discontinued. Of course, frequent communication with your pediatrician and close follow-up will be necessary. Prompt treatment of encopresis in preschoolers is important and usually yields excellent results. When encopresis persists into the school years, it can lead to diminished self-esteem, poor peer relations, family conflict, and social stigma. Sometimes encopresis is related to a stressful family situation, such as divorce, or is linked to an emotional problem in the child. Occasionally, a child will soil and even smear feces as a way to express anger. In such cases, referral to a professional therapist is indicated.

Fussy Feeders and Picky Eaters

Eating is a necessity of life that usually is an enjoyable and highly social experience. Babies quickly learn that eating is accompanied by pleasant sensations—feeling satisfied, secure, and relaxed. Parents typically find newborn feeding to be a rewarding interaction with their baby and a source of fulfillment and confidence in their new caretaker role. By toddlerhood, however, many parents find that mealtimes have disintegrated from a pleasurable experience to a painful battle of wills. They wonder, "How did something so enjoyable become so traumatic?"

The Balance of Power in Early Childhood Feeding

As children grow and develop, eating independence progresses fairly smoothly, as long as the parent and child maintain an appropriate balance of power concerning the control of food. At first, babies are dependent on their parents for food and have no choice in food selection, since they drink milk exclusively. But even newborns, especially those who are fed on demand, are capable of exercising some control over the timing of their meals and the amount of milk they consume at a feeding. Once toddlers start feeding themselves, however, they increase their control over food selection and meal size. This is the point at which many parents become anxious and preoccupied with their child's food intake and at which feedings can abruptly change from a previously mutually rewarding experience to a frustrating battleground of wills.

The Origins of Feeding Problems

Many conscientious parents of children between one and five years of age worry that their child does not eat enough. Their well-intentioned but misguided efforts to make their youngster eat more often result in daily mealtime hassles and can place their child at risk for lifelong eating problems. Several factors contribute to the frequent emergence of feeding problems toward the end of a baby's first year.

• *Decline in appetite and rate of growth.* The first reason parents become convinced that their baby isn't eating enough is simply a misperception. When we begin feeding our newborn, she initially eats a great deal for her size and grows rapidly, doubling her birth weight around four months of age and tripling it by one year. After the first year, a child's appetite decreases and her growth rate declines considerably. She doesn't quadruple her birth weight until around two and a half years and then takes another two years to increase it fivefold. Thus, toddlers and preschoolers need proportionately less food than they required during their rapid growth in early infancy. Meanwhile, we remember feeding our baby relatively large volumes of food in the first year compared to what she feeds herself now. No wonder we are convinced that she doesn't eat enough! The same parent who shoveled baby food into a willing eight-month-old may feel like their eighteen-month-old now leaves more food on the floor than she puts in her mouth.

• *Normal toddler mealtime behavior.* Normal toddler antics can make mealtimes seem more challenging than in early infancy. This doesn't mean a feeding problem exists; it just means that parents need to be better informed about the normal range of toddler behavior they can expect. Toddlers are preoccupied with asserting their independence and individuality and testing whether you really will enforce limits. The same child who once opened her mouth in eager anticipation when you presented a spoonful of food now clamps her jaws and turns her head in defiance. Eating independence is an

Eating independence is an important milestone for young children, and part of that independence involves making choices about which foods and how much of them to eat and experimenting with using food to gain control over anxious parents.

important milestone for young children, and part of that independence involves making choices about which foods and how much of them to eat and experimenting with using food to gain control over anxious parents.

For curious toddlers, eating is a social and developmental activity, as well as the source of vital nutrients. Just as important as eating a food are exploring its texture and adhesiveness; testing the law of gravity when the food is dropped from the high chair; and seeing whether the food rolls, stretches, breaks, or melts. Toddlers love to combine new developmental hand skills with the routine of eating. Between bites, they will roll their peas, stick their fingers in mashed potatoes to see the imprint left behind, and use yogurt or ketchup for finger paint.

• *Erratic eating patterns*. Toddlers are erratic and unpredictable, varying in their food preferences from month to month and in their appetite from day to day. Most experience periods when they refuse one or more foods or binge on another, such as macaroni and cheese or peanut butter and jelly.

• *Initial rejection of new foods*. Young children typically reject new foods at first. This reaction has been called neophobia, or fear of the new. Many parents mistakenly interpret this initial rejection to mean that their child has a permanent dislike for the food, earning the child the label of picky or finicky. In fact, children gradually learn to like initially rejected foods following repeated opportunities to try the new foods. It can take eight to ten exposures to a new food before a child increases her acceptance of it.

Relinquishing Control

Probably the main reason parental anxiety about feeding starts to escalate after the first year is that many parents have difficulty relinquishing control in the feeding arena once their children begin to feed themselves and to regulate their own intake of food. After all, the preparation of food is an act of love, and a toddler's refusal to eat not only feels like rejection but also provokes worry about the youngster's health. We want to take charge and make certain that our child continues to consume proper nutrients. However, once a child starts feeding himself, around age fifteen months, a clear division of responsibility exists. Ellen Satter, in her popular books on child feeding, *Child of Mine* (Bull Publishing, 1991) and *How to Get Your Child to Eat . . . But Not Too Much* (Bull Publishing, 1987), has clarified this role delineation. According to Satter, our job as parents is to take responsibility for making available to our child a variety of healthy food selections. We are not obligated to see that he eats them at every meal. While we can control what foods are offered, the self-feeding child takes control of which and how much of the offered foods he will eat.

> **Our job as parents is to take responsibility for making available to our child a variety of healthy food selections.**

Generally, small children who are offered a healthy diet will eat a proper balance of nutrients over time, even though one or several days' intake may be lopsided. Young children usually are able to self-regulate the amount of food they consume in response to what is offered. While the size and composition of individual meals may vary dramatically, children who are offered a variety of nutritious foods generally will self-select a balanced diet. They will eat more when served low-calorie foods and consume proportionately less of high-calorie foods.

The Pitfalls of Coercive Feeding Practices

It is not only unnecessary but also clearly undesirable for parents to try to control their child's intake of food. When parents respond to a picky eater by force-feeding, coaxing, bribing, or substituting preferred foods, they inadvertently reinforce the problem behavior. Giving excessive attention for refusing to eat ("Just one more bite, please. It will make you strong!") only invites a similar power struggle at the next meal. Pleading, threatening, cajoling, and punishing tend to be counterproductive and do more harm than good. Instead of getting the desired response, such tactics all too often provoke children to escalate their resistance by clenching their teeth, holding food in their cheeks, spitting, gagging, vomiting, or throwing food. Young children also recognize our attempts to influence their intake of food through praise and reward. Rewarding children for eating certain foods can actually cause their preference for those foods to decline. Thus, any type of pressure can cause children to develop dislikes for the very foods we want them to eat.

Not only do coercive feeding practices fuel short-term battles, attempts to control your child's intake can contribute to obesity and other long-term eating problems. A study with preschoolers and their families was undertaken to explore some of the influences on children's eating habits and their weight. Children of authoritarian mothers who used more coercive feeding strategies were less able to control their own food intake and had greater body-fat stores.[3] Twenty-five percent of American children are overweight, and the incidence of childhood obesity has increased more than 50 percent in the last two decades. In addition to genetic tendencies and levels of physical activity, this new evidence suggests that very controlling child-feeding practices—even when they are well intentioned—may contribute to childhood obesity. Later eating disorders also may be linked to early control issues concerning food.

Disengage from Feeding Power Struggles

If you are involved in mealtime struggles with your toddler or preschooler, stop trying to control how much your child eats and remember that your job is simply to offer your child a selection of nutritious foods at meal and snack times. She is in charge of deciding which of the offered foods and how much of them she will eat. If she is on a food "jag," where she wants macaroni and cheese or a peanut butter sandwich at every meal, for example, give a small amount of the preferred food along with the rest of the meal the family is having. Keep portions small; then let her ask for more if she wants it. Turn off the television or CD player, put the paper down, and eliminate other distractions while everyone concentrates on eating and talking together.

Remain matter-of-fact about your youngster's eating behavior, trying to show neither frustration nor delight over what he refuses or accepts. Keep dinner conversation positive and don't make any comments about how much or what your child is eating, such as "clean your plate," "just one more bite," or "try your peas." Let your child feed herself. Don't pick up her spoon and try to entice her to eat something by singsonging, "Here comes the choo-choo train." In fact, don't use any coercive methods at all.

Parents are responsible for preparing and serving a variety of healthful foods, but they should not use coercive measures to influence a young child's intake.

After about twenty minutes, remove the food without comment. Even if she didn't eat anything, don't offer any food until snack time. Repeat the same process at the next meal, without making a fuss or pleading. With a relaxed attitude, chances are good that your "picky" child will soon be eating happily at family mealtimes. Missing an occasional meal or refusing to eat a particular food does no permanent harm. The outer limits of acceptable nutrition are much broader than you might think. As long as your child's growth rate remains within normal limits, you can assume she is getting enough nutrients.

The final message is to remember that healthy, normal children will eat a balanced diet over time if consistently offered a selection of nutritious foods. Parents are responsible for preparing and serving a variety of healthful foods, but they should not use coercive measures to influence a young child's intake. Rather, children should be allowed to decide how much they eat at a given meal. So maintain a low-key approach to mealtimes, trusting your child's natural ability to regulate how much she needs to eat.

Helpful Guidelines for Preventing Mealtime Battles

- Set a good example yourself by modeling healthy eating habits. Whenever possible, eat together as a family. Limit excitement and tone down activity before meals so children won't be so distractible. Make a concerted effort to neutralize mealtimes and to keep meals calm and pleasant. Do not make your child stay at the table after others have been excused.
- Keep serving portions small. Being able to finish a small serving can make a child feel successful. Respect your child's likes and dislikes. We don't judge adults' food preferences. When a new food is introduced, encourage a taste test, but don't require your child to eat all of the new food. Offer new foods repeatedly, even if they are initially refused, as children usually develop a taste for initially rejected foods.
- Offer simple food choices to give your child a sense of control: "Do you want cereal or toast this morning?" "Would you like cheese or tuna on your sandwich?" Let her build her own salad or choose her baked potato toppings. Offer foods that let your young child practice fine motor skills, like dipping fries in ketchup or apple slices in yogurt.
- Avoid making food an emotionally charged issue by using food as a reward or withholding it as punishment: "If you behave in the store, I'll buy you a candy bar." "That's it, young lady! Now, we're not going to stop for ice cream!" Do not categorize food as good or bad. All foods eaten in moderation can be part of a healthy diet. Desserts, when served, should be part of the meal, not a reward for a clean plate.

- Don't let your child eat while watching television or engaging in other activities. This could lead to habitual eating past the point of feeling full. Serve meals in the kitchen or dining room, not in the living room or in front of the television. Snacking while watching television is linked with excessive caloric intake.

Contact your child's doctor if your youngster's feeding problems are not improved by the strategies described here or if you are having difficulty in other parenting areas, such as toilet training or bedtime routines. You also should seek professional help if your child has lost weight or has failed to gain for four months or if her poor appetite is associated with symptoms, such as fever, diarrhea, or frequent gagging, choking, or vomiting.

Habit Behaviors of Early Childhood

Many young children engage in repetitive behaviors that serve to discharge tension and reduce anxiety. These common behaviors, which may be either deliberate or unintentional, can range from hair twirling and thumb sucking to masturbation. Many habits are learned by innocent self-exploration or imitation. Others start out as purposeful movements that get reinforced over time because the behavior is pleasurable or relaxing. The activity is most often exhibited during times of anxiety, boredom, and fatigue.

Instead of harping on the undesirable habit, focus extra attention on the positive aspects of your child's behavior.

Although habit behaviors generally are benign and temporary, they represent a common source of parental concern, confusion, and sometimes guilt. When dealt with harshly, habit behaviors can leave

Additional Strategies for Dealing with Picky Eaters

- If your child refuses everything being served, make it clear that it is her responsibility to find something to eat (if she is old enough) or serve her something simple requiring no preparation, like yogurt and fruit. Don't break down and let her fill up between meals. While regular nutritious snacks are very legitimate sources of between-meal energy for active toddlers and preschoolers, continuous snacking and empty snacks should be limited for children who eat little at mealtimes.

- Exercise creativity in expanding your child's diet. If your child won't eat vegetables, disguise them in casseroles, soups, stews, or omelets, or serve them raw and diced with dip. Use fruit strips, vegetables, or cheese to draw a smiling face on top of a dish. Or create a face on your pancake with berries or bananas. Rename the food, such as "breakfast pizza" or "mighty milk shake." But don't overdo it. You shouldn't be expected to come up with an elaborate display at every meal.

- Remember that children like to eat things they have helped to grow, select, prepare, or serve. Allow your child to accompany you to the grocery and invite him to select a variety of colorful fruits and vegetables. Then let him help in simple chores associated with meal preparation, including washing produce, shelling peas, tearing lettuce, husking corn, or helping mix a colorful salad.

- Give your child a daily vitamin if it will ease your mind about meeting her daily vitamin requirement. Although vitamin supplements are not routinely necessary for healthy toddlers and preschoolers, some mothers will give a daily vitamin supplement (one that does not provide over 100 percent of the RDAs) to assure that their child receives the recommended dietary allowance whether or not she eats a well-balanced diet that day. Please realize that overdoses of iron can be very toxic, so keep vitamins with iron well out of reach, and never refer to them as candy.
- Consider the place of milk in your toddler's diet. Whole or low-fat milk is an important source of protein, calories, fat, calcium, riboflavin, and vitamins. Even if little food was consumed, knowing your child drank milk at every meal can give you some peace of mind. On the other hand, some children fill up on milk to the exclusion of other foods. If this is the case, limit your child's milk intake to sixteen ounces per day to keep milk from diminishing her appetite.

a youngster feeling ashamed and disappointed in himself. Fortunately, with your understanding, acceptance, and support, chances are good that simply ignoring the habit will result in its disappearance. Instead of harping on the undesirable habit, focus extra attention on the positive aspects of your child's behavior. Examine possible sources of anxiety, stress, and tension at home or in the child-care setting and make an effort to provide a secure, relaxed environment for your child. Offer additional comforting, cuddling, and loving interaction to help your little one feel valued.

Thumb Sucking

Nearly half of children in the United States under four years of age are estimated to suck their thumb or finger. Such nonnutritive comfort sucking is considered entirely normal and helps promote independence as a baby learns to soothe herself when a parent can't be there. Thumb sucking usually begins when a baby accidentally discovers her fingers, and the habit easily gets reinforced because sucking is so pleasurable. Preschoolers who continue to suck their thumb or finger are more likely to engage in the habit when they are tired, bored, frustrated, or anxious. The habit is so normal in the first three to four years of life that you should make no attempt to stop it. Certainly, there is no place for punitive measures, criticism, or belittling a child to try to eliminate a thumb-sucking habit. If your child is sucking due to boredom, try distracting her with a play activity that requires both hands.

> Certainly, there is no place for punitive measures, criticism, or belittling a child to try to eliminate a thumb-sucking habit.

Although most children will have stopped sucking their thumb by three to four years, up to 20 percent continue the habit beyond the age of five. Misalignment of the teeth can result if thumb sucking continues after the permanent teeth begin to erupt around age six. In addition, thumb sucking during the elementary school years can result in embarrassment among a child's peers and decreased social acceptance. If your child is at least five and wants help breaking the habit, you can support her with verbal reminders, commercial bitter-tasting solutions applied to the thumb, wearing a Band-Aid or mitten, or a positive-reinforcement star chart. If necessary, a child's dentist can fit her with a simple orthodontic appliance to break the habit by preventing contact between the finger or thumb and the roof of the mouth.

Pacifiers

Although babies discover finger sucking on their own, they learn the pleasures of sucking on a pacifier when their parents introduce it to them. Years later, the same parents who got their baby hooked on the pacifier habit may wonder how to break it! Although pacifier use can contribute to some types of dental misalignment, the habit tends to be less prolonged than thumb sucking. Helping your child discontinue the use of a pacifier will be easier if you start to put it aside once he learns to crawl and is easily distracted by his newfound mobility. After one year of age, it is preferable to restrict the use of his pacifier to bedtime and naptime, if possible. Try to decrease your child's reliance on his pacifier by substituting a stuffed animal or blanket for his security object. Weaning from a pacifier will be more difficult if a toddler is accustomed to walking around with it in his mouth all day. Furthermore, having a child's mouth continually "corked" or "plugged" by a pacifier may interfere with his language development.

Weaning from a pacifier will be more difficult if a toddler is accustomed to walking around with it in his mouth all day.

Unlike a thumb or finger, a pacifier can be removed from your child's presence. However, you will need to get him to agree on how to diminish his pacifier use. Of course, you shouldn't criticize or belittle him for still using a pacifier. And don't ask him to wean from it when he is dealing with other stresses, like adjusting to a new sibling or a new child-care setting. Substitute lots of cuddling and one-on-one time to make up for the comfort he derived from the pacifier. You might mutually decide to leave the pacifier at home when you go out, then to use it only at night or naptime. Eventually you might offer to let your child trade his pacifier for a coveted gift, such as a tricycle or training bike. One mother who made such an arrangement with her four-year-old had him "pay" the cashier with his pacifier. Some especially charitable children have agreed to mail their treasured pacifier to a relative's new baby, now that they were a "big boy" and no longer needed it.

Hair Twirling and Hair Pulling

Hair twirling, twisting, or pulling often occurs while a child sucks her thumb or finger. Parents naturally display less concern over hair fiddling than hair pulling, which can lead to conspicuous bald spots. The irresistible urge to pull out one's hair is known as tricotillomania. Two distinct patterns of the disorder occur in childhood. In the first, hair pulling begins before age five and usually is associated with thumb or finger sucking. Like other tension-relieving habits, it tends to occur during times of boredom, anxiety, or fatigue. The behavior usually disappears when the thumb-sucking habit is relinquished. A later and more severe form of tricotillomania begins around puberty and tends to be a chronic, troubling problem.

If your preschooler pulls her hair, don't punish her or try to prevent the behavior, for example by making her wear mittens over her hands. Trying to bribe her with rewards won't work either. Don't make comments about any evident hair loss. Your best approach is to try to ignore the behavior and reduce possible sources of stress and anxiety in your child's life. Offer additional comforting, cuddling, and loving interaction to help your child feel secure. If she pulls her hair while sucking her thumb, chances are good that she will discontinue the hair-pulling habit when she gives up thumb sucking.

Nose Picking

Virtually all children occasionally put their fingers in their noses and remove the contents, sometimes eating it or wiping it on themselves, on others, or on any available surface. Because this behavior is so socially unacceptable, parents are apt to overreact to it with their words or body language. However, your youngster may misinterpret your intense rejection of the behavior to mean you disapprove of her. Furthermore, an overdramatic response may actually provoke more nose picking by young children who enjoy their ability to upset you.

Instead of using words like yuk or gross, tell your child in a matter-of-fact manner not to pick her nose in public. Offer her tissues to dispose of removed nasal contents.

To reduce the spread of respiratory viruses on your child's hands, wash them often and keep her fingernails trimmed. Nose picking can cause minor nosebleeds. To reduce nasal dryness and help heal and soften irritating scabs, you can daily apply a small amount of petroleum jelly to the center wall inside the nose using a cotton tip swab. While it may not be realistic to try to completely eliminate this distressing habit, you can at least teach your child by age four to five not to pick her nose in public and to dispose of the contents in a hygienic manner. If your child wants help in curbing the habit, she can wear a Band-Aid on her finger to serve as a reminder.

Lip Licking or Chewing

Many habitual behaviors begin as purposeful activities that become repetitive and get incorporated into a child's behavior as an outlet for tension. A lip-licking or lip-biting habit might begin when a child tries to moisten badly chapped lips or smooth their surface by gently chewing off dried, rough tissue. The repeated mouthing actions may then become a habitual behavior that increases when the child is tense, tired, or anxious. The habit is easily perpetuated because the more the lips are licked and chewed, the more uneven and irregular the lip surfaces become and the more irresistible is the urge to nibble the rough edges. Often a telltale ring of red, irritated skin surrounding the lip margins accompanies the habit.

Don't draw attention to the habit or blame your child for the unsightly red ring around his lips that may have spoiled a family photo. Help him apply some lip balm frequently throughout the day and at bedtime. This protective coating will moisten the dry, rough edges on his lips and discourage him from chewing the tissues. Instead of rubbing the lip balm across the lips, apply it with vertical strokes to prevent cracks from reopening.

Tics

Unlike habits, which are deliberate behaviors, tics are repetitive involuntary and purposeless movements or vocal sounds. Tics most commonly involve movement of the eyes, mouth, face, neck, shoulders, and hands. Examples of motor tics include eye blinking, nose twitching, and facial grimacing. Vocal tics, which are less common, include coughing, sniffing, and throat clearing. More boys than girls display tics. Often a tic develops as an exaggeration of normal spontaneous or purposeful movements. For example, an eye-blinking tic might begin when a child's eyes are bothered by an allergy, pink eye, or chlorinated pool water. But the frequent blinking may continue after the irritation is no longer present. A sniffing tic might start when a child is sniffing purposefully due to a cold or allergy. Although tics tend to wax and wane, they usually occur many times each day. In most cases, tics are self-limited and disappear spontaneously within several months of their onset.

> **When a tic has been present for more than a year, it is considered to be a chronic disorder and may persist.**

Tics often become more prominent during times of emotional upset, tension, or anxiety. Stress not only can make existing tics worse but also may precipitate new tics in some cases. Although tics are not deliberate behaviors, a tic may be inhibited voluntarily for a short period of time with considerable concentration and effort; however, this is harder for young children. A tic may diminish or disappear when a child is absorbed in an activity, relaxed, or sleeping. When a tic has been present for more than a year, it is considered to be a chronic disorder and may persist.

Don't nag your child or give frequent reminders about a tic behavior. Excessive attention paid to a tic may cause a child to dwell on it and make the tic worse. A tic is not a bad habit that can be broken; tics are beyond a child's control. Try to reduce the stress in your child's life and increase the praise and encouragement you give your child.

Tourette's syndrome (TS) is a type of chronic tic disorder that begins in childhood, usually in the early school years, but the onset can be earlier. Once thought to be extremely rare and manifest only in severe forms, TS no longer is considered uncommon, as many mild cases recently have been recognized. Boys are affected three times more often than girls. The main symptom of TS is chronic tics, both motor and vocal, that occur many times each day for a period of more than one year. Although the type and frequency of tics change over time, both multiple motor tics and one or more vocal tics are evident during the illness. If your child has both motor and vocal tics or any chronic tics, you should ask your child's doctor about the possibility of TS.

Masturbation

Most parents mistakenly believe that small children should not have sexual feelings and become anxious when they find their child touching or rubbing his genitals. In fact, babies discover their genitals just as naturally as they explore other body parts and quickly learn that they are a source of pleasurable sensations. Babies and toddlers have no understanding that genital touching is "impolite" or requires modesty. It's our reaction to genital touching that imparts a value judgment to the behavior. When parents overreact to innocent genital exploration, a young child can conclude that there is something wrong with these body parts.

> When parents overreact to innocent genital exploration, a young child can conclude that there is something wrong with these body parts.

Whether parents acknowledge it or not, the majority of children do masturbate occasionally, the most common ages being about four years and during adolescence. Because masturbation is natural and almost universal, it doesn't make sense to assume your child won't do it. Despite the numerous myths and misbeliefs surrounding masturbation, it does not cause any symptoms or health problems. However, many adults have strong feelings about masturbation and consider it to be immoral or unhealthy. The greatest risk of masturbation is the emotional harm that can result when children are made to feel guilty or naughty about exploring and enjoying their own bodies. If you are highly conflicted about masturbation, I suggest you talk to your child's doctor about your feelings.

Young children may masturbate by stimulating their genitals with their hand, moving their thighs against each other, thrusting against a straddled hobbyhorse, or by rubbing against an object. They often engage in the habit as a way to relieve tension when they are tired, bored, or watching television. The child may look preoccupied or flushed. As soon as children become aware that such behavior is not appropriate in public, they masturbate only in private. As a result, their parents become less aware of it and are less concerned.

By four or five years of age, your child should be old enough to understand that touching the genitals is something we don't do in front of other people.

Even if it makes you uncomfortable that your child is deriving pleasure from self-stimulation, I urge you not to react negatively or make judgmental comments if you discover your child touching himself. Your strong negative reaction can make your child feel ashamed of his sexual self. To be told that a part of his body is inherently bad or untouchable can be very confusing to a child and may adversely affect his self-image. Don't act suspicious of your daughter by telling her to take her hand from between her legs. And don't convey disgust or dismay when your son absentmindedly strokes his genitals. Overreacting or punishing can provoke increased masturbation and cause your child to feel unwarranted shame. To help children feel comfortable with their whole bodies, give them the proper names for their genitals (penis or vagina rather than weenie or peepee) when you are teaching about body parts.

If you find your preschooler masturbating where others are present, try to distract her with another activity or ask her to go to her room. By four or five years of age, your child should be old enough to understand that touching the genitals is something we don't do in front of other people. It's important that other caretakers be taught to respond to masturbation in a manner that is consistent with your reaction in order not to confuse your child.

Excessive or intense masturbation that interferes with other activities or continues to occur in public is not normal and indicates a possible emotional problem. Excessive genital handling can be a sign of generalized anxiety or exaggerated childhood fears. For example, a little boy who has recognized that his new baby sister doesn't have a penis might worry whether something could happen to his. Inform your child's doctor if your youngster masturbates excessively as a self-comfort habit. You should also consult her physician if your child tries to masturbate others, uses an object to masturbate, or imitates sexual intercourse. It is possible that she has been exposed to sexually explicit material or has been sexually abused by someone.

Other Common Concerns

In addition to common concerns about toilet training, picky eating, and habit behaviors, many parents of preschoolers are bewildered by other worrisome but usually developmentally appropriate behaviors and characteristics of young children. An explanation of these often transient and sometimes puzzling behaviors and attributes will help you respond with sensitivity and understanding as your preschooler navigates the emotional challenges of early childhood.

Breath-Holding

Breath-holding is similar to a temper tantrum—an outward display of intense internal frustration. While older children learn to express their tensions by talking about them, young children do not yet have the means to articulate the internal frustrations they feel over the limits adults must set for them. Instead they tend to resort to emotional explosions in the form of temper tantrums (see chapter 2 and chapter 5) or breath-holding when they are upset or don't get what they want. Typically breath-holding spells are precipitated by an interaction with a parent that causes a child to become angry or frustrated. The child usually cries briefly, then stops breathing after exhaling and does not inhale. It only takes about thirty seconds before the child starts to turn blue. She may become limp or even faint.

Approximately 5 percent of children between six months and five years of age breath-hold to the point of turning blue and 50 percent of these children occasionally pass out. Obviously, this can be very frightening to parents, but it is important to know that if your child passes out after holding her breath, she will start breathing normally again and be fully awake within a minute. Many parents worry that a child can hold his breath long enough to cause brain damage from lack of oxygen. Rest assured that it is not possible for anyone to hold their breath voluntarily to the point of doing any harm. Make sure your child does not injure her head if she falls when passing out from a breath-holding spell. Keep her flat and time the spell, which should last no more than one minute. You don't need to resuscitate your child after a breath-holding spell (unless she doesn't start breathing again quickly), and you should *never* put anything into your child's mouth if she has fainted. This could provoke vomiting and lead to choking.

If your child has breath-holding spells, try to remain calm and ignore them as best you can. If you let her see how upset you are and give in to her demands, she will figure she has won a victory and you will only reinforce her inappropriate behavior. Although your child may not have set out to manipulate you, she will quickly recognize her ability to do so. After the spell, give your child a hug and talk to her about her frustration and anger. You can empathize with her feelings, while still maintaining the limits you have set. Most children outgrow temper tantrums and breath-holding spells by four or five years of age. By that time, children usually have acquired the language skills needed to express their emotions and don't need to resort to acting them out.

You should notify your child's doctor and have her evaluated if breath-holding spells occur more than once a week, if episodes are increasing in frequency, if an attack lasts more than one minute, or if muscle jerks occur during a breath-holding spell.

Nightmares

Dreams and nightmares that we experience during "active" sleep or REM (rapid eye movement) sleep are normal occurrences to help us work out in our minds the emotional stresses and anxieties we face during our waking hours. Nightmares occur in the latter part of the night when dreaming is most intense. Toddlers report dreams and nightmares as soon as their vocabulary is large enough to express them. A child who awakens from a nightmare crying and frightened will need the comfort of your presence and the reassurance of your calming words to feel he is safe. Even when you tell your child that what he experienced in a dream isn't real, he is genuinely frightened by a nightmare. After your child has calmed down, it's best to lead him back to his bed. If your child can remember his nightmare and is still troubled by it, you might have him close his eyes while awake and ask him to change what occurs in the dream to give it a happy ending.

Consider ways you might limit stress and anxiety during your child's waking hours, such as minimizing parental conflict, monitoring the videos and television your child watches, avoiding scary bedtime stories, and reducing the pressure you place on your child. Talk to your pediatrician if your child has frequent nightmares, appears chronically stressed, or has emotional conflicts that are creating behavior problems.

Sleep Terrors

Sleep terrors are different from nightmares. They occur during partial arousal from the deepest phase of non-REM (nondreaming or "quiet") sleep—usually one to four hours after falling asleep. Sleep terrors are seen most commonly in young children two to six years of age. When they begin after age six, sleep terrors may be linked to emotional problems. In young children with sleep terrors, the episodes may occur up to twice a week and usually last five to ten minutes. Unlike a child who awakens crying after a nightmare, a youngster in the midst of a sleep terror is not really awake. Although he may sit up, look around, cry out, thrash about, and appear frightened, the child is only partially aroused and does not recall what happened. Sleep terrors (as well as sleepwalking) are more common in boys and tend to run in families.

Sleep terrors are more upsetting for parents than for children. Your attempts to awaken your child from what appears to be a bad dream only make him more upset. Just cuddle him gently, whisper a brief reassurance, and try not to let him hurt himself. Keep the lights dimmed and stay with him until he has calmed down. He will probably settle back to sleep without ever becoming fully awake. Because sleep terrors sometimes occur when children are overtired, try putting your child to bed thirty minutes earlier or encourage him to take a brief daytime nap. Children gradually outgrow sleep terrors. If sleep terrors occur more than twice a week, last more than half-an-hour, or begin before one year of age or after six, you should notify your pediatrician.

Shyness

Children vary widely in their individual temperaments. Some adjust to new experiences easily, while others need more time to feel safe in an unfamiliar or noisy situation. Many preschool children can be called shy, or slow to warm to strangers and cautious toward new surroundings. They may cling to a parent as they are adjusting to a new experience, take a while to join in with the other children, and make frequent eye contact with the parent as they ease into a new situation.

Although shy youngsters need a longer period of adjustment to new experiences, these children do not differ from others once they are acquainted with their companions and surroundings. Shy children usually enjoy individual relationships or small numbers of children more than larger group situations.

Many preschool children can be called shy, or slow to warm to strangers and cautious toward new surroundings.

Don't limit your child by labeling her as shy. She has so many other qualities in addition to being timid in new situations. Remember that typecasting and stereotyping of children (see chapter 4) can become a self-fulfilling prophecy and can limit your child's sense of possibility. Calling her shy sounds like a criticism and makes her feel like a disappointment to you. Instead, say that she likes to take her time getting used to new things.

Your child will appreciate your introducing her to new experiences gradually without overprotecting her. Tell her what to expect and go with her as she enters an unfamiliar situation. Make her feel comfortable talking about her fears. Remind her that she usually enjoys herself after she gets used to a new experience. Focus on things that are already familiar to her: "Oh, there's an aquarium like the one at Dr. Bowman's office." You can step back once your child has begun to enjoy herself. Remain nearby, without hovering. A periodic nod or wave may be enough to reassure your child from a distance.

Role-play with your shy child how to ask other children to play by saying, "Hi, my name is Shanel. Can I play Barbies too?" Have her practice making eye contact and speaking loudly enough. Help her be more assertive by telling a child who takes her toys, "No. That's mine. I want you to give it back." Praise her for playing with another child or initiating a conversation. Allow her opportunities to be part of a regular small playgroup or to invite one or two friends to your home.

Fears

Irrational fears are a normal part of early childhood, when children have not yet learned to separate fantasy from reality. The clown you find amusing may look frightening to your three-year-old. While it is important to acknowledge your child's fears and display appropriate sensitivity, your over-reaction can actually magnify his fears. Instead, a matter-of-fact response will validate his concern, while reassuring your child, "I know the bug is coming our way, but it won't hurt you." Don't let your voice sound overanxious or strident. Use a neutral, low-key tone.

> While it is important to acknowledge your child's fears and display appropriate sensitivity, your overreaction can actually magnify his fears.

Fears serve many purposes for a preschooler. They can help him gain control over a difficult situation or withdraw from it: "I don't want to hold the frog; it doesn't feel good." A child's fears can be used to get attention ("Hold me; I'm scared") or to feel powerful by manipulating his parents; for example, when he discovers he can get them to remain in his room longer by telling them he is afraid of monsters.

Ultimately, a child learns to replace his fear with courage and confidence, largely through our example. When your child expresses a fear, say of dogs, you can validate his concern ("That's a big doggie"), while providing reassurance ("He won't hurt you"). It's important to maintain your usual limits while your child is dealing with the fear: "No, I won't carry you, but I'll hold your hand." First and foremost, when your child is afraid, he needs you to help him feel safe, and he needs to be convinced that you will protect him. Never trivialize your child's fears, tease him about being afraid, or call him a "scaredy cat." Not only is such mocking mean and hurtful, it will make him reluctant to share his fears with you or reveal his vulnerabilities. Without your support, his fears will not diminish, even if he learns to hide behind a false, tough-guy image.

In addition to your support and protection, your child needs you to help him make a plan for managing his fears. For example, if he has bedtime fears of the dark or monsters, you can visually check his room when you tuck him in, leave a night-light on, post a stuffed animal sentry, or give him a flashlight. Don't dwell too long on his fears, however, or empathize too much. For example, letting your child sleep with you because he says he is afraid of the dark gives your child a great deal of secondary gain as a result of his fear. In addition, you may be conveying the message that you lack confidence in his ability to learn to master his fear.

Model for your child how to draw on his spiritual faith to help manage his fears. Remind him that God loves him and is always watching over him, like a good shepherd watches over his sheep. You also can pray with your child about a specific fear, such as the dark, asking God to help reassure and calm him. Give him a comforting phrase to repeat to bolster his confidence about God's protection, such as "God loves and cares for me" or "God is always watching me" or "Do not fear; I am with you."

> **Model for your child how to draw on his spiritual faith to help manage his fears.**

Common fears of early childhood include animals, loud noises, costumed characters, bugs, and water. A fear of animals can be diminished by reading animal books together or exposing your child to harmless pets or docile animals at a petting zoo. Let your child approach the animals at his own pace and don't force him. You can show him how to gently pet a dog or let him practice petting a stuffed animal. You also can make up encouraging songs to sing to help your child overcome a fear or tell him what worked for you to overcome the same fear. In addition, you should monitor your own fear reactions, for example to bees or spiders, since your child learns a lot about what to fear from watching you.

Help your child learn the difference between caution and fear. For example, warning your child never to go near an animal without the owner present teaches him to be cautious. Caution helps children recognize possible dangers and take appropriate action. Fear, on the other hand, immobilizes us and diminishes our ability to cope with problems.

Imaginary Friends

Between three and five years, preschoolers are learning a great deal about how to relate to their peers as they acquire many new social skills, including interactive play, sharing, and taking turns. Many preschoolers invent pretend friends—who may be animals or humans—to let them use their imagination and practice their social skills. For young children, who love fantasy and make-believe games, creating a special pretend friend is great fun. Don't worry about this normal preschool behavior, feel threatened or jealous about this cherished companion, or tell your child that the friend doesn't exist. Just accept your child's imaginary playmate, appreciate the ways that she helps your child, and play along until your child no longer needs her friend.

> For young children, who love fantasy and make-believe games, creating a special pretend friend is great fun.

An imaginary friend can be a faithful companion, especially to an only child, offsetting fear and loneliness. Your child's imaginary friend can treat her better than others when she is feeling unloved or can be bossed around when she needs to feel powerful. Having a pretend playmate can bring magic into a child's life, allowing her to vicariously experience what she can only dream about, whether it is having a father or no longer having diabetes. An imaginary companion also may serve a valuable role as your child's conscience, helping her learn to distinguish right from wrong. The friend can do the naughty things your child resists or motivate her to set a positive example for her companion. Being able to criticize her imaginary friend for being naughty helps a child begin to reject her own unacceptable behavior as she develops a conscience. Some children rehearse the family rules with their imaginary friend as a way to monitor their own behavior. A child may even send her imaginary friend to time-out as a way of practicing consequences for misbehavior.

Security Objects

Babies and young children develop a variety of comforting behaviors that help them self-soothe when a parent can't be there. Between eight to twelve months, most babies become attached to a "lovey" item, such as a special stuffed animal, soft toy, or blanket. In addition to clutching the object, a child may chew on the edge of a blanket or stroke a stuffed animal while sucking her thumb. By doing so, the child is symbolically clinging to a piece of you when you are out of sight. Clutching a favored object serves as an outlet for tension and a source of comfort when a child is anxious, lonely, frightened, or tired. The attachment to this special item often continues through the preschool years. Your child may need to take her security object to the store, on a trip, and to bed.

Clutching a favored object serves as an outlet for tension and a source of comfort when a child is anxious, lonely, frightened, or tired.

Although some people frown on a child's need for her "blankie" and view it as babyish, being able to partially rely on such a parent substitute to provide a measure of self-comfort is actually quite adaptive. Trust me, anything that helps your child cope more readily in stressful situations will make both your lives easier. Because the child's attachment to the favored object helps smooth her transition from dependence to independence and improves her coping skills, it has come to be known as a security object or transition object. Its reassuring familiarity and comforting softness helps her feel safe in new surroundings, say good-bye to Mommy at the child-care center, and fall asleep at night. As a child gets older, she can take increasing responsibility for remembering to bring Teddy or Lambie or Doggie with her when she needs him.

A child's security object is so important to her that many parents keep two identical items in case one accidentally gets left at Grandma's house or needs to be washed. You will want to rotate the two objects regularly so one is not conspicuously less worn. There is no need to attempt to wean your child from her dependency on the object. Don't tease her about it, tell her she's too old to need it, or threaten to take it away. Her interest in and attachment to "blankie" will gradually diminish. By five years of age, she probably will no longer need it, although she may always feel nostalgic toward her "lovey" and want to keep it in her room. Some parents try to decrease their child's dependency on the item by taking it away to wash it and "forgetting" to return it until the child asks. Others have gotten their child's permission to cut her security blanket in half, and later half again, until she can carry it around inconspicuously. However, such measures are unnecessary, as your child will give up her security object on her own when she no longer needs it.

Separation Anxiety

Late in the first year, babies who have made an appropriate strong attachment—usually to the mother—will become distressed, anxious, and clingy when their mother exits the room or leaves them in the care of someone else. Separation anxiety is a normal developmental phenomenon and a positive sign of a healthy parent-child attachment. From the baby's perspective, when the parent is not in sight, he fears she will never return. Separation anxiety may cause a year-old child to refuse to be held by a stranger, to have trouble going to bed at night, or to cry out for his mother when he wakes in the middle of the night. Games like peek-a-boo help a baby learn that something can be out of sight and still exist. Later, games of hide-and-seek will reinforce the same lesson for preschoolers. Eventually a child learns that not only will you return from your absences, but he will survive the intense feelings that separation provokes.

> Separation anxiety is a normal developmental phenomenon and a positive sign of a healthy parent-child attachment.

Although separation fears are greatest between ten months and two years, children retain some level of anxiety about losing their parent or worrying whether their parent will return after a separation. Such anxieties intensify when children are exposed to new surroundings, for example when they enroll in a child-care program. Separation anxiety can become accentuated for five-year-olds, who absolutely adore their mothers and are very attached to their fathers as well. Many children who attend Sunday school, preschool, or kindergarten—even those who look forward to it—will experience temporary distress and may even become teary at the prospect of separating from their parents. (See chapter 6.) Pray with your child about these concerns and explain that God is always with her, even when you are not there. You can smooth your child's initial adjustment to new situations by remaining in the background until she is happily engaged in an activity. Adhering to familiar good-bye rituals also helps your child separate from you each day. Parents can be reassured that few children remain upset for more than a few minutes after you depart. An oversolicitous parent only makes her child more anxious. Tell your child when you will return ("right after playground time") and be sure to keep your commitment.

Children who have exaggerated, persistent separation anxiety that interferes with their daily functioning are said to suffer from Separation Anxiety Disorder. Such children are consumed with worry about their parents' health and well-being and are preoccupied with other exaggerated fears. The disorder can cause chronic anxiety and problems with school attendance as children get older. Referral should be made to a child psychiatrist or other therapist experienced in treating childhood anxiety disorders.

Death of a Loved One

The death of someone close to a child is one of the most stressful events in a youngster's life. A child should be told about a death honestly, using age-appropriate explanations. Sharing your own grief reaction—shock, disbelief, guilt, sadness, and anger—is both normal and helpful. Young children need to be reassured that they will be well cared for, especially if they have experienced the loss of a parent. Often parents are so consumed by their own grief that the child may temporarily feel abandoned.

> Children under six do not understand the finality of death and think it is reversible or temporary.

Because young children think "magically," they may believe that they are responsible for the person's death. For example, a child who was angry about her parents' divorce and her father's departure may believe that her hostile thoughts caused her father's death. Children under six do not understand the finality of death and think it is reversible or temporary. They also may perceive death as punishment. A child needs to be reassured that she did not cause the death, could not have prevented it, and cannot do anything to bring the person back. Avoid the use of euphemisms, such as sleep, when discussing death, as this can be highly confusing to young children and make them fearful of going to sleep at night. Similarly, saying a deceased person has "departed" or "gone from us" makes it sound like they will return again.

Share your faith with your child and help her understand death in light of that faith. You can explain that people go to be with God after they die and will always continue to be under his care. Explain that God shares our sorrow and comforts us in our times of loss and sadness. Help your child appreciate that loved ones live on in our memories. She can commemorate the life of the deceased by drawing a picture, making a scrapbook, planting a tree, or giving away a favorite object at the funeral service. The decision whether to have a young child participate in a funeral service is an individual one. Parents may be so concerned about protecting their child from the emotional reaction of others that they neglect to let her express her own legitimate sadness. If a child is to be present at the funeral, she must be prepared for what to expect, and a trusted person should support the child throughout the process.

Young children may display a wide variety of grief manifestations, including behavior problems, physical complaints, sleep disturbances, anger, clinging, withdrawal, crying, regression, decreased appetite, being good or bad, or keeping their concerns inside. The stages of grief can span weeks or months, eventually leading to acceptance and readjustment. Prolonged or severe behavior change suggests the need for therapeutic intervention. Books for children can help with the grieving process. Even when a child seems to be adjusting well, be prepared for her concerns to resurface at holidays or during times of other losses.

Attention Deficit Hyperactivity Disorder

The activity levels and attention spans of young children vary widely. Some normal children are more active, impulsive, distractible, irregular, and unpredictable than others. In addition to innate differences between the sexes, cultural traditions and parental gender expectations powerfully shape the play and behavior of boys (noisy, adventurous, rambunctious) versus girls (quiet, composed, compliant). External reinforcers, including the kinds of toys provided to a youngster (a police car versus a puzzle), also influence the activities children choose and can contribute to a rowdy, aggressive style of play. In general, little boys do tend to roughhouse more than girls and make more motoric sounds during their play.

A child's behavior also can vary considerably depending upon his developmental abilities, physical environment, and family circumstances. For example, exposure to acts of violence on television increases aggressive behavior in young children. Restlessness can result from overcrowded living conditions without adequate play areas. Delayed language and social skill development can cause frustration outbursts and noncompliant behavior. Inconsistent parental discipline and a disorganized and chaotic environment may aggravate symptoms of hyperactivity or aggressiveness. Hunger, fatigue, overstimulation, illness, or stressful life events can produce irritability and uncooperative behavior in a child.

Boys are several times more likely to be diagnosed with ADHD than girls, perhaps because overtly hyperactive or aggressive behavior is less common among girls.

Parents react differently to similar behaviors in children, depending on their experience, expectations, emotional reserve, and coping abilities. When a parent's temperament proves a poor match for the child's, such a misfit can negatively influence the parent's perception of the youngster. An inexperienced or overly stressed parent may perceive the normal oppositional behavior of a toddler or the high activity level of a preschooler as abnormal. Parents who consider their child's behavior as difficult may be too quick to label their youngster as hyperactive, a subjective and imprecise term.

Attention deficit hyperactivity disorder (ADHD) has been estimated to affect as many as 5 percent of all American children, making it one of the most common childhood developmental disorders. However, critics argue that this popular diagnosis is overused. Boys are several times more likely to be diagnosed with ADHD than girls, perhaps because overtly hyperactive or aggressive behavior is less common among girls.

> Despite ongoing controversy, stimulant medication is undoubtedly the most effective treatment for school-age children with ADHD.

To be diagnosed accurately with ADHD, a child must have problems with hyperactivity, act impulsively without considering the consequences, and have difficulty paying attention. Several of the following behaviors usually are present: restlessness, fidgetiness, inattention, poor concentration, distractibility, impulsivity, disorganization, disruptive behavior, trouble following directions, emotional immaturity, poor social skills, and noncompliance. The diagnosis of ADHD should be reserved for children whose problem behaviors start in early childhood, have been present for more than six months, and are reported by child-care personnel and teachers in addition to parents. Early recognition of the problem is important. Delayed diagnosis places a child at a great disadvantage since attention deficits can influence behavior, learning, social acceptance, and emotional adjustment. Learning disabilities are often present in children with ADHD, placing children at risk for poor academic performance.

If you think your child may have ADHD, begin with a thorough evaluation by his pediatrician. Unrecognized medical problems, such as mild hearing loss, impaired vision, or allergies, can cause a child to have difficulty with attention and activity. Developmental pediatricians, and some general pediatricians, are experienced in evaluating children for ADHD using standard behavioral questionnaires. Behavior rating scales to evaluate a child have been developed for both teachers and parents, since many of the symptoms of ADHD are most evident in classroom settings, where a child is required to focus his attention.

Despite ongoing controversy, stimulant medication is undoubtedly the most effective treatment for school-age children with ADHD. The majority of treated children experience significant improvement in attention span, impulsiveness, and hyperactivity. The number of preschoolers being treated with stimulants and antidepressants has increased significantly in recent years, although little research is available concerning the effectiveness of such drugs on young children. In addition to the use of medication, children with ADHD may need special help for learning problems. Counseling also may be necessary to help parents manage behavior problems related to impulsivity.

Delayed or Inarticulate Speech

"Slow to talk" can simply be a variation in normal development for some children, but it also can point to a serious problem in acquiring language, an impaired ability to learn, a communication disorder, severe hearing loss, or other significant problem. Normal language development proceeds in a predictable order and at a predictable rate, although each child develops at his own unique pace, with characteristic spurts and plateaus. Still, it is appropriate to be concerned when your child seems to lag behind in a certain area.

By two years of age, a child usually has about a fifty-word vocabulary, can speak in two-word sentences, points to pictures and body parts, listens to simple stories and rhymes, begins to use plurals, and follows simple commands. Thereafter, a child's vocabulary rapidly increases, as well as his ability to speak in more complex sentences. By three years of age, most children can put several sentences together and carry on a conversation. Approximately 5 percent of children have some type of impairment in speech or language.

Expressive-language delays are quite common in toddlers, particularly boys. Children with expressive-language delay understand what is said, but they have difficulty expressing themselves with words. They follow directions well, but point to what they want instead of asking for it. Although most children with this type of problem eventually catch up, toddlers who are slow in expressive-language development are at increased risk for ongoing delays in acquiring language skills throughout the preschool period. They also are at risk for future academic learning difficulties once they start school.

With an overall language delay, a child not only has a limited vocabulary for his age but also understands little of what is communicated to him. He is unable to follow directions and can't play interactive games, like "show me your nose," because he doesn't grasp what is being said. Other aspects of the child's development are likely to be delayed, and the youngster should have a comprehensive evaluation.

A child who appears to understand and use language properly for his age but is poorly understood by parents and others may have an articulation problem, or difficulty pronouncing words intelligibly. The problem commonly results from impaired hearing or chronic ear infections. About 30 percent of preschoolers have trouble pronouncing some words or sounds. An articulation problem should be suspected when a child's speech is unintelligible at two and a half years, or less than 50 percent intelligible by three years. Difficulties with articulation can be very frustrating for children who know what they want to say but can't be understood.

Abnormal speech and language development, together with impaired social skills, occurs in children with serious communication disorders, known as pervasive developmental disorders (PDD), including autism. These children often parrot or echo what was just said or repeat jingles or phrases without being aware of their meaning. They lack interest in interpersonal interactions or imitative play, largely ignore others, and frequently engage in repetitive behaviors like twirling, rocking, or hand flapping. The problem usually becomes evident by two and a half years of age.

If you have any reason to think that your child may have delayed speech, contact your pediatrician right away.

If you have any reason to think that your child may have delayed speech, contact your pediatrician right away. Your child's doctor can perform simple screening tests in the office to confirm your observations. When delayed speech is present, a child should have his hearing tested by an audiologist experienced in evaluating young children. In addition, he should have a comprehensive assessment of his language skills by a certified speech and language pathologist to determine the exact nature of his problem. When a language delay is identified, early speech therapy should be provided. The longer a child's speech is delayed, the more frustration he will experience trying to communicate with others. This can set the stage for behavior problems, low self-esteem, and poor social skills. Early intervention will help reduce such problems and also give a child the best chance of remedying his speech delay before he enters school, where he might be singled out as "special." Children usually find speech therapy to be enjoyable and fun. It's also a good idea to enroll a child with delayed speech in a preschool program where he can hear youngsters his own age speak their simplified language. He might make a greater effort to express himself verbally in this setting than at home.

When a speech delay is present, there are lots of ways a parent can help stimulate their child's speech development: reading books to him, singing simple songs together, playing interactive games ("Where's Eddie's belly button?"), naming objects for him, listening patiently when he does speak, and helping him express what he is trying to communicate. Fortunately, most children experience a virtual explosion of language development during the third year, when many slow talkers catch up.

Stuttering

Stuttering is the interruption of the natural flow of speech due to repetition and prolongation of sounds, syllables, or words. Learning to speak fluently is a highly complex task, and it is quite normal for children between two and five years of age to have some repetitions and hesitations in their speech. Temporary stuttering occurs in up to 25 percent of all children, and the vast majority of those who begin to stutter will completely outgrow it by early school age. Other children will need help from a trained therapist, while some young stutterers will be afflicted for life.

Most stuttering begins after age two, once children are using sentences to express their ideas. A child with a mild stutter problem repeats sounds more than twice and may elevate the pitch or loudness of his voice or have "blocked" speech for several seconds. In addition, he may display obvious tension in the facial muscles, especially around the mouth. A child is considered to have a severe stuttering problem requiring speech therapy if he stutters on more than 10 percent of his speech, displays considerable effort with obvious muscle tension, has frequent blocks of speech, or changes words and uses extra sounds in order to avoid stuttering.

Stuttering is four times more common in boys than girls, and there appears to be a genetic predisposition toward stuttering. Although the cause is still not known, a great deal has been learned about some of the factors that can aggravate and perpetuate stuttering, such as excitement, stress, fatigue, apprehension, and feeling rushed, self-conscious, or on display.

If your preschooler has begun to stutter, there are many ways you can support fluent speech simply by your style of interaction with your youngster. First, foster his confidence and help him feel emotionally secure by spending individual time with him each day and by offering liberal praise and encouragement. Talk to him in a calm, slow, relaxed rate of conversational speech and eliminate background noise from the television, radio, or stereo. Make eye contact and listen patiently and attentively whenever he is speaking, using smiles, nods, and "uh-huh's" to let him know that you hear what he is saying. Never hurry your child's speech by interrupting him or by completing his sentences, and don't reveal your own frustration, either through words, concerned looks, or body language. There's nothing wrong with occasional comments about obvious difficulty, such as "Everyone gets stuck on words sometimes." However, don't try to correct your child's speech. Don't make him repeat words or start over each time he stutters. Instead, ignore his stuttering, convey a patient, accepting attitude, and focus on his message, not his words. Pause a few seconds after he finishes speaking before responding. Ask fewer questions and pose no more than one at a time.

Learning to speak fluently is a highly complex task, and it is quite normal for children between two and five years of age to have some repetitions and hesitations in their speech.

Don't make your child self-conscious by discussing his speech in front of him and try not to convey your anxiety through comments, concerned looks, or other body language. Be patient and allow him ample time to express himself without making him feel he has to rush. Don't correct his speech, tell him to slow down, ask him to repeat words, or put him on the spot by requiring him to answer questions or recite in public if he doesn't want to.

Professional therapy should be sought whenever a child stutters on more than 10 percent of his speech, when stuttering has been present for more than six months and is occurring more frequently, or when a child is concerned about his speech and avoids talking in some situations. Arrange to have your child evaluated by a qualified speech-language pathologist who specializes in working with children who stutter. While there is no known cure for stuttering, it does not have to be a lifelong problem. Many forms of therapy are available, and most children who stutter can be helped by early treatment. In general, the sooner therapy is started, the better chance a child has for full recovery.

The information provided in this chapter should prepare you to deal with a host of common concerns in your preschooler and enable you to distinguish between normal and problematic behavior. Remember to work *with* your child to successfully handle each challenge. By viewing our youngster's behavior from a child's perspective, we can partner with her as we shepherd her through the emotional challenges of the preschool years. When appropriate, be prepared to seek essential expertise in overcoming specific concerns.

Although sorting through the maze of early childhood behaviors is a daily challenge, do not lose heart. Instead, remember that God has promised to "equip you with everything good for doing his will" (Heb. 13:21).

Parting Words
from Dr. Mom

In the preceding pages, I have shared my prescription for effectively parenting preschoolers, using the model of seven essentials for your child's formative years. Appreciating that parenting must be a high priority can motivate you to make necessary lifestyle changes in order to say yes to your children's needs. Your basic understanding of early child development should enable you to optimize your child's social, emotional, and intellectual outcome. Nurturing your youngster's innate spirituality will help her cultivate a living faith in our loving God that will give purpose and meaning to her life. Promoting your child's sense of identity, worth, and competence will equip her to handle life's challenges and reach her full potential. Modeling desired behavior, promoting cooperation, and consistently enforcing limits with love and affection teaches children self-control and how to live with mutual respect for others. Knowing how to recognize high-quality child care will give you the assurance that your child is physically safe, emotionally secure, and intellectually stimulated when being cared for by others. Finally, being knowledgeable about common and perplexing behaviors of young children will empower you to support your child's emotional needs in the preschool years.

The foundational elements I have emphasized are based on my professional expertise as a pediatrician, my personal experiences raising five precious children of my own, and my Christian perspective of parenting as a divine mandate to become cocreators with God. By keeping these seven essential elements in the forefront as you raise your child, you will increase your parenting effectiveness and enjoy greater fulfillment in your role. Although the preschool years are a particularly challenging period for both children and their parents, each believer can claim the many assurances of God that he will be with you and empower you in every situation. As I juggled parenting my own children with other competing priorities, I trusted God's Word: "I can do everything through him who gives me strength" (Phil. 4:13). When I didn't always know what to do, I repeated God's promise: "Trust in the LORD with all your heart and lean not on your own understanding; in all your ways acknowledge him, and he will make your paths straight" (Prov. 3:5–6).

May God bless you richly in your parenting role. Don't just enjoy the journey; savor it!

Notes

Chapter 1: The Essential Need to Make Parenting a Priority

1. Joseph P. Shapiro and Joannie M. Schrof, with Mike Tharp and Dorian Friedman, "Honor Thy Children," *U.S. News and World Report,* 27 February 1995, 39.

2. David Blankenhorn, "The Unnecessary Father," in *Fatherless America* (New York: Basic Books, 1995), 65–83.

3. Shapiro, et al., "Honor Thy Children," 39.

4. Blankenhorn, "Fatherless Society," in *Fatherless America,* 25–48.

Chapter 2: The Essentials of Early Child Develpment

1. Sharon Begley, "Your Child's Brain," *Newsweek,* 19 February 1996, 55–58; Madeline Nash, "Fertile Minds," *TIME,* 3 February 1997, 48–56; Special Issue: "Your Child From Birth To Three," *Newsweek,* Spring/Summer 1997.

2. Sharon Begley, "How to Build a Baby's Brain," *Newsweek* Special Issue, 28–32.

3. Begley, "Your Child's Brain," 55–61; Nash, "Fertile Minds," 55–56.

Chapter 4: The Essential Ingredients of Healthy Self-Seteem

1. American Academy of Pediatrics, Committee on Communications, "Media Violence," *Pediatrics* 95, no. 6 (1995): 949.

2. Jane F. Knapp, "The Impact of Children Witnessing Violence," *Pediatric Clinics of North America* 45, no. 2 (1998): 356.

3. American Academy of Pediatrics, Committee on Injury and Poison Prevention, "Firearm-Related Injuries Affecting the Pediatric Population," *Pediatrics* 105, no. 4 (2000): 888.

4. American Academy of Pediatrics, "Firearm-Related Injuries," 892.

Chapter 5: The Essentials of Discipline: Love and Limits

1. American Academy of Pediatrics, Committee on Psychosocial Aspects of Child and Family Health, "Guidance for Effective Discipline," *Pediatrics* 101, no. 4 (1998), 723–28.

2. American Academy of Pediatrics, "Effective Discipline."

3. James Dobson, *The New Dare to Discipline* (Wheaton, Ill.: Tyndale, 1992), 61–62.

4. Dobson, *Discipline,* 62–63.

Chapter 6: Those Essential Others: Alternate Caretakers

1. U.S. Department of Health and Human Services, National Center for Education in Maternal and Child Health, with the Maternal and Child Health Bureau, "Healthy Child Care America: Blueprint for Action" (Washington, D.C.: GPO, 1996), 1.

2. W. Steven Barnett, "Long-Term Effects of Early Childhood Programs on Cognitive and School Outcomes," *The Future of Children* 5, no. 3 (1995), 25–50.

Chapter 7: Essential Answers for Common Concerns

1. Ann C. Stadtler, Peter A. Gorski, and T. Berry Brazelton, "Toilet Training Methods, Clinical Interventions, and Recommendations," *Pediatrics* 103, no. 6 (1999): 1359.

2. Julian Wan and Saul Greenfield, "Enuresis and Common Voiding Abnormalities," *Pediatric Clinics of North America* 44, no. 5 (1997): 1118.

3. Susan L. Johnson and Leann Birch, "Parents' and Children's Adiposity and Eating Style," *Pediatrics* 94, no. 5 (1994): 653–61.

Index

We want to hear from you. Please send your comments about this
book to us in care of the address below. Thank you.

GRAND RAPIDS, MICHIGAN 49530

www.zondervan.com